RELIGION SINCE THE REFORMATION

RELIGION SINCE THE REFORMATION

Eight Lectures

Preached before the University of Oxford in the year 1922, on the Foundation of the Rev. John Bampton, M.A., Canon of Salisbury

BY

LEIGHTON PULLAN, D.D.
Fellow and Tutor of St. John Baptist's College, Oxford

WIPF & STOCK · Eugene, Oregon

Wipf and Stock Publishers
199 W 8th Ave, Suite 3
Eugene, OR 97401

Religion Since the Reformation
Bampton Lectures, 1922
By Leighton Pullan
ISBN 13: 978-1-5326-6995-8
Publication date 9/13/2018
Previously published by Oxford University Press, 1924

EXTRACT

FROM THE LAST WILL AND TESTAMENT

OF THE LATE

REV. JOHN BAMPTON,

CANON OF SALISBURY

——" I give and bequeath my Lands and Estates to the
" Chancellor, Masters, and Scholars of the University of
" Oxford for ever, to have and to hold all and singular the
" said Lands or Estates upon trust, and to the intents and
" purposes hereinafter mentioned ; that is to say, I will and
" appoint that the Vice-Chancellor of the University of
" Oxford for the time being shall take and receive all the
" rents, issues, and profits thereof, and (after all taxes,
" reparations, and necessary deductions made) that he pay
" all the remainder to the endowment of eight Divinity
" Lecture Sermons, to be established for ever in the said
" University, and to be performed in the manner following :

" I direct and appoint, that, upon the first Tuesday in
" Easter Term, a Lecturer be yearly chosen by the Heads
" of Colleges only, and by no others, in the room adjoining
" to the Printing-House, between the hours of ten in the
" morning and two in the afternoon, to preach eight Divinity
" Lecture Sermons, the year following, at St. Mary's in
" Oxford, between the commencement of the last month in
" Lent Term, and the end of the third week in Act Term.

" Also I direct and appoint, that the eight Divinity Lecture
" Sermons shall be preached upon either of the following
" Subjects—to confirm and establish the Christian Faith, and
" to confute all heretics and schismatics—upon the divine

"authority of the holy Scriptures—upon the authority of the writings of the primitive Fathers, as to the faith and practice of the primitive Church—upon the Divinity of our Lord and Saviour Jesus Christ—upon the Divinity of the Holy Ghost—upon the Articles of the Christian Faith, as comprehended in the Apostles' and Nicene Creeds.

"Also I direct, that thirty copies of the eight Divinity Lecture Sermons shall be always printed, within two months after they are preached; and one copy shall be given to the Chancellor of the University, and one copy to the Head of every College, and one copy to the Mayor of the city of Oxford, and one copy to be put into the Bodleian Library; and the expense of printing them shall be paid out of the revenue of the Lands or Estates given for establishing the Divinity Lecture Sermons; and the Preacher shall not be paid, nor be entitled to the revenue, before they are printed.

"Also I direct and appoint, that no person shall be qualified to preach the Divinity Lecture Sermons, unless he hath taken the Degree of Master of Arts at least, in one of the two Universities of Oxford or Cambridge; and that the same person shall never preach the Divinity Lecture Sermons twice."

PREFACE

THESE lectures make no pretence of being a history of the Church during the last four centuries; for such a history could not well be compressed within so small a compass. They are only a few studies and sketches which I hoped might be useful in present circumstances to members of the University.

When the lectures were delivered it was explained that the phrase 'Modern Protestantism' bore no reference to English Evangelicalism. The words were used in the technical sense employed in Germany and Holland, signifying a form of Theism which respects Jesus Christ but denies His essential Deity. It was also explained that the word 'Modernist' was not used in the sense which it bears in Rousseau, but in the more recent sense brought from France into England; namely, to denote one who holds that he is morally justified in repeating the ancient creeds and prayers of the Church while repudiating the meaning of important phrases in those creeds or prayers. I have criticized Modernism solely in that restricted sense; for I believe that it is possible to combine all modern learning with a loyal adherence to the great Catholic truths for the defence of which the Bampton lectures were founded.

In preparing this work for the press I have been largely indebted to the care and interest of the Rev. F. E. Brightman, Fellow of Magdalen College, and of my brother, Mr. P. D. Pullan.

SYNOPSIS OF CONTENTS

LECTURE I

THE COUNTER-REFORMATION AND THE DOCTRINE OF GRACE

                                                                                   PAGE

1. The year 1521 a turning-point in history. The history of the Indulgence system. Luther's teaching on Indulgences and Justification. His practical influence 1
2. The Counter-Reformation organized in Italy . . . 8
   Theological importance of the Council of Trent.
       i. Protestant doctrines as to the Bible, sin, and grace condemned, but
       ii. The exact relation of the Pope to the Church left undefined.
3. The reform of clerical life in Italy 13
   St. Charles Borromeo in Milan.
   St. Philip Neri in Rome. Reaction against infrequent communion.
4. The so-called golden age of the Church of Spain . . . 16
   Mystical writers.
   St. Ignatius de Loyola. The revolution in Monasticism. Influence of his ' Spiritual Exercises '.
   St. Francis de Xavier. Missions in Asia.
   St. Teresa and the Carmelites.
5. France and the revival of sacred learning 23
   St. Francis de Sales and the Calvinists.
   Fénelon. Bossuet, a symbol of his epoch.
6. Jansenists and Augustinianism. Jesuits and Probabilism. Moral principles at stake. Pascal. His opposition to Probabilism and Scepticism 26
7. Evolution in the resistance to Protestantism. Failure of the Gallicans to preserve a middle path between Lutheranism and Ultramontanism. Need of such a path 31

SYNOPSIS OF CONTENTS ix

LECTURE II

RELIGION IN GREAT BRITAIN FROM 1550 TO 1689

PAGE

1. By 1550 the position of the English Church defined. General condition of religion between 1550 and death of Elizabeth. England and the Popes. Strength of Romanism in the northern counties . 34

2. Puritanism and the sects 42
    a. Presbyterians within the Church.
    b. Anabaptists break up the mediaeval conception of religion.
    c. The English and the American Congregationalists. All Calvinistic and oppose Episcopacy.

3. The attempt to reconstruct 44
    Parker.
    Hooker, Donne.
    Andrewes.
    Laud.
    A reformed Catholicism.

4. Scotland. The Reformation. Knox, Melville . . . 52
    Introduction of Episcopacy.
    The so-called Laud's liturgy.
    The National League and Covenant. Collapse of Episcopacy in the south of Scotland.

5. Cromwell and the Church 58

6. Charles II and the Church 60
    Renewed troubles in Scotland.
    Was reconciliation between Anglicans and Nonconformists in England possible ?
    Calvinism of the Nonconformists. Its later tendency to Unitarianism.

7. The Prayer Book of 1662 : 'lex orandi, lex credendi.' Ecclesiastical art (Wren) an index to that harmony between the ancient and the modern which marked the beginning of the English Reformation . . 66

x RELIGION SINCE THE REFORMATION

LECTURE III

CONTINENTAL PROTESTANTISM FROM 1520 TO 1700
PAGE
1. The common features of the reforming movements . . 68
2. The divisions of Continental Protestantism.
    a. Luther's attitude to Catholicism and the Bible . 70
    b. Zwingli, humanist, splits Protestantism by his anti-sacramentalism 74
    c. Calvin. Predestination. Attempt to rebuild belief in Church and Bible 77
    d. Socinus, anti-Trinitarian. 'Tota iacet Babylon' . 80
3. Deep religious and ethical differences between Lutheranism and Calvinism. Patriarchal system *v.* Theocracy. Calvinism gains 81
4. Development of Lutheranism. Scholasticism, worship, hymns, mysticism 83
    Calixtus in England.
    Grabe in England.
5. Development of Calvinism. Geneva and scholarship. The learned abandon strict Calvinism. Cameron . 89
    Casaubon in England.
    Voss in England.
    Study of Continental Protestantism leads to an appreciation of the Anglican position.
6. Protestantism in Holland. Calvinist, but modified by wealth and enterprise. Arminius defends free-will. The State controls the Church. Amsterdam a centre of art and toleration. William III . . . 92
7. Pietism in Holland and Germany. Its origin international, largely English. New devotion to the Bible . . 95
    Voet, Spener.
    Pietism goes from England (Bayly) back to England (Wesley).

LECTURE IV

THE ROMAN CATHOLIC CHURCH FROM 1700 TO 1854
1. Strong position and gradual extension of Roman Catholicism *c.* 1700. Would it become universal? . . 98
2. Relation of national Churches to the Universal Church. Gallican *v.* Ultramontane theory of the Papacy. The Bull *Unigenitus* divides the French Church . 100

SYNOPSIS OF CONTENTS

PAGE

3. Attempted reunion of Gallicans and Anglicans. Louis XV. Defeat of those who appealed to the primitive Church. Ecclesiastical art significant of this defeat 105
4. National and reforming movements in the Church outside France 108
   a. Febronianism limits papal claims.
   b. Reforms of Maria Theresa.
   c. Joseph II and Leopold II : a State Church.
   Suppression of the Jesuits by the Pope in 1773. Its futility.
5. Missionary work of Spain. Serra in California . . . 113
6. Roman Catholicism in England. Bishop Challoner. 'The old religion': its moderation. English Roman Catholic bishops deny papal infallibility . 115
7. The French Revolution. Increasing persecution of the Church. French bishops in England. Pius VII. Napoleon I and the Papacy 118
   The Concordat. Reorganization of the Church.
8. The authority of St. Augustine replaced by that of Alphonsus Liguori. Pius IX his disciple. Triumph of Ultramontanism 125
   a. In doctrine.
   b. In moral theology.
   A French prelate, Mgr. d'Hulst, estimates the result . 128

LECTURE V

RELIGION IN GREAT BRITAIN AND AMERICA FROM 1689 TO 1815

1. The secession of the Nonjurors. Survey of religion: strength of the Church c. 1700 130
2. The quest for 'another Gospel, which is not another'. The revolt against the Creeds 132
   a. Deism and the 'Religion of Nature'. The opponents of Deism: Law, Leslie, Butler 134
   b. Arianism. Should Christ be worshipped if His Deity be denied? English Dissent becomes Arian. Clarke, Taylor, Priestley 137
3. Hoadly the latitudinarian and Law the mystic . . . 142

xii   RELIGION SINCE THE REFORMATION

PAGE

4. The revival of religion. Could the Methodist organizations have been kept within the Church ? Wesley made schism inevitable 144
Extraordinary gifts of Wesley and Whitefield.
Danger of antinomianism (seen by Fletcher).
The effect of the Evangelical movement.
5. Profound effect of the fall of the Stuarts on religion in Scotland and America 149
In Scotland Episcopacy stronger than Presbyterianism but gradually crushed by persecution. A remnant survived. Diary of Bishop Forbes.
Consecration of Bishop Seabury for Connecticut.
Sir Walter Scott.
6. Survey of religion in America. The Church strangled by the British Government 155
 a. The Connecticut converts strengthen the Church.
 b. Among the Puritans Calvinism led to Unitarianism. 'The Boston religion.' Its failure.
Religious value of the doctrines of the Incarnation and the Trinity 159

LECTURE VI

ASPECTS OF LUTHERANISM AND CALVINISM SINCE 1700

1. Pietism (continued). The Moravians : Zinzendorf. Missions in America. Protestant monasticism in America : Beissel, Miller 161
2. Opposition to Pietism at Halle. Wolff's philosophy. Frederick the Great 166
Influence of English Deism. Toland.
Influence of Voltaire and French sceptics.
The result is the 'Illumination' (1751). Protestantism without Christianity.
3. Lessing and Reimarus : Pantheism and Deism. Theology of Semler and his contemporaries: victims of their predecessors 169
4. Kant. Rationalism supreme. Mutilation of Church services and hymns. Rousseau's challenge to the Arian ministers of Geneva. Protestantism in Holland. Bilderdijk 172

SYNOPSIS OF CONTENTS xiii

PAGE

5. Partial opposition to Rationalism on part of leaders of German culture *c.* 1800. Klopstock, Herder, Schiller, Goethe 176

6. Romanticism, philosophic and literary, becomes religious. Leads to Romanism in reaction against Rationalism. Vain attempt to strengthen Protestantism by the forcible union of Lutherans and Calvinists in 1817. Genius of Schleiermacher. Value attached to the idea of a Church 179

7. Ritschl follows Schleiermacher. Their merits and defects . 184
Tübingen criticism; Harnack.
Disintegration of Continental Protestantism. ' Modern ' or ' Liberal ' Protestantism summarized by Troeltsch 189

LECTURE VII

THE EASTERN ORTHODOX CHURCH

1. Retrospect. The separation between the Eastern and the Western Church in 1054. Its effect upon religion . 192

2. The fall of Constantinople in 1453 left Moscow as the great centre of Orthodoxy; but the Patriarch of Constantinople retained his position 196
Outline of Turkish policy towards the subject Christian population.

3. The Reformation affects the Eastern Church (Lutherans: Cyril Lucaris and Calvinism). The reaction: Peter Mogila. The official Greek theology remains that of 1672 199

4. Easterns and Anglicans. Eastern teaching as to : . . 202
    a. The procession of the Holy Spirit from the Father.
    b. The Eucharist: Russians modify Greek doctrine.
    c. Icons and the reality of Christ's manhood.
    d. Saints prayed to and prayed for.
Value of the Eastern conception of the Church . . 210

5. After 1700 the Church in the Turkish Empire under difficulties caused by 211
French diplomacy.
Phanariot Greek domination.

xiv   RELIGION SINCE THE REFORMATION

PAGE

6. The Non-Greek Churches once under the Turks free themselves from Phanariot Greek rule . . . 216
   a. Bulgarians.
   b. Arabs of Antioch.
   c. Rumanians.
   d. Serbians.
7. The Russian Church since Peter the Great. Holy Synod. Missions. Revival at the revolution. Persecution under Bolshevism. The Patriarch Tikhon. Certainty of new life 221

LECTURE VIII

ASPECTS OF CHRISTIAN THOUGHT SINCE 1815

1. .The downfall of Napoleon and the growth of Romanticism (continued). A new emphasis on the Church and the Kingdom of God in France, Germany, and England 225
2. The Oxford Movement and its critics : Pattison and Stanley v. Newman and Pusey. The movement essentially religious 229
   The Church as ' home for the lonely '.
   Newman on development of dogma.
3. The year 1835. Scientific Rationalism, starting from the ' Illumination ' of the eighteenth century, brings criticism to bear upon 238
   a. The origin of Christianity.
   b. The authenticity of the New Testament.
   Collapse of the Tübingen theory. Evil legacy of that theory in present treatment of the works of St. John and St. Paul 240
4. Superstition the reaction against scepticism. The Vatican Council of 1870. Success of Manning . . . 243
   The Pope made infallible.
   The excommunication of Döllinger.
   The protest of ' Old Catholicism '.
5. Reunion of Christendom. Value of the Anglican position for such reunion. Modernism as a ' *modus vivendi* between scepticism and superstition ' . . . 249
6. Effective union not possible without fundamental agreement as to the Person of Christ. Historical exegesis proves that the Church has correctly interpreted 252
   a. The nature of Christ's claim.
   b. The fact of the Resurrection.

APPENDED NOTES

LECTURE I

		PAGE
NOTE 1.	The Council of Trent on Indulgences	257
2.	The Council of Trent on Episcopacy	257
3.	The hymn attributed to St. Francis Xavier	258
4.	St. Francis Xavier's exposition of the creed	259
5.	The Five Condemned Propositions attributed to Jansenius	260
6.	A moral reason for supporting the Jansenists	260

LECTURE II

NOTE 7.	The First Prayer Book of Edward VI and the Canon of the Mass	261
8.	The excommunication of Queen Elizabeth	262
9.	British Calvinism	263
10.	The Pope as Antichrist	264

LECTURE III

NOTE 11.	The Position of the Church of Sweden	264
12.	The languages spoken by the Sephardic Jews in Amsterdam and London	266

LECTURE IV

NOTE 13.	Roman Catholicism in Amsterdam	267
14.	The Sephardic synagogue in Bevis Marks, London	267
15.	Medals commemorating the suppression of the Jesuits	268
16.	The Protestation of the English Roman Catholics in 1789	268
17.	The cultus of the hearts of Jesus and Mary	270

LECTURE V

NOTE 18.	The Wesleyan Methodist and Calvinistic Methodist Schisms	272
19.	Political Principles of the Scottish Episcopalians in the time of George I	273
20.	Early American Church Architecture	274
21.	The Lapse of American Congregationalism into Unitarianism	275

LECTURE VI

NOTE 22.	Goethe on the Sacraments	276

LECTURE VII

		PAGE
NOTE 23. The Greek rite in Italian Churches	.	277
24. Constantinople and Anglican Ordinations	.	279

LECTURE VIII

NOTE 25. Newman on the Anglican Position	.	281
26. Newman on Transubstantiation	.	281
27. The Return to the traditional Dates of many Books of the New Testament	.	282
28. The 'Jesus of History'	.	284
INDEX	.	285

I

THE COUNTER-REFORMATION AND THE DOCTRINE OF GRACE

Romans iii. 24: Being justified freely by his grace, through the redemption that is in Christ Jesus.

LET us think of that memorable year, the year of our Lord 1521. In that year the terrible army of the Turks began to threaten central Europe. In that year a European empire first annexed a great part of the new world. In that year died Pope Leo X and with him the Papacy of the Renaissance began to descend into the grave. And in 1521 Martin Luther was finally excommunicated, and Ignatius de Loyola was converted. On the one side was the German friar who had burnt the Pope's bull with theatrical display in front of an enthusiastic mob. On the other side was a soldier of Spain lying sick, taking a turn for the better when almost at the point of death, reading the life of Christ and resolving to be His penitent servant.

Now Martin Luther and Ignatius de Loyola did what they did, and we are what we are, because Leo X had been in want of money. The late Pope Julius II had determined to rebuild the venerable basilica which Constantine erected near to the circus of Nero where St. Peter was crucified; and to raise funds for a grandiose new church Leo 'published indulgences throughout the Christian regions'. *Indulgentia* in Christian Latin meant forgiveness or remission, or, as our forefathers called it, a 'pardon'. And Luther in Germany and Zwingli in Switzerland separately began a revolution by attacking, not indulgences, but the granting of indulgences as a means of raising money. Leo X had previously offered an indulgence for all sins and 'reconciliation with the most High' without even mentioning confession or contrition, and, if not in intention, yet in effect, the preaching of indulgences in Germany by Tetzel meant that the pardon won by the precious blood of Christ could be secured for the souls in purgatory by a piece of money and a paper certificate.

It is evident that the whole question of the Pope's authority is involved in the theory of these indulgences, whether that theory be unimpeachable or not. And it is now freely stated by Roman Catholic writers that indulgences were converted into 'money transactions' and a 'traffic', and that the greatest abuses prevailed. In fact the discipline which had originally existed for the purpose of deepening repentance for sins had been made into a system for doubling the revenue of the Papal States. We must briefly notice some stages in this miserable decline.

In the primitive Church a Christian who had committed a heinous sin, especially such sins as fornication or idolatry, and then repented and confessed his sin to his bishop or a priest appointed by the bishop, had to undergo a course of penitential discipline of prayer and fasting before he received absolution and was once again permitted to receive the holy communion. So high was the moral standard demanded by the Church that it was not until late in the fourth century that the question was even raised whether a person who had sinned against the second or the seventh commandment should receive absolution for a second offence. It rested with the local Church to determine whether the spiritual condition of the penitent demanded a long discipline or justified some indulgence and a comparatively early absolution and remission of this temporal chastisement.[1]

By the end of the Middle Ages this wholesome system

---

[1] For the early history of Penance see Pierre Batiffol, 'Les Origines de la Pénitence' in *Études d'Histoire et de Théologie Positive* (Lecoffre, Paris, 1902).

had become seriously corrupted by a combination of different evils. It was not a corruption that the Keltic practice of treating the whole process of confession and penance as strictly private had gradually spread from the British Isles to the south of Europe.[1] But it was a corruption that absolution for heinous sins was granted before the penitent had undergone any adequate testing or discipline and that donations in money were sometimes regarded as a suitable reparation for ill-doing. Moreover, the whole subject became involved in a very precarious doctrine concerning purgatory and the merits of the saints.

The penitent was taught that though he was forgiven as Moses and David were forgiven, yet, like them, he must be prepared to suffer some temporal punishment. He must make amends to God whose majesty had been outraged. If he did not pay to God this satisfaction while he lived, he must after death before he entered heaven pay it by suffering the torments of purgatory. And this was understood to mean that he must undergo something more than the discipline, the formative trials, which God sends us for the good of our character even when a sin has been forgiven. It meant the payment of an expiation by bitter suffering, an agony like the agony of hell, although the Roman canon of the mass, full of primitive doctrine, speaks of the faithful departed as resting in the sleep of peace. Could this awful punishment be mitigated or escaped? Rome said 'Yes; the Church has an inexhaustible treasure, not only in the infinite merits of Christ, but in the works which the saints have done over and above what was necessary for their salvation. Part of this overplus might be credited to the repentant sinner.' And in 1343 Pope Clement VI announced in virtue of this treasure a full pardon of sins to pilgrims who were truly penitent and had confessed.

[1] See O. D. Watkins, *A History of Penance*, vol. ii, pp. 750 ff. (Longmans, London, 1920).

Then the question arose, May an indulgence be sought for a father, a mother, a child no longer living? Again Rome said 'Yes'. In 1476 Pope Sixtus IV wrote that if parents and friends who wished to help those who were exposed 'to the fire of purgatory for the expiation of sins' would pay 'a certain sum of money' for the repair of the church at Xanten, he willed that the money should avail *per modum suffragii* for the souls aforesaid. The donation was to be considered as a recommendation to the Almighty for a plenary remission of punishment. This is the first known instance of an indulgence being applied to the souls in purgatory, and it gave rise to dreams of avarice which in the next century hardened into one of the worst scandals in Christian history.

When Julius II died, 70,000 ducats had already been spent on the new basilica of St. Peter and it was still far from completion. Leo X, a patron of the arts, wanted to complete it, and Albert of Brandenburg had been elected to the great position of Archbishop of Mainz. Albert had to pay a huge sum before the Pope would give him the pallium, the narrow scarf which had originally been a decoration given as a compliment, but had become a symbol of metropolitan jurisdiction. He had to borrow money through bankers in Augsburg, and it was arranged that in consideration of a cash payment to the Pope of 10,000 ducats, Albert's agents might dispose of indulgences. Half the proceeds were to go to the Pope and the rest was to be retained by the Archbishop. The bargain was concluded on April the 15th, 1515. The Dominican John Tetzel was entrusted with the task of preaching up the indulgences, and he was accompanied by an agent of the bankers. Among the blessings promised to the donors of money was a plenary remission of all sins and all punishment due to sin. For this an expression of penitence was necessary. But for the souls already in purgatory a plenary indulgence *per modum suffragii* was also offered, and for such an indulgence nothing was required except, as Tetzel said, 'the rattling of the penny in the box'. He simply put into crude German what the Popes had written in scholastic Latin. He did it with the zeal of a revivalist and the acuteness of an auctioneer, and in due time he was rewarded with the degree of Doctor of Divinity.

Luther was resolved to test the real doctrine of Rome on the subject, and for this purpose he nailed up on the door of All Saints' Church in Wittenberg, the University church where notices were usually posted, ninety-five short theses concerning Penance and Indulgences.[1]

The theology of the theses into which Luther flung his indignation, and the history of the subsequent controversies, I cannot explain at length. But there are two facts which must be borne in mind if we are to understand the religious significance of his action. They are quite apart from the scandal that a money payment had been taken for the release of souls already in purgatory. The first is that throughout his early protest against indulgences Luther held that a Christian who has truly repented and has been truly absolved is by grace in union with Christ and shares in the benefits of the merits of Christ and of His whole mystical body, the Church—and that therefore the Pope can give him no further indulgence except a remission of ecclesiastical penalty: an argument which appears to be unanswerable unless it be openly stated by papal authority that any indulgence beyond a remission of ecclesiastical penalty is not a pardon, but a prayer for more abundant grace. The second fact is that it is proved by his conference with Cardinal Cajetan that Luther had to defend himself

---

[1] These theses and all the important documents of the Indulgence controversy are printed in B. J. Kidd, *Documents Illustrative of the Continental Reformation* (Oxford, 1911).

against the charge of having maintained that it is necessary for a person who approaches the sacrament of penance to believe that he is obtaining grace. It is possible that in this connexion a heterodox meaning might be put upon his words *sola fides verbi Christi iustificat*. But his statement as a whole is an attempt, not to disparage sacramental confession to a priest, but to make it more serious and less perfunctory, to treat it as a real means of grace in which the penitent takes Christ at His word.

It is one of the greatest tragedies in history that a man with such an overwhelming force of character, a born leader of men, did as a result of the unmeasured violence of his language and the one-sided nature of his doctrine bring no moral deliverance to his people. Luther's more patient friend Melanchthon tells us how at Ratisbon in 1541 he and the other Protestant representatives came to an agreement with the Roman theologians on the central doctrine of justification by faith. And in the joy which he felt at that agreement our Cardinal Pole wrote, 'I give thanks to God through Christ'. But Luther was implacable. His own doctrine of justification by faith was an eager and passionate attempt to revive the doctrine of St. Paul. But his doctrine is by no means purely Pauline. He was familiar with the scholastic distinction between *fides informis* and *fides formata cum charitate*. But while the schoolmen said that only a faith formed with love rendered a man acceptable to God, Luther said that this love was not necessary for justification, and that it would introduce the idea of winning acceptance by good works. This inadequate and unscriptural view of faith, a view which finds expression in his contemptuous reference to the Epistle of St. James, was attended by other no less serious mistakes. From his experience of the power of sin and of the miserable weakness of the human will, and his deep sense of the need of a Saviour, Luther concluded, like the later Calvinists, that human nature has been totally corrupted by Adam's fall, a theory which in time prompted men to deny that there is any inherited defect in the nature that is ours by physical descent. Next he denied the freedom of the human will, and thereby lessened man's sense of responsibility. Thirdly, he took a most pessimistic view of the character, or rather the nature, of even the converted Christian. He held, and the Calvinists did the same, that the tendency to wrong desires within us, the *concupiscentia* from which no Christian is wholly free, is in itself sin. The infirmities which cannot be avoided are confused with the sin which can be avoided, and the fundamental distinction between the mere feeling of an incitement to sin, and a deliberate consent of the will to that feeling, is destroyed. And the sinner is then consoled by the doctrine that when he believes, and so long as he believes, all his sins are as venial sins. It was therefore, though rhetoric, not mere rhetoric, when Luther wrote, 'Be a sinner, and sin lustily, but be more lusty in faith and rejoice in Christ. . . . Sin will not pluck us away from Him, even though a thousand times, a thousand times a day, we commit fornication or murder.'[1]

What is that but an indulgence—an indulgence no longer purchased by money but by an emotion? And what was the effect of this teaching? It is needless to quote his enemies. It is enough to read his own words, and the evidence is thus summed up by an admirer: 'In passage after passage Luther declares that the last state of things was worse than the first; that vice of every kind had increased since the Reformation; that the nobles were greedy, the peasants brutal; that the corruption of morals in Wittenberg itself was so great that he contemplated shaking off the dust of his feet against it; that Christian

---

[1] *Epistolarum D. M. Lutheri*, tom. i, a Jo. Aurifabro collectus, p. 345 b. Jhenae, 1556, Bodl. Tratt. Luth. 370; and Enders, *Dr. M. Luthers Briefwechsel*, iii. 208 (Kalw u. Stuttgart, 1884).

liberality had altogether ceased to flow; and that the preachers were neither held in respect nor supported by the people.'[1]

For the whole study of Continental Protestantism it is of the first importance to remember that by minimizing human freedom, and by teaching that there is only one effective Will in the universe, Luther prepared for Pantheism as well as for Antinomianism, and the Pantheism of the classical German writers has been one of the greatest barriers in the way of any revival of Christianity in modern Germany.

The beginning of Church reform in Italy shows a consciousness of the antagonism which existed between the Italian Renaissance and the Gospel. This antagonism some of the Popes had tried to disguise by uniting paganism and Christianity in their own persons. Other men saw more deeply and understood what an abyss had separated life and faith. And before we consider the important part which was taken by Spain in promoting the Counter-Reformation, we must recall what Italian brains were able to accomplish.

Italy was not only the cradle of the Renaissance which became the torchbearer of the Reformation. It was also the home of a reformed Papacy which was able to arrest the progress of the Reformation. Italians were able to set in motion the gigantic machinery which at the end of the sixteenth century affected the whole world then known to civilized mankind. A religious reaction had begun in Italy several years before the Papacy had thoroughly roused itself to reform. Almost immediately after Luther's excommunication we find in Italy itself a growth of new religious orders, some of which were concerned directly with the education and improvement of the clergy. Such were the

[1] Charles Beard, *The Reformation of the Sixteenth Century*, Hibbert Lectures, 1883, p. 145 (Williams & Norgate, London, 1883). See too J. Chevalier, *Revue Catholique des Églises*, Mai 1908, p. 287 (Paris, 83 Rue des Saints-Pères).

Theatines and the Barnabites, with whom may be mentioned the Capuchins, who endeavoured to bring back the Franciscans to their primitive severity of life. Other orders were devoted to the instruction of the young. To these belong the Somaschans, founded for the care of orphans, and the Ursulines, a sisterhood founded for the education of girls, famous at a later time for their work in Quebec and New Orleans.

We find also in Rome, in Venice, in Padua, and especially in Naples, little groups, little societies of well-educated ecclesiastics, literary men and noble ladies, animated by a really religious spirit, disturbed by the thought of the moral disorder and theological degeneracy which weakened Christianity. They were deeply interested in the nature of faith and justification through the redemption won by Christ. Interest in these questions gradually developed three distinct tendencies. The first tendency was that of the men who went not only as far as Luther but far beyond him in their negation of traditional Christianity, a tendency represented by Peter Martyr, Bernardino Ochino, and afterwards by the Sozzini whose teaching was merely on the frontier of Christianity. The second tendency appears in John Valdes, a Spaniard who lived at Naples and was the author of several original mystical writings;[1] and we find in sympathy with the same central tendency Morone, Bishop of Modena, Cardinals Pole and Sadoleto, and Gaspar Contarini, the leader of the party. They represented the highest and the most uncorrupt Catholicism of Italy, and for a time their fervour seemed likely to become a fashion. But the programme of Contarini was abandoned amid the tangle of political events and the tightening grip of Spain upon a distracted Italy. The movement for a reformation

[1] Among them the *Hundred and Ten Considerations*. All copies of the original edition were suppressed by the Spanish Inquisition. It is of special interest to English Churchmen as it was translated from Italian into English by Nicholas Ferrar at the instigation of George Herbert and published at Oxford in 1638.

without rebellion, and for discipline without despotism, failed also for another reason. It did not fail because its leaders were utopian. To succeed greatly it is necessary to dream dreams and to see visions. The failure was caused by the fact that the movement was too exclusively aristocratic and academic. It made no effort to reach the common people, and its labours became isolated and individualistic.

The third tendency in Italy met Protestantism with the whole force of resistance and reaction. Paul III, the Pope who favoured Pole and Contarini, gave his sanction in 1540 to the newly formed Spanish Society of Jesus, and by the introduction of the Inquisition in 1542 he definitely checked the circulation of books of a Protestant character. And in his honest anxiety for reform he summoned in 1545 the Council of Trent which laid the dogmatic and the disciplinary basis of the Counter-Reformation.

The sessions of the Council were prolonged for more than eighteen years. Its beginning was feeble, and serious doubts were entertained as to its ultimate issue. But the issue left the Roman Catholic Church presenting a compact united front to the teaching of Luther and Calvin though still containing different schools of thought. Among the numerous reforms effected must be mentioned the abolition of the office of *quaestors* or indulgence preachers, the better education of candidates for the priesthood, and the prohibition of the accumulation of benefices in the possession of the same ecclesiastic. Strange to say, the doctrine of indulgences was left indeterminate, although the use of indulgences was said to be 'very salutary' and recent abuses were strongly condemned.[1] Otherwise there was a great consolidation of dogma. At the Fourth Session (8 April 1546) the written books of Scripture and the unwritten traditions 'received by the apostles from the mouth of Christ himself, or from the apostles themselves' were put upon the same level of

[1] See app. note 1, p. 257.

authority. At the Fifth (17 June 1546) a moderate view was taken of concupiscence diametrically opposed to the Lutheran and Calvinist views that it is truly and properly sin. At the Sixth (13 January 1547) it was affirmed that free will was not extinguished by the fall and that a man can accept or refuse grace, so that he can by God's help take a real share in preparing for his justification. It was also affirmed that no one can have an absolute assurance that he possesses grace, and that a man who commits mortal sin loses grace even if he has faith. Thus was Protestantism definitely excluded.

Hardly less important was the question discussed during the later sessions of the Council. It involved the whole problem of the relation of the episcopate to the Papacy. If the manners of bishops were to be reformed, what was to be done with the officials who had been rewarded for their services by the gift of bishoprics in which they never intended to reside? The existence of this abuse, an abuse which had a parallel in England in modern times, found ingenious defenders. They said that though the order of a bishop is an ordinance of Christ, the jurisdiction which he exercises over his diocese is given by the Pope, and therefore if a bishop is truly consecrated but receives no jurisdiction from the Pope, he is not obliged to visit his see. The energetic bishops of Spain vigorously defended the ancient view that the powers of a bishop are derived from Christ independently of the Pope. They were opposed by their fellow countryman the Jesuit Laynez, who thus inaugurated the policy which Cardinal Manning is said to have summed up in the saying that the Pope is the only plank left between the Jesuits and the Presbyterians. The Council finally adopted certain skilfully drafted canons which left the question open, though their tenor is rather in favour of the Papacy.[1] The bishops failed to secure a clear recognition

[1] See app. note 2, p. 257.

of their rights, and the result was that though the Council did allow some privileges to certain national Churches, these Churches which remained in union with Rome gradually became less national and more Roman. However, the question as to whether the Pope is infallible and can himself decide without the episcopate what is the true tradition of the Church was left untouched. It was still quite permissible to hold that the bishops had independent rights apart from the Pope and to deny the Pope's infallibility.

Compared with the more recent developments and accretions in Roman Catholic teaching, the decrees and canons of the Council of Trent are moderate and well balanced. The doctrine of grace and of the seven sacraments as means of grace is in its main outlines, though not always in detail and in language, in harmony with the teaching of the New Testament. The Nicene Creed, which states nothing which the Gospels do not imply, was left in itself intact. And though it is an exaggeration, it is not a violent exaggeration, on the part of the most distinguished of German Protestant theologians, when he says, 'The mediaeval Church went forth from the Council of Trent as still substantially the ancient Church'.[1] And it went forth strong. Henceforth all religion and all life, all arts and all sciences, were to be brought more closely than ever under the rule of the Papacy. There could be no better emblem of this reformed Papacy than the new basilica of St. Peter with its immense façade rising at the end of the wide square and its embracing colonnades. The proportions of the church are faulty, and it has none of the mystery of sorrow and thirst for God that many older churches appear to voice. But it offers a welcome to the world, and the spirit of it is militant, expectant, and all but triumphant.

---

[1] 'Die mittelalterliche Kirche ging aus dem Tridentinum wesentlich als die alte hervor.' Adolf Harnack, *Lehrbuch der Dogmengeschichte*, vol. iii, p. 616 (Freiburg i. B., 1890).

Before the Council closed, there had appeared in Mexico the first important work of an American printing press. It was a superb edition of the Roman Missal.

Italy, Spain, and France may be considered in turn as respectively centres of the reform of clerical life, the revolution in monasticism, and the revival of Christian learning.

'These most illustrious lords require a most illustrious reform', remarked the good Archbishop of Braga concerning the cardinals. And that reform was exemplified by St. Charles Borromeo (1538-1584), Cardinal Archbishop of Milan. He is the connecting link between the Italian episcopate of the Renaissance and that of the Christian reaction. He was a member of a noble family whose seat was amid the Italian lakes. According to the custom of the period, he received the tonsure at the age of eight, and at the age of thirteen became the titular abbot of a monastery at Arona which was regarded as a mere dependency of his family. His uncle, Pope Pius IV, whose coronation took place on January the 6th, 1560, promptly summoned his nephew to Rome to enter his diplomatic service, and even the unpleasant experiences of his predecessor did not keep the new Pope from loading a youthful relative with every conceivable dignity. He was soon made a cardinal and then administrator of the vast diocese of Milan, though he was not yet a priest. A young man of twenty-two, he was not only surrounded with almost royal magnificence, but even exposed to temptations which remind us of the Roman debauchery of the previous generation. He kept his head and he also kept the issues of his heart. He had distinguished himself at the University of Pavia, and he now worked with a will at his diplomatic correspondence and made his house a centre of refinement and philosophic discussion. He loved to take part in Latin debates and confesses that he found it one thing to deliver a speech in Latin and another thing to answer questions in that language. The Pope, wishing his noble family to be saved from extinction, desired him to abandon a clerical career, but in spite of the Pope's wishes he was ordained priest in August 1563, shortly before the close of the Council of Trent. He had displayed great skill in acting as an intermediary between the Pope and the Council. He helped to smooth away the differences between the papal and the episcopal party. He edited the celebrated Roman Catechism of the Council of Trent, and he supervised new editions of the Vulgate, the Missal, and the Breviary.

On the death of his uncle in 1565 he took possession of his see, to which he devoted his whole future. His private life was one of severe simplicity. He improved the character of the clergy, organized the diocese, and set to work to reform the monasteries.[1] He met with the strongest opposition, especially from the order of the Humiliati, who hired an assassin to shoot him at the altar. The shot only grazed his skin, and during the famine of the next year, 1570, and the great plague of 1576 his unsparing devotion to the sufferers finally won the hearts of the turbulent Milanese. Included in the large library which he bequeathed to his successors are no less than ninety-six treatises on medicine, which were probably bought at the time of the plague. In matters of art he had good taste, and he studied the ancient basilicas that the new churches of his diocese might be simple and dignified in their architecture. What was equally important for future generations, he was the means of saving the ancient Ambrosian liturgy for his diocese. Theologians of to-day know that the history of Christian worship must be studied if we are to understand the history of Christianity itself. And with the exception of two solitary churches in Spain, no ancient non-Roman Latin rite survives anywhere

---

[1] The advice given by St. Charles Borromeo to his clergy is summarized in his *Pastorum Instructiones* (nova editio, Rothomagi, 1767).

except in the archdiocese of Milan. We owe it to St. Charles that in spite of strong pressure he refused to introduce the Roman liturgy and secured the survival of the venerable prayers and ceremonies at which we can still assist in the vast cathedral where he worshipped.

St. Charles visited Switzerland in 1570, often travelling on foot through the hamlets in the mountains. His visit resulted in the establishing of a nuncio at Lucerne and in the foundation of a league which two years after his death bound the Roman Catholic cantons to take arms against those cantons which tolerated heresy. He was a man of his own period. He was not opposed to coercion in religious matters, but he nipped in the bud the plan of Philip II to introduce into Lombardy an Inquisition of the pitiless Spanish pattern. He spent much time in private prayer and often went on pilgrimage to hallowed shrines. It would be absurd to blame him if he believed that at Turin he saw the winding sheet in which the body of Christ was laid, and that at Loretto he saw, encrusted with goodly offerings, the original holy home of Nazareth. He was generous to his family, but he did not try to enrich his kindred with gold and titles. And as he lived in the sixteenth century, we may venture to think that one of the best proofs of his real goodness is the fact that when his beloved sister was left a widow, and wished to retire into a convent, he persuaded her to stay at home and look after her children.

With the name of St. Charles must be linked that of St. Philip Neri (1515–1595), who came to be regarded as the new apostle of the eternal city.[1] He refused the help of a rich relative who wished him to devote himself to commerce, and gave his care to the poor and the sick and the pilgrims who came to Rome. He had a great influence with young people and horrified the over-good by encouraging

---

[1] Life by P. G. Bacci with additions by G. Ricci, *Vita di S. Filippo Neri* (Roma, 1745).

dances and games. Like some other great Italians, he teaches us that it is not necessary to be sanctimonious in order to become a saint. The centre of his activities was a hall turned into an oratory for sermons, lectures, prayer meetings, and music, the word *Oratorio* being taken from the musical exercises that he fostered. Like St. Charles, he obeyed the wish expressed by the Council of Trent in urging upon others the duty of frequent communion, the neglect of which had proved one of the most fruitful causes of misapprehension and superstition with regard to the sacrifice of the mass. From the priests who associated themselves with his work St. Philip formed the congregation known as the Oratorians, not an order of monks, but a voluntary association of secular priests. The Oratory anticipated our modern parochial life with its clubs and societies radiating from the altar. In 1611 there was founded an Oratory in France, and among the many great French Oratorians is to be numbered the famous preacher Massillon (1663–1742) and in more recent times Gratry (1805–1872), a writer of exquisite simplicity and depth. It was the Oratory of St. Philip that proved a home to one, who, as old men have told me, spoke in this church words that came to them like a revelation, the man whose sensitive intellect and moving arguments are typified by his own motto, *Cor loquitur ad cor*—John Henry Newman.

Spaniards reckon the age of the Counter-Reformation as the golden age of the Church of Spain. The country was revelling in new wealth and knowledge. The Castilian language had just passed from youth to manhood. The Church was more episcopal and less papal than it became in later times, and was in the forefront of the work of education. The faith of the people was fanatically Catholic, tempered hard by their long struggle with the Moors and sharpened by their hatred and suspicion of the Jews. A few

Protestant books, now of excessive rarity, were printed in Castilian, but the majority of the people were in no mood to inquire into new religions; they were enthusiastically eager to express what they already believed. And this enthusiasm produced leaders of religion as original and as bold as the Spanish writers of imaginative literature. Some of the Spanish theological writers themselves show a literary capacity of the highest quality. Such are St. John of the Cross and Luis Ponce de León, of whom it has been said that he united the Hebrew thirst for righteousness with pagan serenity and the Christian charity which resists evil only with forgiveness. Time would fail me to speak of them or of St. Peter of Alcántara or Alfonso Rodríguez, whose book on 'Christian Perfection' might well be abbreviated for English use. But no reference to the religion of Spain could pass over St. Ignatius de Loyola and St. Francis de Xavier, though neither of them was strictly a Spaniard. Both were Spanish Basques, and these two members of that obscure primaeval race did more than any other men to make Rome to be once again 'maxima rerum'.[1]

And here let us give honour where honour is due. The subsequent decadence of the Jesuits gives us no more right to condemn St. Ignatius and his six companions than the corruption of the Franciscans gives us the right to blame St. Francis of Assisi. Ignatius founded his society in 1534 for the conversion of the heathen. When this work appeared for the present to be impossible, the Jesuits adapted themselves to preaching, pastoral visiting, and the instruction of youth. The society was a religious order founded upon military obedience, a principle which had appealed to St. Pachomius the Egyptian who founded monastic com-

---

[1] The literature dealing with the early history of the Jesuits is very large. The early Spanish Life of St. Ignatius is by Ribadeneira, 1594. An interesting Life in English is Francis Thompson's *Saint Ignatius Loyola* (Burns & Oates, London, 1909). Of importance are *Monumenta Historica Societatis Jesu* (Madrid, 1894–1914).

munities in the fourth century, and to General Booth who
founded the Salvation Army in the nineteenth. But Ignatius
revolutionized monasticism. It was an innovation for monks
to dress like the secular clergy. It was a startling innovation
to dispense monks from the duty of singing the long daily
and nightly services in choir, a custom which has survived
in a modified form in our cathedrals. It was a momentous
innovation to divide his disciples into six grades of which
only the highest took the most solemn and irrevocable vows.
The idea of a college for training young men in religion and
learning was not a novelty in Spain, but Ignatius gave it
fresh vitality. The success of the new order was amazing.
When the founder died in 1556 there were about a thousand
Jesuits grouped in twelve different provinces. Most of the
principal towns in Europe had Jesuit halls, and Ignatius himself had founded not only the great Collegium Romanum
for the teaching of philosophy and theology, but by a master
stroke of policy the Collegium Germanicum for carrying war
into the land of Luther.

But the ability of Ignatius was not confined to organization. He gave a new direction to the life of the soul. His
book of meditations and prayers called 'Spiritual Exercises'[1]
won an immediate and permanent success. The book is
penetrated by three ideas. The first is that Christ is a king
and the general of an army going forth to conquer. Here
we see a thought of chivalry subtly suggested, as it is subtly
suggested in a very different manner in the great romance
of Cervantes. The second idea is that we cannot conquer
unless we fight. There are some men who wish to be saved,
but will not destroy the obstacles that hinder their salvation. They like the end but not the means. We must
choose both the end and the means, discerning the real
nature both of the pleasures that weaken and of the pains

---

[1] *Exercicios espirituales.* A good translation into English with notes
is that by W. H. Longridge (Robert Scott, London, 1919).

that fortify. And the third idea is the need of finding a path in life, or if we have already entered upon a path, the need of making the best use of it.

The book is simple enough, but it contains such a variety of subjects treated with such vivacity that the interest of the reader is never allowed to flag, and the peculiar skill of the author is shown by the way in which he makes the reader use his imagination as a tonic to his will. Its inspiration and its energy do not come from the books which the biographers say that Ignatius had read. They come from the fact that, like the works of Thomas à Kempis and John Bunyan, this book was lived before it was written. If we would understand Roman Catholicism as an organization between 1520 and 1700, we must study the Council of Trent; if we would understand it as a religion, we must study the 'Spiritual Exercises' of St. Ignatius de Loyola.

Added to these exercises are certain *Rules for thinking with the Church*. These rules comprise some excellent advice as to a reverent caution in speaking about predestination, faith, and free will, and the usefulness of even a servile fear of God if filial fear has not yet been gained.[1] But they also contain a praise of scholastic theology which might be interpreted as encouraging a blind adherence to the views of the greater schoolmen, and the still more unfortunate phrase in Rule XIII, ' we ought always to be ready to believe that what seems to us white is black, if the hierarchical Church so define it '. Such sayings, together with the abject obedience to superiors which is enjoined in the Constitutions of the Society, tended to make every Jesuit a wheel in a great machine, a machine which might indeed be directed towards noble ends, but might also be equally harmful to the world and to the individual soul of every member of the Society.

[1] This last point is unfairly represented by M. Philippson, who does not quote the passage in full in his *La Contre-Révolution religieuse*, p. 116 (Paris, 1884).

St. Francis de Xavier (1506–1552) was an embodiment of the spirit of adventure.[1] That is why he is so intelligible to Englishmen, for we still have ears open to the call of adventure. Recent criticism has destroyed the belief that he was the author of the hymn that endears his name to so many of our people:

> My God, I love Thee, not because
> I hope for heaven thereby,
> Nor yet because who love thee not
> Are lost eternally.

But it has left us a convincing portrait of one of the greatest missionaries since the days of St. Paul. He set out in 1541 in a ship for the Portuguese colony of Goa. A loathsome fever broke out in the filthy ship, and this fastidious gentleman washed the linen and cooked the food of the sufferers. Goa itself needed an apostle. In spite of its flaunting wealth and fine new cathedral, it was a graveyard physically and morally. Even among the Portuguese of Goa he was able to witness to Christ. But he went on and onward in his tattered gown and old black hood along Travancore, the Fishery Coast, Malabar, Ceylon, and the Spice Islands. In Travancore alone he planted forty-five Christian settlements. He planted a mission among the Japanese, whose abilities he recognized and whose character he cleverly delineates. He died on an island near Hong-Kong in 1552 attended by a faithful Chinese servant, but his intense desire to enter China was unfulfilled. When he was dying and unconscious he spoke in a language neither Latin nor Spanish nor Portuguese. Doubtless it was the ancient Basque that he had talked in his mother's tapestried room when he was a child in their old castle below the Pyrenees. He was every inch a man,

---

[1] Life with full Bibliography by Edith Anne Stewart, *The Life of St. Francis Xavier* (Headley, London, 1917). For the hymn, see app. note 3, p. 258.

able to make himself at home with a Brahmin or a pirate, and as for the Indian children, they sometimes left him time neither to read his prayers nor to go to sleep. There is one fruit of his missionary zeal which has not received all the attention that it deserves. He wrote for the benefit of his converts a long instruction in the Malay language, an exposition of the Christian faith following the lines of the Apostles' Creed. It is quite as remarkable for what it omits as for what it contains. There is a mention of the Pope and a few lines about the torments of purgatory, but the absence of peculiarly Roman Catholic doctrine is almost complete. The guide of innumerable souls, a man whose faith became ' a passionate intuition ', he put the first things first.[1]

In St. Teresa (1515–1582), the reformer of the Carmelites, we see the essence of the old Castilian spirit. It is something both distinguished and distinctive. It is a peculiar union of idealism and homeliness, of mysticism and common sense, of courage and submission to God. It is distinctive, and in her case it is marked by a special experimental knowledge of God. And yet it is not remote from that which all men, except the very worst, hope to find in a good woman.[2]

Her writings enable us to understand her from her childhood, when she was handsome and vivacious, well educated and well dressed. At an early age she discerned the difference between good and evil and resolved to lead a virtuous life, partly from the fear of God but still more because she respected the current laws of a woman's honour. Slowly the fear of God began to soften into the love of God. She read the letters of St. Jerome, those piquant Latin letters which praise virginity and throw such a cold hard light upon the semi-Christian society of Rome in the fourth century of the Christian era. She resolved to be a nun, and at the

---

[1] See app. note 4, p. 259.
[2] *Vida de la Santa Madre Teresa de Jesús* (Administración del apostolado de la prensa, Madrid, 1911).

age of eighteen she entered the Carmelite convent of the Incarnation at Avila, an embattled city built on a rock set in a treeless tableland of Old Castile.

It was not until Teresa's fortieth year that she found real peace with God. She dated her true progress in the spiritual life from a day when she saw in an oratory a statue of our Lord covered with wounds. She was smitten with intense grief at the thought of her want of gratitude for the love of Christ. She knelt down, weeping abundantly, and prayed for strength never to offend Him henceforth. Soon afterwards she read for the first time the 'Confessions' of St. Augustine, and she remained deeply influenced by his teaching. Like Augustine, she was convinced of the power of God's grace, and made her own his words, 'Lord, command what thou wilt, and give what thou commandest'. From the time of her conversion she became subject to trances and visions which her confessor regarded with suspicion and the sisters of the convent ascribed to devils. At first she thought that their explanation might be correct, and she never appealed to visions as a proof of her own sanctity. But she became sure that Christ was often especially near to her, and believed that once an angel pierced her heart with a dart tipped with fire. Whatever be the value of these experiences, the hardest sceptic cannot question her extraordinary humility, and the most critical Christian cannot doubt that she understood the secret of communion with God.

Meanwhile the rebellion of Luther and Calvin caused Teresa to reflect upon its cause. She saw the cause in the relaxation of the religious life, and she formed the project of reviving all the original rules of the Carmelites. Encouraged by some earnest priests, she procured the necessary bull from Rome, and in 1562 mass was said in a house where four women were installed as members of a new order. They were to be Barefooted (i.e. wearing rough sandals), as distinguished from the older relaxed order (sometimes nicknamed the Barefaced). The small convent of St. Joseph at Avila remains as in her own day, strict and gracefully severe. In spite of threats and calumnies and even two years spent under arrest, she persevered in her work of reform. Sixteen convents and fourteen monasteries were the result of her untiring efforts and her skill in organizing. Her troubles did not end until 1580, when Pope Gregory XIII made the reformed Carmelites into a separate province distinct from the unreformed. Two years later she died at Alba de Tormes. Certainly she was an heroic woman. And her greatness is not diminished by her masculine contempt for ' silly devotions ' and her motherly uneasiness when her young disciples forgot how to laugh.

Let us change the scene from Spain to France. The religious revival in France had its own distinct characteristic, the unity of piety with sound learning which for a time made the Church of France the most illustrious in Christendom. In the person of St. Francis de Sales (1567–1622) this revival found its first great exponent. He had a somewhat cosmopolitan education, having studied at Paris and at Padua. As a student he was modest, brilliant, and devout, and not the milksop that he was supposed to be by some of his fellow students who, when they tried to insult him in the streets of Padua, found to their cost that he had a capital knowledge of the gentle art of fencing. He was ordained priest in 1593, and before his ordination made a resolution which illumines his whole subsequent life. It was simply to remember all day that he was preparing to say mass the next morning.

He was sent to Thonon, the principal town of the Chablais in Savoy, and began his ministry amid circumstances of extraordinary difficulty; the population was strongly Calvinist, and certainly not likely to change their views in deference to a dissolute Roman Catholic garrison stationed among them. Francis first converted his own co-religionists and then turned to the native population. When criticized for his gentleness towards heretics he said, 'I have never permitted myself to use invective or reproach without repenting of it. . . . Love has a greater empire over souls than, I will not say strictness, but even force of arguments.' He was absolutely fearless, he went everywhere, even when his enemies were planning his assassination, and one winter he spent a night up a tree surrounded by a pack of wolves who were waiting for the fall of their expected prey. When almost the whole population had returned to the Roman obedience he determined to banish the Calvinist ministers whose religion had been imposed upon the people by the Bernese some sixty years before. Delegates from Bern finally requested that he would leave three ministers in the Chablais; he said he would consent on condition that they would receive the priests whom he would send to Bern. The offer was not accepted.

He was made Bishop of Geneva in 1602, though he was unable to reside in that Protestant citadel. He lived at Annecy, where he did his utmost to raise the intellectual level of his clergy, and founded the first convent of the order of the Visitation. He felt at one with nature. And it was nature in her beauty, the beauty that he could watch at Annecy, that coloured his devotions. His treatise on the 'Love of God' and his 'Introduction to the Devout Life' remain as masterpieces to teach the Christian how to love God and how to love his neighbour. They show a delicate and intimate knowledge of the human soul. St. Francis de Sales is at his best when describing Christian patience in contrast with the corresponding Stoic virtue, and that Christian humility which lies in a valley that few men can enter without slipping.

St. Francis de Sales, by his eloquence, devotion, and culture, anticipated that outburst of religious learning which marked the latter part of the seventeenth century. It was the age of Malebranche the subtle metaphysician, of Mabillon who created the science of Latin palaeography, of Montfaucon, of Ducange, of the magnificent group of sacred orators who remain unequalled in the annals of Christendom. Of these it was Archbishop Fénelon who said to the son of King James II of England, ' Never force your subjects to change their religion '. His literary style and taste are admirable. His character had many facets and therefore he has had many critics. He has been called an Ultramontane, a heretic, a hypocrite, and a sentimentalist. But it is hard to believe that these words would ever be applied to him by a modern student who had read even a few lines of his letters or spent even half an hour over his short ' Meditations for every day in the month '.

In Bossuet (1627–1704), Fénelon's contemporary and theological opponent, we see not only the most eloquent of all French preachers, but also a great symbol of this great epoch. His sermons are the work of a theologian, an artist, a combatant. His mind united the knowledge of sacred and of profane antiquity. It was a practical active mind. And yet by some strange paradox, in his dispute with Fénelon concerning the spiritual life, he considered that the soul might be even in this world so firmly established in grace as to be beyond the liberty of choosing, while the gentler Fénelon, in his conception of the more advanced states of prayer, held that the soul at every stage of its spiritual career retains the kind of freedom which is characteristically human. Such a soul will always retain the liberty of choice. In prayer, in love, in devotedness, it will enjoy a life that is supernatural but not miraculous. Here the general mind of Christendom has been with Fénelon and not with Bossuet. But it has been with Bossuet in repudiating Fénelon's view that the saint's love of Christ can be so disinterested that he no longer loves Christ as his own Redeemer but as the Redeemer of the world. And Christian common sense has inclined to side with the Pope who summed up their controversy about this disinterested love of the saints for God by saying that Fénelon had erred by loving God too much and Bossuet had erred by loving man too little.[1]

We are now touching that great controversy which had never been lulled to sleep since the beginning of the Reformation. What is the grace of God, and how is the freedom of the human will compatible with the grace of Him who is almighty and is also love? In the New Testament grace is the undeserved lovingkindness of God to man. It comes from the divine Christ to man, giving to man the assistance necessary for his salvation. And for some four centuries after the birth of Christ His followers in opposition to the fatalism of the Gnostics emphasized the truth that every man is free to accept this grace and thereby to gain salvation. Then St. Augustine, conscious that God had pursued him through the years of his sin and of his doubt, and had converted him almost in spite of himself, came to the opinion that grace is sometimes irresistible and that God gives to some men the grace necessary for their salvation but withholds it from others. He was opposed by the Pelagians who, falling into the opposite extreme, exaggerated human merit and minimized our need of the help of God in ' all holy desires, all good counsels, and all just works '. Luther and Calvin adopted and even exaggerated the Augustinian doctrine of irresistible grace and absolute predestination, and the controversy extended to the University of Louvain, where Bajus tried to revive the doctrine of St. Augustine in order to refute the ultra-Augustinianism

[1] Fénelon's deepest mystical teaching is in his *Explication des Maximes des Saints sur la Vie intérieure.* This is usually omitted in editions of his works. There is a critical edition of it by Albert Cherel (Bloud, Paris, 1911).

of Calvin. He was opposed by two Jesuits, Molina and Lessius, who advocated a theory which was nearer to Pelagianism, maintaining that the gift of God's grace to man depends upon the meritorious use which God has foreseen that they will make of His gift.

Then Cornelius Jansenius, professor at Louvain and Bishop of Ypres, followed in the steps of Bajus. He died in 1638, and after his death there was published his important book on grace, called *Augustinus*. It was a learned attempt to revive the full teaching of the great Latin father, emphasizing the corruption and weakness of human nature and the irresistible character of the grace bestowed by God upon the elect. The controversy which followed the publication of this book involved the use of much ink and not a little gall. Within the Roman Catholic communion widely different views prevailed concerning the doctrines in question, and extraordinary interest was taken in the discussion. The Jesuits were determined to secure the condemnation of a book which struck so heavily at the principles of Molina. They succeeded in raising a controversy in Paris which caused the French bishops to appeal to Rome. The result was that in 1653 Pope Innocent X condemned five propositions of a strongly anti-Pelagian character which had previously been laid before the theological faculty of Paris by an ex-Jesuit. It should be noted that four of the five propositions are not in so many words contained in the book, and that the remaining proposition is not a maxim of Jansenius, but occurs in his book as an objection raised by an opponent. Nevertheless the condemnation was confirmed in 1656 when Pope Alexander VII drew up a form of oath which was included in his Bull of February the 15th, 1665. Those who took the oath had explicitly to condemn the five propositions as taken from the *Augustinus* and 'in the sense of the author'.[1]

[1] See app. note 5, p. 260.

The solemn attraction of the writings of St. Augustine and the authority of so devoted a servant of God have not prevented the Church from avoiding some of his dogmatic conclusions. Those conclusions cannot fairly be reconciled with the truth that every man is born into a world redeemed by the blood of the Lamb, and the general orthodox doctrine that to all mankind, even to the heathen, there is given grace sufficient for avoiding eternal death. Then why, it may be asked, did some of the best men and women in France side with the Augustinian party? The reason was a moral reason.[1] On that side, to take a most notable instance, was the famous convent of Port-Royal, for ever associated with the name of Blaise Pascal (1623–1662). Port-Royal represents a school of thought which has been called by no mean critic ' the greatest religious birth of the French Church, before whose heroic and sublime singleness of mind, and thoroughness of purpose, and hatred of pretence and display, even the majesty of Bossuet, and the grace of Fénelon, and the sweetness and tenderness of St. François de Sales, and the grand erudition of the Benedictines, fall into a second place '.[2] That school stood for strictness in the moral life. It knew the beauty of Christian austerity, and therefore found itself in conflict with the prevalent Jesuit casuistry. For the same school of Jesuits, who in their dogmatic theology exalted human merit, did in their moral theology lower the standard of human duty. They illustrate the truth that creed does affect character, and that to live rightly one must think rightly about God and about oneself.

Since the fifteenth century there had been a gradual development of moral theology in special connexion with the hearing of confessions. The greater complexity of life

---

[1] See app. note 6, p. 260.
[2] R. W. Church, *Pascal and other Sermons*, p. 5 (Macmillan, London, 1896).

increased the need for a practical discussion of difficult cases of conscience and the conflict of different duties. Books embodying the result of these discussions were published for the use of the clergy. It was perhaps inevitable that some authors tended to be more severe, others to be more lenient, in their views as to the best methods of checking sin and training character. And the word *casuist*, which might reasonably have been applied to any trained theologian who had written about cases of conscience, came to denote a theologian who used his subtilty in the service of laxity. To casuistry of this type the Jansenists, and all who were in sympathy with St. Augustine, were absolutely opposed. And the Gallican theologians, who believed that a Pope is subject to an Oecumenical Council of the Church, joined with the Jansenists in opposing certain prominent Jesuits who defended so lax a system and maintained propositions so scandalous that they treated hardly any sin as really guilty and were taunted with taking away the sins of the world by treating them as non-existent.

Bossuet, and even the head of the Jesuits, Tirso Gonzalez (d. 1705), did, like Pascal, attack the fundamental principle upon which this laxity was based. It is the principle known as Probabilism, according to which, when it is only probable and not certain that a particular law applies in a particular case, it is lawful to give a penitent the benefit of the doubt if the reasons are serious, even though they be less serious than the reasons for a stricter course. And the so-called laxists held that even the slightest doubt was sufficient to dispense the penitent from taking the stricter course.

Pascal was a man who knew that a knowledge of the truth is impossible without moral purity. He began life with all the promise of becoming one of the most brilliant scientists of his age, he experienced a wonderful conversion and did not give himself to God to lead a life based on Probabilism. His *Provincial Letters* directed against the

Jesuits form one of the most telling indictments ever written to expose hypocrisy. They strike and they flash. Simple words are joined in brief sentences strong in their eloquence, carrying conviction by their rigid sequence of argument. No irony could excel the irony with which he demonstrates how different Jesuit casuists indicate how little and how seldom it is necessary for the Christian to love God, or teach the advantage of having two confessors, one for mortal sins and one for venial sins, or find reasons for justifying homicide. The book is a masterpiece of French prose because of the deep earnestness of the author and the quick light touch with which he handles the gravest of subjects.

Pascal died after much physical suffering in 1662. Eight years afterwards appeared a volume of his *Pensées*, incoherent fragments collected and arranged by his friends. Fragmentary though the collection is, it remains of great value. It is a battle against scepticism, a battle brilliantly conducted by one who sees the difference between reason and religion, and refuses to relinquish either. Pascal looks out upon mankind, and he puts side by side the two extreme views of human life which exist outside the limits of Christianity. There is the view held by those who, like Epictetus, think of man's greatness, his moral strength, his mastery over those ideas and appearances which present themselves from without, his fellowship with God. And there is the view of those who, like Montaigne, are concerned with the comedy of life, the vanity of man's business and pleasure and opinions, who select and catalogue our failures.

Pascal discerns the right and the wrong in both these views. He sees man's capacity for greatness. The weakness of human nature caused Montaigne to smile and to doubt. It caused Pascal to grieve and to seek. He wishes to ignore nothing, whether it makes for or against religion. He faces the anomalies and the perplexities of life and all the multitude of human errors, and beyond them all he sees God and certainty. It is a God who says 'Thou wouldst not search for me, if thou hadst not already found me'. And man's greatness is fallen greatness, greatness disinherited. The disaster of the Fall is a fundamental supposition of Christianity, and it gives us a key to the anomalies of our present condition. He is careful to tell us that revelation does not banish all our difficulties; but he has an overwhelming conviction of its truth, because of the profound correspondence of Christianity with what he knows of himself and of the whole complex nature of man.

The great preachers of France had much in common with Pascal. They, too, were fine analysts of the soul. They were haunted by the necessity of bringing a moral revival into the midst of a society corrupted by idleness, by a paganized literature and a lascivious monarch. In exposing the depravity and the atheism of their contemporaries they knew the value of a definite creed. And when they saw the fluctuations of infidel philosophy and 'the variations of Protestantism', they thanked God that they could point their hearers to an infallible rule of faith, the same in all times and in all places. And yet that rule of faith was changing, though they knew it not.

At the outbreak of the Reformation on the Continent, the two contending parties, Roman Catholic and Protestant, were not fully conscious of their differences. Their disputes turned upon the mode whereby fallen man can be justified by grace and gain peace with God. But from that centre the opposition spread backward and forward with astonishing rapidity, touching the whole course of human conduct, and reaching the two terms of human history, man's creation and fall and his entrance into eternity. And as we look back upon five generations of the resistance offered to Protestantism by the Counter-Reformation, we can detect a steady evolution in the development of that resistance. It was not uniform. There existed within the Roman Catholic communion grave divergences of opinion and practice. Quite apart from the Jansenists with their sincere if one-sided devotion to St. Augustine, we find a school, of which Bossuet is the great representative, always turning to the Bible and the Fathers for the purest sources of Christianity. And on the other hand there is the party of the Ultramontanes and later Jesuits, who rather than leave open any door of reconciliation with the Protestants, lay new burdens upon the conscience of their own co-religionists. They oppose the Lutheran doctrine that the corruption of our nature is 'intima, pessima, profundissima' by an attitude towards worldliness and sin which inclines to easygoing optimism. To Protestant individualism and anarchy they are ready to oppose an infallible Pope; to the blind rejection of tradition they oppose unhistorical legend, and to the neglect of the communion of saints they oppose an ever-increasing worship of God's servants that finally culminated in such prayers as 'Jesus, Mary, Joseph, I give you my heart and soul', where the same words are addressed to the Creator and the creature. And it was the latter school, and not the school of Bossuet, that eventually proved victorious.

Reflexion upon the distinctive doctrines of Lutheranism and Ultramontanism, doctrines which, however harmful they may be, never extinguished the light of the Gospel, will, I think, suggest to us that there was room and there was need for another path of Christian life and thought, a middle path between those two extremes. The leaders of Gallicanism strove to find and to keep that path. If they failed, they did not fail ingloriously. They represented within the Roman Catholic communion a grave and inward religion, reasonable and manly, which preferred sense to sensibility, and thoughtfulness to the lures of imagination, active in good works and watchful against every appearance of evil, loyally attached to the Church, and devoted to the incarnate Word who is ' full of grace and truth '. As we have already seen, a different party was not only in existence but was striving for the mastery. It would tolerate no enthusiasm but the enthusiasm of exaggeration and excess. It has gradually rendered more difficult and more impossible within the Roman communion that moderation which Ultramontanes regard as a kind of contraband heresy, a moderation which is both more Catholic and more apostolic than the two extremes which it has endeavoured to avoid. Pure Catholicism and undefiled, like perfect holiness, is for none of us a present possession but an ideal. And the path where that ideal can be approached most worthily will be a mean in relation to some other paths, but in itself it will be the best and the most heroic.

II

RELIGION IN GREAT BRITAIN FROM
1550 TO 1689

Ps xvi. 7: The lot is fallen unto me in a fair ground: yea, I have a goodly heritage.

THE heart of mediaeval English religion was not superstition. It was devotion to our Lord Jesus Christ and His Passion. But it was enfeebled by superstition, and in England as in Italy it was right to purge that superstition. A reformation was necessary, and in the year 1550 the English Reformation, as a Reformation and considered apart from the royal adulteries, murders, and thefts by which it was unhappily accompanied, was essentially complete. In no other country was the work done equally well. Nowhere else had the ancient and the modern spirit been so wisely combined. The claims of the Pope to govern and to tax the dioceses of other bishops had been repudiated. An official translation of the Bible had been issued. A good statement of doctrine, called the *Erudition for any Christian Man*, a book now too much neglected, had been published with the full authority of the Church. The standard of private prayer was a Primer based on mediaeval books. The new Book of Common Prayer contained the order of the Mass and other public services of the Church carefully simplified and excellently translated.[1] And lastly there was the new Ordinal. It asserted that the orders of Bishops, Priests, and Deacons had been in the Church 'from the Apostles' time' and that these orders are to be 'continued'. While preserving the apostolic succession of the ministry Cranmer severely reduced the clumsy accumulation of old

[1] See app. note 7, p. 261.

Roman, Gallican, and later mediaeval forms in the ordination of priests, and the services were brought back to a form fundamentally the same as that of the older Roman books.

With the creeds and with the apostolic succession of the ministry, the whole ancient sacramental system of the Church was in essence retained, while also freed from mediaeval innovations. In Confirmation the primitive laying on of the bishop's hand was again made of paramount importance. Penance was freed from the incubus of indulgences. Extreme unction, instead of being used chiefly as an aid to the dying, became a means towards the recovery of the sick, as enjoined in the New Testament. And the chalice, which in some parts of the Continent had only been finally withdrawn from communicants in the fifteenth century, was restored to all the faithful.[1] In one and the same system new learning and light were united with the language and teaching of ancient saints and Fathers. In substance, though not in every detail, this system corresponded with the faith and practice common to the whole Catholic Church in East and West before the great schism of the eleventh century. And that is a common ground, a basis, which will have to be seriously considered in any comprehensive scheme for the future reunion of Christendom.

Time and patience would have commended these English services to the people, when reverently performed and wedded to the beautiful Church music of the Tudor period. Haste and impatience hindered their acceptance; and the arbitrary manner in which changes were enforced was noticed by Bucer, one of the most moderate of the foreign reformers, who observes, 'all is done by ordinances, which

---

[1] For the history of the withdrawal of the chalice, see Julius Smend, *Kelchversagung und Kelchspendung in der abendländischen Kirche*, p. 27 (Vandenhoeck & Ruprecht, Göttingen, 1898), and Edm. Martene, *De antiquis ecclesiae ritibus*, tom. iii (1737), p. 489.

the greater part of the people obey very grudgingly'. The majority of the people did obey, but the mind of many seems to be revealed in the articles drawn up by the rebels in the west of England. They say nothing about the Pope or indulgences. They want Mass without any one communicating with the priest except at Easter. They want the eloquent old ceremonies of Ash Wednesday and Palm Sunday. They want the reserved Sacrament to be hung over the high altar, and there to be worshipped. They want celibate priests. And they say 'we will not receive the new Service, because it is but like a Christmas game'. They did not like English at the altar. To them it savoured of mummery, for it made them think of the mummers playing St. George and the Dragon as they still do in some country villages at Christmas. Cranmer poured upon these luckless rebels the vials of his learning. He was correct when he said that ancient canons forbid priests to separate from their wives, correct when he maintained that ancient rules required the laity to communicate at least three times a year, and that the canon of the Latin Mass implies the communion of the people as well as the communion of the priest. And he was quite correct when he affirmed that in Italy the holy Sacrament was not hung up in a pyx above the high altar, a custom which had become common in France and England in spite of the canonical rule that the reserved Sacrament should be kept in an aumbry in the wall.[1]

Rapidly the religious confusion grew worse. The vacillation of Cranmer, blown about by every wind of doctrine from the Rhine, the publication of a second Prayer Book before the people were accustomed to the first, the

---

[1] It was revived in the seventeenth century in the gorgeous chapel erected at St. James's for Queen Henrietta Maria. 'Behind the altar was a dove holding the Blessed Sacrament.' See Johanna H. Harting, *Catholic London Missions*, p. 9 (Sands & Co., London, 1903).

destructive controversial propaganda encouraged by the Government, the rapacity and hypocrisy of the Duke of Northumberland, combined to make religious peace impossible. And when the boy king died and Mary came to the throne, the nation was willing to be reconciled with Rome. Mary, however, wanted more than peace with Rome. At first she had been disposed to show clemency towards her restive Protestant subjects. But the rising in Kent under Sir Thomas Wyatt in 1554 made her think that clemency was a mistake; and there is another reason which must be taken into account. She expected a child, and no child arrived. Tortured by disease and disappointment, she sought to propitiate God. She was half a Spaniard, and deep in the heart of a Spaniard is the belief that in religion and in politics there cannot be an honest compromise, and also the belief that physical suffering is a punishment from God. In Spain and Portugal the burning of Jews was a solemn normal function, an 'act of faith'. And to Mary the burning of heretics seems to have been a real 'act of faith', an oblation to the Almighty. Between three and four hundred victims of lower rank and four bishops suffered this appalling death. And Mary died neglected by her foreign husband, hated by the English people, and only successful in disseminating sympathy for the opinions which she longed to extirpate.

Elizabeth (1533–1603) saw the necessity of steering a middle course. In the language of the Book of Proverbs we may say that her royal heart is unsearchable. Her beauty, her Byzantine splendour of attire, her immense physical endurance, her English energy and Welsh duplicity, her fluent French and Latin, help to create in our minds an impression of one of the greatest of queens and most finished of actresses. We know that she liked a learned, and disliked a married clergy, that she wished the Church to be governed under the royal supremacy by its proper convocations, that she was resolved not to allow England to come under the Papacy again, that she disliked Knox and Calvin. But we cannot tell the exact relation of the religion of her heart to the religion of the father whom she frequently resembled.

Elizabeth's task was difficult. She tolerated the introduction of the Second Prayer Book of Edward VI, but tried to deprive it of its Protestant sting by combining the new formula for giving the holy communion with the older Catholic words of administration, and she secured the nominal restoration of the Mass vestments. The vast majority of the clergy acquiesced in the use of this English rite. But the new bishops soon compromised with regard to the vestments. She repudiated the title of Supreme Head of the Church, knowing that it was equally distasteful to men of the most opposite religious convictions. But Parliament, though not the Church, reasserted it in the plainest terms. Papal authority was abolished and an offensive phrase about the Bishop of Rome's 'detestable enormities' was expunged from the Litany. Clergymen and office-holders might be required to swear that the Pope's authority was nothing, and if any one advisedly upheld that authority he was to forfeit his goods. Legally the Roman Catholics were at the Queen's mercy. But she was too wise to hurry, and for some time the new oath was not tendered to the judges and hesitating priests were treated with forbearance. If the country could have been preserved from entanglements abroad, the malcontents and their immediate descendants might have been soon absorbed into the existing *Ecclesia Anglicana*.

Such isolation, however, was impossible. Scotland, France, the Netherlands, and Spain provided a problem which had to be solved if England was to be saved. It was a problem of which politics formed the web and religion the woof. With consummate sagacity Elizabeth and Cecil began by cutting the connexion between France and the majority of the Scottish people, with the result that the nation which in 1550 was grateful to France had in 1560 transferred its friendship to England. The Pope sent to Elizabeth a courteous letter by the hands of a nuncio. Philip of Spain suspected that this move was the result of French intrigue and persuaded the Pope that he had made a mistake. The nuncio was stopped at Brussels and the breach between England and Rome became a little wider. A second nuncio was sent with Philip's approval, but was stopped on his way by Cecil's work, and Elizabeth refused to send bishops to the Council of Trent. The Council reopened, 1562, and that year Pope Pius IV forbade attendance at English Mattins and Evensong, without even considering the lawfulness of attendance at holy communion. The next year, 1563, the English Thirty-nine Articles of Religion were passed by a Convocation of the province of Canterbury. Like the decisions of Trent, the Thirty-nine Articles are not free from ambiguity but nevertheless powerfully contributed to a consolidation of doctrine. They adroitly avoid all distinctively Lutheran or Calvinist doctrine, and though less defiant than the Forty-two Articles of the previous reign, they cannot be accused of seeking reunion with Rome by retrogression towards mediaevalism.

So the knocks and blows went on, but still Pope Pius IV, a genial diplomat, did not anathematize the Queen of England. There came the long duel between Elizabeth and Mary Queen of Scots, the imprisonment of Mary in England in 1568, then the rising of Roman Catholics in the north of England, its failure followed by the murmurs that if only the Pope had excommunicated Elizabeth the rising would have been better supported. The Pope was now Pius V, the zealous and austere pontiff for whose election Charles Borromeo had laboured. He decided that a supreme effort was needed on his part and on May the 15th, 1570, the Bull *Regnans in excelsis* was found nailed to the gate of the Bishop of London's palace.

What the Bull lacks in strict veracity, it gains in vigour. It accuses the 'pretended Queen of England' of the monstrous usurpation of the place of Supreme Head of the Church and of turning bishops, rectors, and other Catholic priests out of their churches and benefices. Further, that 'she has abolished the sacrifice of the Mass, prayers, fasts, distinction of meats, celibacy, and Catholic rites; has commanded books containing manifest heresy to be put forth throughout the kingdom and that impious mysteries, and institutes according to the order of Calvin received and observed by herself, be also kept by her subjects'.[1] He therefore excommunicates and anathematizes Elizabeth, deprives her of her rank, and absolves her subjects from their oaths of allegiance. Pius V hoped to bring about the dethronement of Elizabeth and he failed completely. Gradually Philip II came to the same certainty as Pius that the haughty island kingdom must be broken if his empire was to be secure. And his Armada, like the Pope's Bull, failed, and infected the English with hatred of Rome and of the missionary priests who came hither from the Continent restrained by no obstacle and daunted by no defeat.

In 1571, the year after Elizabeth's excommunication, Archbishop Grindal issued Advertisements which throw considerable light on English religion. The north was then intensely conservative, clinging to old customs, some of which were harmless and even edifying.[2] And the Archbishop worried his flock with inquisitive tyranny. He reduced the majority to subjection. But many definitely threw in their lot with the Pope, though in the time of

---

[1] See app. note 8, p. 262.
[2] J. Strype, *History of Edmund Grindal*, pp. 164 ff. (London, 1710).

Edward VI the English feeling against the Pope was so strong that the Venetian envoy wrote that 'no one, either of the old or new religion, can bear to hear him mentioned'. A hideous persecution of the Roman Catholics of the north of England followed in the latter part of Elizabeth's reign. The Gunpowder Plot was manipulated from abroad; but Guy Fawkes and the other Yorkshire gentlemen who helped him in his desperate adventure had bitter memories to goad them into crime. The story of the bishops whom Mary burnt in Oxford is indeed terrible. But for a hundred Englishmen who have read that story there is perhaps hardly one who has read the tale of the execution of Robert Bickerdike of Farnham, or of Margaret Clitheroe of York, who was slowly crushed to death naked on the bridge across the Ouse. If ever there was a bridge of sighs, it was that ancient bridge at York which at last the more ancient river swept away.

In Oxfordshire during the time of Elizabeth and for many years of the seventeenth century, Roman Catholicism was strongly represented among the country gentry and their dependants. There was little hostility between the two rival communions. Cases are recorded where recusants, whether they attended their parish church or not, were shown leniency when they were not satisfied in their conscience that they might receive the holy communion. And as late as 1660 Mr. Thomas Stonor, a recusant, presented a bell to the parish church of Watlington.

Though at the beginning of the seventeenth century the Church of England had begun to recover, the opposition to it had been and continued to be dangerous in the extreme. Every day the Church of Rome was growing intellectually more formidable, as it was growing practically more formidable. The time past might suffice for the common sense which had ridiculed false relics and even obscene relics, pretended miracles and magical images, and the taxing of Englishmen to support boy cardinals and Roman harems. But something more than common sense was needed to confront a Baronius who spent thirty years in collecting materials for his ecclesiastical history; a Bellarmin who not only wrote copiously but tried to quote his opponents fairly; a Mariana who loved what was true, and, though a Jesuit, dared to criticize the Society of Jesus.[1] To meet such men learning was necessary.

And learning was required to meet the Puritans. They had come back from Geneva and Zürich fiercely opposed to the religion of Queen Mary who had driven them into exile, completely under the spell of Calvin, and with Calvin's passion for convincing others and forcing others to obey. The year after the Pope's excommunication of the Queen, the Puritans began a violent and well-organized attack upon the English hierarchy and the Prayer Book.[2] The main body had no intention of separating from the Church of England. They opposed separation. They were determined to transform the Church after the Calvinist and Presbyterian model, and the great ability of Thomas Cartwright enabled them to start the working of their scheme, a scheme to be imposed on the Church by the State. At the other extreme of sectarianism were the Anabaptists. They had no creed of general binding force and they differed greatly among themselves. But they united in breaking up the ancient conception of the Church by opposing the baptism of infants; and they also broke up the whole mediaeval conception of the relation between

---

[1] In his work *Discours des grands defauts qui sont en la forme du gouvernement des Jesuites, Traduict d'Espagnol en François*. No printer's name, or place, 1625. It was printed in Latin at Bordeaux and reprinted by order of Charles III when he expelled the Jesuits from Spain in 1767.

[2] W. H. Frere and C. E. Douglas, *Puritan Manifestoes* (Society for Promoting Christian Knowledge, London, 1907). These manifestoes are most important for any real understanding of Puritanism.

Church and State by maintaining that each congregation of believers should be independent of all external control, civil or ecclesiastical, and that no believer should hold the office of a magistrate.

Between these extremes were the Congregationalists or Independents who retained infant baptism while rejecting the Church's doctrine of baptism. The left wing of the Congregationalists was associated with Robert Browne and approximated to the Anabaptists. All authority of the civil magistrate in matters of religion was denied, the necessity of separating from the Church of England was upheld, and it was taught that each local congregation must be independent and founded upon a covenant which the believers make with God and with one another. The tendency of this left wing was strongly democratic, and Browne is the parent of modern English Congregationalism.

The right wing of the Congregationalists was that led by Henry Barrowe. The Barrowists agreed with the Anabaptists and the Brownists in regarding the Church of England as too inclusive and comprehensive, and refused to look upon all baptized and non-excommunicate persons as members of the Church. But they differed from the Brownists in being less democratic and in allowing a more substantial authority to the elders chosen by the congregation. The elders were a ruling class, and the distinction between them and the rest of the congregation was more marked than in the Brownist system.

Let us bear in mind that whereas English Congregationalism is the work of Browne, American Congregationalism in New England was in its origin mainly a blend of Barrowism and the original Puritanism. It is true that the men who on Christmas Day 1620 planted New Plymouth on the site of an Indian village depopulated by disease were Separatists. But the men who settled in Massachusetts Bay in 1628 were not. They were Puritans who had been determined to reform the Church till it should be without spot or wrinkle, without a college cap or a 'Babylonish' surplice. Seeing that it was impossible to get what they wanted in England, they determined to go to America. The polity of the Church was held to be immutably prescribed by the word of God. Each local congregation was autonomous, but the civil magistrate had the right to interfere in doctrine and in practice so that the State might itself become more perfect. The alliance between Church and State was of the strictest kind, and the American Congregationalists, so far from being the friends of religious equality, made their Church an established Church and a persecuting Church, and in Massachusetts it remained established until the nineteenth century was well advanced.

The Congregationalists, like the Elizabethan Puritans, were Calvinists.[1] The British Westminster Confession of 1646, the American Cambridge Platform of 1648, the English Savoy Declaration of 1658, are all in substantial agreement in teaching a strict Calvinism, powerfully summarizing the doctrines which had been held by the respective parties for two generations. We see therefore that apart from the more ignorant sectaries, such as were most of the Anabaptists, the English Church was threatened by three Protestant parties which were united by their acceptance of Calvinism and their repudiation of episcopacy. Their two darling convictions were first that Christ brings salvation only to those who are irresistibly predestined, and, secondly, that the Pope is Antichrist.[2] Those two convictions form a key to the history of this entire period.

The work of defending and reconstructing religion in England was in a peculiar degree accomplished by Archbishop Parker, Richard Hooker, Bishop Andrewes, and Archbishop Laud.

[1] See app. note 9, p. 263.   [2] See app. note 10, p. 264.

Elizabeth in choosing Matthew Parker (1504–1575) to succeed Cardinal Pole chose a scholar of learning and moderation. In his younger days at Cambridge he and some kindred spirits used to meet for the discussion of theological questions at an inn which was nicknamed 'Germany'. He nevertheless rose to be Vice-chancellor of the University and with rare wisdom prevented it from being plundered by a royal commission of Henry VIII. Under Queen Mary he lived a life of study and retirement in England, and therefore retained a more impartial mind than the Marian exiles who became imbued with the extravagances of Zürich and Geneva. A man of weak health, he would have preferred to devote himself to his university, but Elizabeth summoned him to London, and on December the 17th, 1559, he was consecrated to the see of Canterbury in Lambeth Palace chapel. The evidence for his consecration is complete, and it was not until more than forty years later that certain Jesuits floated the notorious 'Nag's Head Fable', according to which he underwent a mock ordination at a tavern in Cheapside.[1]

During the fifteen years of his primacy Parker led an arduous conscientious life. Every kind of dull dreary thankless work that a prelate could do, came into his hands, and he did it steadily, carefully keeping good ancient precedents. He reformed his own courts, reformed hospitals, prevented benefices being held by children, insisted that registers should be carefully kept. He found his solace in books. He not only collected them judiciously, but loved them, new and old, and encouraged printing and bookbinding. England owes to Parker the revival of the study of Anglo-Saxon, and the translation of the Scriptures

---

[1] The literature dealing with Anglican Orders is immense. The best short account of the controversy is given by F. E. Brightman, *What Objections have been made to English Orders?*, published by the Society for Promoting Christian Knowledge for the Church Historical Society, London, 1896.

known as the Bishops' Bible, a work which prevented the Genevan translation from becoming the official Bible of the Church of England. He took an interest in the proceedings of the Council of Trent, translating and criticizing certain decrees of the Council. Under his presidency the Thirty-nine Articles were passed by Convocation in 1563, and he issued in 1566 Advertisements for regulating the services of the Church.

In the midst of much that is sombre and serious we find from Parker's own pen a delightful account of a visit from the French ambassador De Gonnorre together with the Bishop of Coutances and a retinue of young gentlemen. Of course he knew that they had come as spies, and they knew that he knew. But every one was affable and friendly. The French, who arrived on a Friday, were surprised to find that the English had fast days, fixed prayers, and holy orders. They even professed that 'we were in religion very nigh to them . . . they were contented to hear evil of the Pope, and bragged how stout they had been aforetimes against that authority'. But in spite of all this, Parker let them see that his house contained an armoury, and after the departure of his guests he was much relieved to find that they had not purloined 'even the worth of one silver spoon'.[1]

In Parker we find already that appeal to Christian antiquity which, side by side with the appeal to nature and reason, the nature that God made and the reason which is God's image, played so large a part in Anglican apologetics. It was imperatively necessary to investigate the creed and the ritual of the early Church or to leave undisputed the challenge from Rome, 'Whose are the glory and the covenants . . . whose are the fathers?' Did the passages in the Fathers which had been assumed to justify the universal

[1] *Correspondence of Matthew Parker*, p. 216 (Cambridge University Press, 1853).

jurisdiction of the Bishop of Rome, or the full later cultus of the saints, or a material conception of purgatory, or of the real presence, really signify these things when studied in their true context? The Anglican divines made repeatedly an appeal to antiquity in opposition to theologians who said that Rome was always the same. This appeal when wisely made is no hindrance to development but its help and safeguard. It is a necessary element in scientific criticism, as legitimate as the restoration of the true text concealed in a corrupt Greek manuscript. It is a sign of progress. It is no mere appeal from the living to the dead, for the Church does not die. So Parker wrote, 'We will proceed in the reformation begun and doubt not by the help of Christ His grace of the true unity to Christ's Catholic Church and of the uprightness of our faith in this province'.

The reasonableness of this upright faith, this orthodoxy, was specially vindicated by Richard Hooker (1553–1600), a humble parish priest, and his younger contemporary John Donne, Dean of St. Paul's (1573–1631). Few men have done more than Hooker to raise controversy to the high level of courteous and profitable discussion. His great work on *Ecclesiastical Polity* is an English classic. His prose is flowing, majestic, brightened with the occasional sparkle of half-concealed humour, prose fitted to carry forward great ideas. He has been influenced by St. Augustine and St. Thomas Aquinas, but he has also felt the air of the revival of learning and of ancient Greek Christianity. If we look for the fundamental principle on which his argument is based, we quickly notice a similarity to the principle selected in the very oldest Christian book outside the canon of the New Testament, the Epistle of St. Clement of Rome dealing with the ministry of the Church. Hooker builds his work on the all-embracing character of law, 'whose seat', he says, 'is the bosom of God, whose voice the harmony of the world'. God's law is to be discovered by reason, and reason teaches us to strive after a triple perfection, sensuous, intellectual, and spiritual or divine.

Applying such an argument to man, Hooker teaches that all men are governed by the law of God and of reason, and are also governed by other laws of human origin. These laws include rules as to both temporal and ecclesiastical matters, and all these must be obeyed if they do not contravene the law of God or of nature, for new articles of faith and doctrine are unlawful. Obedience is not unreasonable because the law really rests upon consent express or implied. It is the act of the whole body politic, and this body politic includes both Church and State. One and the same society is termed 'a commonwealth as it liveth under whatsoever form of secular law and regiment, a church as it hath the spiritual law of Jesus Christ'. Among infidels the commonwealth and the Church were independent societies. Under the sway of the Bishop of Rome there is really one society, but he divides it into two diverse bodies. Within this realm of England there is one society which depends upon 'one chief Governor'.

According to Hooker, the Jewish monarchy fully justifies this view of the royal supremacy and with it the prohibition of Nonconformity. He says, 'Our state is according to the pattern of God's own ancient elect people, which people was not part of them the commonwealth, and part of them the Church of God, but the selfsame people whole and entire were both under one chief Governor, on whose supreme authority they did all depend '.[1]

That was a cogent argument to use against the early Puritans who thoroughly believed in religious uniformity and idolized the Old Testament. It was at the same time a barrier against the Papacy, while itself closely connected with mediaeval ideas and institutions. The supremacy of

[1] *Ecclesiastical Polity*, Book VIII, i. 7.

the King is, according to Hooker, held 'by divine right'. But this does not imply absolutism, nor did Hooker and the Tudor sovereigns assert that divinity of hereditary right which was asserted after the accession of James I. The King has no 'right divine to govern wrong'. In the first place he is subject to divine law, and in the second place he depends upon 'that whole entire body, over the several parts whereof he hath dominion'. Hooker's *Ecclesiastical Polity* is a work of extraordinary value.[1] It is of historical importance because it explains the principles of the Tudor policy in Church and State. It is of constitutional importance because it marks a halting place before the outbreak of the struggle between the supporters of the King and the supporters of Parliament in the seventeenth century. It is of theological importance both because of Hooker's explicit teaching and because there is a remarkable parallel between his moderate theory of the divine right of a king and the Gallican theory of papal authority. The doctrine of royal absolutism and the doctrine of papal infallibility replaced these theories by giving to the King and the Pope respectively an uncontrolled power.

Hooker and Donne believed that the traditional forms of Christian worship are reasonable, and not accepting the Puritan doctrine that man by the Fall became 'wholly defiled in all the faculties and parts of soul and body', they saw not harm, but good, in the ceremonies which correspond with the wholesome instincts of rational human nature. 'Quench not', says Donne, 'the light of nature, suffer not that light to go out; study your natural faculties, husband and improve them; and love the outward acts of religion, though a hypocrite or a natural man may do them. He that cares not though the material church fall, I am afraid is falling from the spiritual. . . . He that undervalues outward things in the service of God, though he begin at cere-

[1] See W. S. Holdsworth, *Columbia Law Review*, June, 1921.

monial and ritual things, will come quickly to call Sacraments but outward things, and Sermons and Public Prayers but outward things in contempt. . . . Beloved, outward things apparel God, and since God was content to take a body, let us not leave Him naked and ragged.'

Lancelot Andrewes became the most influential bishop and theologian who represented matured convictions as to the Catholic heritage and position of the Church of England.[1] At Cambridge he was admired as a catechist; in London he was revered as a guide in difficult cases of conscience; his sermons were valued above any others of that period. And though men might steal his sermons, none could steal his preaching. He knew fifteen languages, and Bacon submitted his writings to the judgement of Andrewes. He cared far more for Christianity than he cared for controversy, but he could not stand aside when King James wished him to enter the lists against Bellarmin. In opposing Bellarmin he defended unequivocally the Catholicity of the English Church as judged by the standards of antiquity. To him this Catholicity was no matter of dry-as-dust speculation. In his teaching he always fixed his thoughts on the certainties which the Christian world believes to be known through Christ, and not on the mysteries of predestination about which men were wrangling in the market-place and the pulpit. He tried to bring a breath of sweeter, fresher air into the hot and narrow rooms of pamphleteers and plotters. He spoke respectfully of Calvin, and fond as he was of the outward adornments of worship, the copes, the incense, the tapers, he did not enjoin these things on others as vital. In his *Devotions*, the book which carried his influence to modern times, he appears as a wide-hearted

---

[1] The one and only blot alleged to exist on his character is that he was one of the majority which decided that the marriage of Robert Devereux, third Earl of Essex, with Frances Howard, was null. The marriage, however, was not consummated, and it is doubtful if it could have been. See *Dictionary of National Biography*, vol. xiv, p. 440, article 'Devereux'.

saint, interceding for all classes and conditions of men. He refused to forget, and he taught others to remember, that as there is a universal historical Church, we have our duty towards the whole body, a duty suggested by the very title-page of the English Prayer Book where the Church is placed first and the Church of England is placed second. Therefore, in his own words he prayed ' for the Catholic Church, its confirmation and enlargement; for the Eastern, its deliverance and unity; for the Western, its adjustment and peace; for the British, the supply of what is wanting, the establishment of what remains '.

Archbishop Laud, who revered Andrewes as ' a light of the Christian world', was equally convinced of the continuity of the Church of England, a spiritual and not a merely legal continuity, with its life in past ages. He, too, was obliged to defend the Anglican against the Roman position. And he did this on a logical and intelligible ground. He maintained that a national Church has the right to reform itself while yet remaining a part of the Catholic body. And it may do so without the Pope if necessary, because papal jurisdiction is not indispensable. Following a line suggested by some great mediaeval writers, and one in close agreement with Eastern Orthodox theology, he denies that the earthly government of the Church is monarchical,[1] and asserts that power does not flow into the Church from the Pope, but from Christ, the Head, into the whole body, a body most adequately represented in an Oecumenical Council. His theory leaves room for the rights of the whole Church and of a national Church, and of both clergy and laity as active members of the same.

Laud's ecclesiastical policy was to enforce a moderate uniformity in the conviction that out of this uniformity a unity of spirit would be generated. It would come with the gradual formation of habit. He did not expect immediate

[1] *Works*, vol. ii, p. 252 (Parker, Oxford, 1849).

success, but he had the courage to work for it. He made a disastrous mistake in trying to use force, and especially the force of royal authority, to secure discipline in the Church. But that mistake was in that age almost universal, and in England we have only seen it vanish during the last twenty years. It is a malicious misunderstanding which has prompted the saying that 'the one element in the Church which to him was all essential was its visibility'. And the question whether he or his opponents attached the greater importance to outward details of worship should not be decided by any one who has not studied the Puritan discussion concerning the wearing of the hat during divine service. The very first thing which his enemies demanded was 'uniformity in religion', and their confederacy, as Heylin remarks, was 'cemented with blood'. It was the blood of Laud, in whose trial there was no semblance of real justice. He was cheerful and loyal, a liberal patron of learning and upholder of good morals, and he resembled John Knox in his unselfish disregard of money. If he made some of the mistakes of a martinet, it is equally true that he had the virtues of a martyr.

Let us now turn to Scotland. In Scotland the Church of the later Middle Ages had been as corrupt as the Church in Rome itself. Typical of the religious condition of the country is the fact that David Beaton (d. 1546), who succeeded his uncle as Archbishop of St. Andrews, attended the marriage of one of his illegitimate children and heavily dowered her out of the Church's patrimony. Bishoprics were like 'Pocket-boroughs' in the hands of great noble families, and great ecclesiastical revenues were held by so-called spiritual peers who were merely lay commendators. But the country was backward, and bishops and abbots felt at ease in Zion and were slow to see the coming storm. There had been in Scotland a little Lollardy and a little

Lutheranism; but in 1550 Scotland had no sympathy with Protestantism and was attached to France and opposed to England. But a change came fast and furious. The Scots began to suspect the French policy of their regent, Mary of Lorraine, Protestantism spread, great lords signed a 'Covenant' opposed to Rome; the bishops burnt Walter Milne, an aged Protestant, and the same year, 1558, on St. Giles's Day, when the saint's image was carried in procession through the streets of Edinburgh, the rabble broke the image in pieces. At the beginning of the Reformation there existed a small body of intelligent and religious men who wished for reform, a reform of the kind that found expression in the first Prayer Book of Edward VI. The Church might still have been saved, but at the last moment the bishops did nothing to rescue the sinking vessel. At their final Provincial Council in 1559 they gave only a halting answer to a demand for reasonable changes, and the next year when Parliament assembled and the doctrine of the Church was called in question, they remained ignominiously silent. The Pope's authority was then abolished, and the saying of Mass was forbidden under the most extreme penalties, the third offence being punishable by death. By their cowardly inaction the bishops left the way clear for one who, if he had not the creative genius of Calvin, could fight as few but Calvin fought.

John Knox, a man hardened by vicissitude, fervid, disinterested, with a personal magnetism that reminds one of St. Ignatius de Loyola, had been a chaplain of Edward VI. His views were those of an extreme Swiss Protestantism, and when in England he had striven to prevent the custom of kneeling at holy communion. On the death of Edward he fled to Geneva. He returned to Scotland in 1555 to preach and to organize, and found powerful supporters. He left Scotland again in 1556, thinking discretion the better part of valour, but he came to his kingdom when the

Parliament of Scotland repudiated the Pope. He must in a large measure be regarded as responsible for the fact that in no country was the change of religion accompanied by more violence than in Scotland. At Perth, at St. Andrews and elsewhere, the populace indulged in a veritable orgy of destruction. A pleasant contrast is to be found farther north. In Inverness there seems to have been no animosity against the Church. A Protestant minister of very dubious character was appointed in 1560, but the old chaplains were still allowed to enjoy their stipends and for many years priests filled the office of town clerk.[1]

Knox, with five other ministers, was commissioned to draw up a new Confession of Faith. Its character is Calvinistic. The doctrine of predestination is stated temperately; but it is taught that in consequence of the Fall the image of God was utterly defaced in man. Like other documents of the Scottish Reformation its language is that of concentrated vituperation, the unreformed Church being described as ' the filthie synagogue ', ' the horrible harlot ', ' the kirk malignant '. The same six ministers drew up the First Book of Discipline which organizes the ministry in agreement with Calvin's ordinances. Public worship was regulated by a crude Book of Common Order, of which the formulae can be traced back to Calvin and Farel. It provides fixed forms of prayer, but it is an astonishing fact that in the ministration of the Lord's Supper, which was to be celebrated quarterly, no form is provided for the consecration of the bread and wine.

In considering the subsequent religious troubles of Scotland it is worth remembering that Knox neither banished fixed forms of prayer nor rigidly maintained a strictly Presbyterian form of the ministry. In 1572, after twelve years' experience, he actually wrote in favour of the organization, closely copied from episcopacy, recom-

[1] See William Mackay, *Life in Inverness in the Sixteenth Century*, p. 51 (Aberdeen, Their Majesties' Printers, 1911).

mended by the Convention of Leith. But he had already sown the seeds of that religious strife which divided Scotland for nearly two hundred years. The novel and most unprimitive type of service which he had introduced prejudiced the people against anything resembling the English Prayer Book which had been for some years employed in Scotland and in 1560 was used even in Glasgow. His coarse gibes at the bishops, the laying on of whose hands in ordination had been contemptuously rejected, had done their work. The new attempt to change the government of the Church merely resulted first in the institution of nominal bishops, unconsecrated, and the tools of the nobility, and then in the establishment of a strict Presbyterian polity in 1592. That was the work of Andrew Melville, one of the ablest men of the time, who destroyed the old educational routine of the Scottish universities and made them the handmaids of the new ecclesiastical system.

James VI of Scotland and I of England (1566–1625) was an astute and ingenious monarch. Though he was vain, he loved peace, and before he became king of England he had displayed considerable wisdom in establishing constitutional relations between the Scottish Crown and the ministers of religion. He had set his heart on effecting a closer spiritual union between the two countries, and for that end he determined that the titular episcopate which already existed in the north of Scotland should be made into a genuine episcopate for the whole country. He secured, not altogether by honourable means, the almost unanimous assent of the General Assembly held at Glasgow in 1610, and three ministers from Scotland were then consecrated bishops in London. It was wisely arranged that no part in the consecration was taken by the Archbishops of Canterbury and York, and in this way any suggestion of subjecting the Church of Scotland to the Church of England was avoided. The king afterwards bought back with his own money alienated Church lands to support the bishops. Some of the new bishops were men of real piety and learning, and they promoted the parish school system which proved so great a benefit to the country.

Charles I (1600–1649) was more sincerely religious than his father, but he was less clever. He secured for the Scottish clergy the teinds or tithes which are still enjoyed by the ministers of the Established Church. But he alienated the nobility by an attempt to make them restore their ill-gotten lands to the Church, and this, no less than his unwise attempts to regulate the ritual of the Church on his own authority, led to the downfall of episcopacy in southern Scotland. The introduction of a new Book of Common Prayer for the use of the Church of Scotland, July the 23rd, 1637, was the occasion of that downfall.

With regard to this Prayer Book grave misconceptions are still prevalent. It is still supposed that it was primarily intended to supplant extempore prayers, and it is still described as 'Laud's liturgy' and, because Laud's, 'Romish'. It was intended to replace existing books, that of Knox and a book mixing the English service with that of Knox. To call it ' Romish ' is to pay the Church of Rome an undeserved compliment which that Church would be the first to repel. And though Laud gave the book his help and his approval, he had not originally wished for it, because he desired that the English book itself should be used in Scotland. And he says explicitly, ' I would have nothing at all to do with the manner of introducing it '.[1] It was prepared on the basis of English books by two Scottish bishops, John Maxwell of Ross, and a gentle scholar, James Wedderburn of Dunblane, and apart from the royal declaration which precedes it, it is a book of which Scotland may be justly proud.

Mythology has supplemented ' alliteration's artful aid ' in blackening ' Laud's liturgy '. It is more than doubtful

[1] *Works*, vol. iii, p. 336 (Parker, Oxford, 1849).

that Jenny Geddes hurled a stool at the Dean of Edinburgh when he began to read the collect, and the tablet erected to her honour in St. Giles's Church is only a monument of modern credulity. The historical facts are that serious riots, apparently planned four months earlier, took place in the churches of Edinburgh, and the bishop was brutally assaulted in the streets. The populace became frantic, and the nobility, determined to keep what they had got, fomented the opposition to the king and the bishops. A 'National League and Covenant' was craftily drafted in the form of a protest against Popery, a protest which many dared not refuse to sign though they knew that it was really intended to inflame the people against the Scottish episcopate. Large numbers of all classes did sign, often under serious threats of violence. The university of St. Andrews refused the covenant, and at Aberdeen, which for generations was a stronghold of episcopacy, the commissioners were politely offered a collation but not signatures. As we know that even a century later no language but the Gaelic was spoken over at least half of Scotland, we may reasonably conclude that in 1638 there were comparatively few who understood the relation between the Pope and the Prayer Book, a book which not one person in a hundred could possibly have seen.

After the Edinburgh riots the Covenanters proceeded to make preparations for a General Assembly at Glasgow. It met in the cathedral church November the 21st, 1638. At first the disorder was so great that a contemporary Presbyterian wrote, ' we might learn from Canterbury, yea from the Pope, yea from the Turks or pagans, modesty and manners '.[1] A series of charges of the most abominable kind, including adultery and incest, had been drawn up by the presbytery of Edinburgh to libel the bishops. These disgusting calumnies having been read and approved by the

[1] *Letters and Journals of Robert Baillie*, vol. i, p. 123 (Edinburgh, 1841).

Assembly, all the fourteen bishops were deposed, and eight suffered the sentence of excommunication, which carried with it the loss of every civil right. It so happened that the reader had opened the Bible at the words, ' They shall put you out of the synagogues, yea the time cometh that whosoever killeth you will think that he doeth God service '. He was told to choose another lesson, and after a virulent discourse from the Moderator, the Assembly sang a psalm and departed, we are told, ' with humble joy casting ourself and our poor church in the arms of our good God '.

Oliver Cromwell (1599–1658) strove to replace the Church of England by an efficient Calvinistic organization meant to include Presbyterians, Baptists, and Independents. He believed in his cause. And his extraordinary capacity for dealing with events and opponents is shown in every line of his face. Sometimes he resembles Mohammed and sometimes he resembles Mazarin. His ferocity in Ireland is revolting, and in his dealings with France and Spain the salesman is as conspicuous as the saint. His small kindness to the Jews and the Socinians, who were too weak to hurt him, gratified his conscience as much as his persecution of the Church that he feared. The use of the Prayer Book was prohibited under heavy penalties, churches were desecrated, the clergy ejected from their livings, forbidden to keep schools, preach, or administer the sacraments. The story of the manner in which Cromwell's Puritan spirit came to make room for secular enterprise forms part of the history of Great Britain. To the history of the Universities belongs the fact that he protected them from the assaults of the more extreme fanatics, while Heads of Colleges and Fellows were expelled by the score.

It was when Cromwell was *Serenissimus Dominus Protector* that Dr. Brian Walton, the great Orientalist, produced the Polyglot Bible, for which nine languages were employed.

Deprived of his preferments by the Government and forbidden to officiate publicly, he was allowed to have the necessary paper free of duty, and toiled in Oxford and London till the work was done. He had reason to believe that his great book would be suppressed if it were not dedicated to the usurper who, in spite of all, was a friend of learning. He therefore composed two different endings to the preface. In one of these the Protector and his Council are courteously mentioned. In the other the book is dedicated to King Charles II who was still ' over the water ', and the Protector and his Council are not explicitly mentioned but included under the simple description of ' those by whose favour we have received the paper duty-free '.[1]

The *Spectator* of September the 26th, 1712, has preserved a diverting story in which there figures the good Puritan divine who attended Cromwell on his death-bed, Dr. Thomas Goodwin, President of Magdalen College.[2] ' A young adventurer in the republic of letters with a good cargo of Latin and Greek ' waited on the President in order to be examined. He hoped to be admitted as an undergraduate of the college. A gloomy servant conducted him to a long gallery, darkened at noonday and illuminated by a single candle. After a time he was led into a chamber hung with black, until the Head of the College came out to him from an inner room with half a dozen night-caps upon his head, and religious horror in his countenance. The young man trembled, but his fears increased when instead of being asked about his Latin and Greek he was examined how he abounded in grace—' Whether he was of the number of the elect; what was the occasion of the conversion; upon

---

[1] H. J. Todd, *Life of Brian Walton*, vol. i, p. 84 (Rivington, London, 1821).

[2] He has been wrongly supposed to have originated the worship of the Sacred Heart of Jesus. See app. note 17, p. 270.

what day of the month, and hour of the day it happened; how it was carried on, and when completed? The whole examination was summed up with one short question, namely, "Whether he was prepared for death?" The boy, who had been bred up by honest parents, was frighted out of his wits at the solemnity of the proceeding, and by the last dreadful interrogatory; so that upon making his escape out of this house of mourning, he could never be brought a second time to the examination, as not being able to go through the terrors of it.' He was afterwards known to the learned as Anthony Henley.

With the Restoration of Charles II the contention between Episcopacy and Presbyterianism began afresh. The king had no love for the religion which had been a means of dethroning his father, and not only were the English bishops restored to their rights, but four new bishops, all Scots, were chosen for Scotland (1661). They included Robert Leighton, the saintly peacemaker, and James Sharp, the diligent diplomatist and persecutor. Both were men of learning and ability. But the Government bound up its own existence with a particular form of ecclesiastical establishment. It was a stiff and arid form of Episcopacy under which it was endeavoured to make the clergy the slaves of the crown, and in which liturgical worship was almost unknown. This Erastian Episcopacy was forced upon the people by Scotsmen whose action makes the policy of Charles I and Archbishop Laud appear by contrast both dignified and enlightened.

The three Commissioners who in turn represented the King's authority, John, Earl of Middleton, John, Earl of Rothes, and John, Earl of Lauderdale, aggravated 'the troubles' in the five western shires which were most strongly Presbyterian until they were past remedy. Lauderdale and Sharp have had to bear the heaviest load of adverse criticism.

Both had shown signs of a spirit of conciliation at the beginning; both were driven by fear or fury to cruel coercion. And although some four-fifths of Scotland were almost untouched by the struggle between the Government and the Covenanters, that struggle was itself so serious and was soon described in colours so lurid, that it could not fail to leave behind it a legacy of hatred.

In 1663 more than two hundred ministers in the southwest of Scotland were compelled, against the wishes of Archbishop Sharp, to resign their benefices because they would not comply with the Patronage Act, which required that they should seek presentation from the lawful patron of their living and collation from their bishop. Their places were filled with young men inexperienced and often from some northern diocese. Some of the former ministers continued to live in their old parishes and held conventicles. Thus began the history of the later Covenanters, the quartering of soldiers upon the people to dragoon them into a preference for Episcopacy, more laws, insurrections, tortures, and summary executions. Times were no better and manners no milder than they had been one hundred years before. A few ministers availed themselves of the 'Indulgences' offered by the Government in 1669 and 1672, but they were scorned by their brethren who refused all compromise. It was proved in 1681 that dislike of sheer Erastianism was not confined to the Presbyterians, for eighty clergymen then gave up their livings rather than accept the Succession Act and the Test Act intended to prepare the way for a Roman Catholic monarch.

Before that year Archbishop Sharp had been foully murdered on Magus Moor within sight of his cathedral city of St. Andrews, and at Bothwell Brig the Duke of Monmouth had routed an army of Covenanters who, in anticipation of victory, had erected a gigantic gibbet and piled around it several cart-loads of ropes. Broadly speaking, neither side gave or expected mercy. And as the 'Highland host' had been quartered on the people of Ayrshire in 1677 to quell their opposition, so in 1688 the peasantry revenged themselves by beginning on Christmas Day the cruel sport of evicting from church and home two hundred Episcopal clergymen with their families to find food and shelter where they might. It is one of the little ironies of history that in Scotland the only time when real freedom of worship existed before the middle of the reign of George III was for a few months under the zealous Roman Catholic King James VII.

Against this gloomy background shines the character of Robert Leighton, Bishop of Dunblane and afterwards Archbishop of St. Andrews, the Fénelon of Scotland. He endeavoured for years to promote a religion which was pacific and not polemic, and advocated a system whereby the rights of bishops, ministers, and Church synods should be harmoniously recognized. His task was wellnigh hopeless, but it was not wholly without effect in his lifetime, and it has won him the sincere respect of posterity. Nor will the same respect be denied to William Carstares, the able, generous, and fearless Presbyterian who influenced William III and thereby secured for Presbyterianism both establishment and liberty.

In England, at the Restoration of Charles II, about three hundred and ninety Congregationalist ministers [1] and more than two thousand Presbyterians held benefices of the Church of England. The question immediately arose whether the Church could be so remodelled as to include them or not. The King's behaviour was bad, even base. In his declaration from Breda he had promised liberty of conscience. As to the organization of the Church he

[1] *Transactions of the Congregational Historical Society*, vol. vi, 1913–1915, pp. 25 ff. (F. S. Thacker, London).

offered improvements which gratified the Presbyterians and would have also strengthened Episcopacy. As to the services of the Church he offered concessions, which, he must have known, the bishops could not tolerate. A Bill in Parliament, founded on the King's declaration, was rejected, apparently with his approval.[1] Nevertheless, there took place by royal commission the conference for the revision of the Prayer Book which the King both promised and promoted. At this, the Savoy Conference, the Nonconformists, whose behaviour towards the King had been tactless, not to say impertinent, proved themselves intelligent, conscientious, and irreconcilable. It would be a great mistake to suppose that their difficulty was a mere matter of such things as the surplice or the sign of the cross in baptism. They were, as we have already noticed, strict Calvinists, believing in absolute predestination and adjusting all other Christian doctrines to that central error. Richard Baxter, one of the best of their number, called the Prayer Book 'a dose of opium', and their hostility both to the language of the book and to the sacramental doctrine which it implied was thorough and unsparing. Their plan of action is evident. It was first to get the book drastically revised so as to become patient of a Calvinist interpretation, and secondly to have the use of even this depraved Prayer Book left so optional that the ordinary Calvinist services might be held in our churches. They objected to ' re-ordination ', as they termed it, by a bishop,[2] and they opposed the necessity of confirmation before admission to holy communion. The bishops charitably dispensed from the absolute necessity of confirmation before communion in the

[1] R. W. Dixon, *Essay on the Maintenance of the Church of England as an Established Church*, p. 352.
[2] When the hierarchy was restored in Ireland, Archbishop Bramhall insisted on the ordination of the Presbyterian ministers who were in possession of ecclesiastical benefices, but the ordination was conditional. See Daniel Neal, *History of the Puritans*, vol. iv, p. 348 (London, 1738).

case of those 'ready and desirous to be confirmed'. But they refused to surrender their principles; and with regard to confirmation in particular they said quite truly 'it is the apostolic ordinance', and 'our Church doth everywhere profess to conform to the Catholic usages of the primitive times, from which causelessly to depart argues rather love of contention than of peace'.

What would have been the immediate result if the bishops had yielded? Calvinism would have been firmly entrenched within the Church and the loyal members of the Church would have felt that their position had been fatally compromised. To permit officially the denial of baptismal regeneration, to dispense without necessity from an apostolic ordinance which the primitive Church regarded as fundamental, to accept as valid a ministry created in opposition to that ministry through which the primitive Church believed the same sacramental gifts were conferred as the apostles had conferred, and then to claim to be both Catholic and Apostolic, would have exposed the Church of England to the whole artillery of Rome.

But there is a further result to be considered. In the minds of early Christian theologians like St. Irenaeus, there existed a close connexion between the freedom of the will, the potential consecration of what is physical, the real incarnation of our Lord and the sacraments. The Church had maintained this connexion in the face of the tremendous opposition offered by the great Gnostic sects on the outskirts of Christianity, sects which taught that matter is evil and substituted fatalism for freedom, a phantom for the incarnation and magic for the sacraments. And in the time of Queen Elizabeth Richard Hooker touched the core of the problem. He urged the Puritans to consider what does Christianity teach as to the relation between the soul and the body, what in the sacraments is the relation between the things that we see and the gift which is unseen, and if through them Christ extends to the faithful the power of His incarnate life, how is God incarnate in Christ ? Thus we are led step by step to the divine Unity in Trinity. Hooker wrote more prophetically than he knew or his own contemporaries understood. We shall see in the fifth lecture how Calvinism in England and America was dogged by Unitarianism. The divorce from nature, the depreciation of outward things in the service of God, the reduced value attached to sacraments, combined to deprive the doctrines of the Atonement, of the Incarnation, of the Trinity, of their proper lines of defence, and minister after minister, congregation after congregation, abandoned the Christ of the New Testament for the idols fashioned by Arius, Socinus, and Priestley.

There is room in the Church for all that is noble in the Puritan's view of the sovereignty and the majesty of God, but it needs combining with the truth that He declares His almighty power most chiefly in showing mercy and pity to all His children. There is room for the fear of the Puritan that attention to things that are seen may divert us from the things that are eternal, but this fear must be balanced by the assurance that our Lord Jesus Christ has made all this visible world a Holy Land, and that, as the Fathers so often taught, His redeeming work is not in opposition to the original creation. The best Catholicism has always contained, and must contain, what we may call a Puritan element. But is there one among us who would say that Archbishop Laud and the other Caroline divines were wrong in refusing to believe that God has created multitudes who are not ethical agents and must inevitably be damned ?

Free or not free, that is the question. Our bishops, in appealing to the faith and practice of the primitive Church, were appealing to certain great principles of permanent authority. It is quite true that we find many and serious diversities of opinion in the ancient Fathers. But we also find a noble unity as to the nature of Christian life and salvation, and the character and object of Christian worship. This unity in experience and worship gradually expressed itself in a growing unity of creed, *Lex orandi, lex credendi.* And our present Prayer Book, that of 1662, is a fine exponent of that law. It was faithful to the best religious thought of that time and has continued to exercise a beneficent influence on a multitude of Christians. If our enlarged knowledge makes us conscious of its very rare defects, and desirous of its future enrichment, let us remember that the Scripture ascribes the power of rightly divining things to come only to that Wisdom which is conversant with God and ' knoweth things of old '.

English ecclesiastical art of the end of the seventeenth century, like all real ecclesiastical art, is an index to the religious sentiment of the time that gave it birth. If we turn back to the earlier years of that century we can see in the beautiful chapel of Wadham College a Gothic survival; it is just archaic, intentionally so, because its archaism has a spiritual value. But in the work of Sir Christopher Wren we find the same art taking a new form developed by a distinct individual talent. If his fame mainly rests upon the great cathedral church that he built in London, his smaller churches have the same quality of dignity and fitness; they show the same mastery of conditions, the same skill in harmonizing the old and the modern. The chapel of Trinity College, probably designed by Aldrich, but certainly modified to meet the suggestions of Wren, has the same excellence. A portion of Wren's mantle fell upon his immediate successors. There are provincial towns and poverty-stricken districts in outer London containing refined and vigorous churches designed by this school, churches with towers and spires that recall the unique beauty of the work of Wren. The elements of their design are Roman, but Rome has no spires like these spires of England. As they lift themselves from and above the noisy streets, with their white stone against the grey sky, let them tell us of a worship which is not the worship of Mammon, and remind us not only of the inheritance which we have already by grace received, but also of an inheritance incorruptible, reserved in heaven for all who will.

III

CONTINENTAL PROTESTANTISM FROM 1520 TO 1700

Ps. cxix. 105: Thy word is a lantern unto my feet and a light unto my paths.

THE different forms which the Reformation assumed in different countries followed at first the national and political characteristics of those countries. The Reformation is therefore as complex as the Church life of the later Middle Ages, and it would be misleading to speak of it in England and Scotland, Germany, Switzerland, Holland, and Scandinavia, as if it were in each case the result of the same causes or led everywhere to the acceptance of the same principles. Yet one main cause was everywhere the same; it was the determination to submit no longer to a rule which constantly invoked God's sanction for actions which were not religious and sometimes not moral. Everywhere therefore there was a denial of the alleged right of the Pope to exercise such an authority as was claimed for him by the early mediaeval False Decretals which Rome now acknowledges to be false, and a repudiation of the late mediaeval indulgence system which Rome acknowledges to have been connected with grave abuses.

Everywhere there was a fresh appeal to the Scriptures, a revival of translation of the Scriptures into vernacular languages, and a use of the Scriptures to which the Roman Catholic Church is now extending a rather belated toleration.[1] Together with the revival of Bible study came a wide

[1] See G. G. Coulton, *The Roman Catholic Church and the Bible*. Published by the author at Great Shelford, Cambs., 1921.

CONTINENTAL PROTESTANTISM 69

though not quite universal use of the language of the people in the services of the Church. Communion in both kinds was everywhere asserted to be the right of all communicants and was permitted after the Council of Trent in several dioceses of the Roman Catholic Church, though it was afterwards withdrawn from all those of the Latin rite.[1] It was everywhere permitted to the clergy to marry either before or after ordination, whereas the Roman Catholic Church only permits marriage, and that before ordination, to priests of the Oriental Churches which are united with Rome. This brief list nearly exhausts the common features of the Reformation in matters strictly religious and of serious importance. The practice of asking the saints now with Christ for their prayers, a practice which the Council of Trent too feebly safeguarded against the recrudescence of grave abuses, became almost entirely abandoned in all countries where the Reformation prevailed. This abandonment formed no part of the original English Reformation. And if these requests for the prayers of Christ's friends had been maintained, together with prayers for the faithful departed, within the limits laid down by our Church in the time of Henry VIII, less injury would have been done to the doctrine of the communion of saints and less stimulus would have been given to the unwholesome necromancy which has led so many dupes from the medium to the madhouse.

The Reformation in Great Britain we have already considered, and some features of the Reformation on the Continent now demand our attention.

The Lutheran Reformation embraced a very large part of what was recently the German Empire, including East Prussia from which it spread farther east along the Baltic.

---

[1] Papal briefs of April the 16th, 1564, to the Archbishops of Mainz, Köln, Trier, Salzburg, Prague, and Gran, permitted the chalice to the laity.

It was accepted with some variations in Denmark, Norway, Iceland, and Sweden. Its most conservative form survives in Sweden where the episcopal succession was maintained.[1] The distinguishing religious feature of Lutheranism was the insistence upon the doctrine that men are forgiven, 'justified', by faith only, that is, 'when they believe that they are received into God's favour and their sins remitted for the sake of Christ, who by His death made satisfaction for our sins'. This was sometimes stated in language similar to that of St. Paul, who in the very centre of his great epistle to the Romans demonstrates that his doctrine does not imperil but secure morality. But it was sometimes stated by Luther himself in terms which disparaged good works and sound morality. That the danger did not pass away with Luther can be illustrated from the career of his indefatigable disciple Matthias Flacius (d. 1575) who assailed George Major, formerly professor at Wittenberg, for maintaining that good works are necessary for salvation though not for justification. The storm aroused by this reasonable statement was so violent that Major was obliged to retract.

Luther's own theology is so torrential, and sometimes so inconsistent, that it is most difficult to understand or condense. But modern Continental writers, both Protestant and Roman Catholic, are agreed that there is a large Catholic element, both ancient and mediaeval, in Luther's belief and teaching.

It was to a mystical work of the fifteenth century, *Theologia Germanica*, that Luther owed much of his conviction that he needed a conscious union with God. It was to his confessor Staupitz that he owed his belief that the Christian is truly free when he believes in Christ. It is to the late mediaeval hymnology and devotion to Christ's Passion that he owed something that is best in his talent for sacred song. In fact his debt to the Catholicism of the

[1] See app. note 11, p. 264.

Middle Ages is so great that he has been called 'a mediaeval heretic'. His attitude towards the earlier Catholicism of the undivided Church is no less interesting and is more important. To determine it accurately we must observe that the external forms of the authority of that Catholicism were three. They were, first, the gradually formed canon of the New Testament with which was united the Jewish canon of the Old Testament; secondly, the rule of faith expressed at first in local creeds such as the Roman Apostles' Creed, then in the Oecumenical Creed of Nicaea; and, thirdly, the episcopate, it being believed that the bishops were divinely commissioned to teach others to 'hold the traditions' and to be the instruments of conferring the same sacramental gifts as the apostles had conferred.

Now Luther, without any necessity for so doing, dropped episcopacy, and as early as 1520 said that the sacrament of orders was 'nothing else than a ceremony for choosing preachers'. His doctrine of the Church is vague, though he says that the outward marks of the Church are 'baptism, sacrament, and the Gospel, and not Rome'.[1] His doctrine of the ministry is destructive, and the rapid deterioration of Lutheranism was hastened by these doctrines concerning the Church and the ministry. They put Lutheranism under the heels of the German nobility. With regard to the rule of faith, he accepted the three ancient creeds. In a foolish moment he wrote that he hated the word *homoousion*, but in spite of that his theology and his religion are inseparable from his Christology. His own best convictions are expressed when he says, 'Wilt thou go surely and meet and grasp God rightly, so finding grace and help in Him, be not persuaded to seek Him elsewhere than in the Lord Christ. Let thine art and study begin with Christ, and there let it stay and cling.' Luther's Christ is perfect,

---

[1] See F. Loofs, *Leitfaden zum Studium der Dogmengeschichte*, p. 363, third edition (Halle, 1893).

sinless, born of a Virgin, with a risen and ascended body. But though he uses the ancient language of the Church, he sometimes quotes it with an accent which the great Fathers would have rightly regarded as a false accent. In his eagerness to 'grasp God' in Christ, he taught a fusion of the Deity and the manhood of Christ in a manner which threatened the verity of that manhood. He taught, and his followers taught, that Christ's manhood was given the properties of His Godhead, a theory akin to the Apollinarianism of the fourth century and to the Monophysite heresy of the fifth and sixth centuries. His doctrine of consubstantiation confirmed him in the same unfortunate opinion. Though he rejected the ancient doctrine of the ministry, he believed firmly in the real mysterious presence of Christ in the Eucharist. He was determined not to abandon the words of Scripture, *Hoc est corpus meum.* He agreed with the Zwinglians that the body of Christ is at the right hand of God, but in opposition to them he affirmed that the right hand of God is everywhere, and that the body of Christ and His whole manhood are present everywhere simultaneously. Since therefore Christ's manhood like His Godhead is properly omnipresent, ubiquitous, it can be given to us with and under the sacramental bread and wine. Some of Luther's followers even ascribed to our Lord's manhood the divine attribute of infinity, and thus a sincere desire to be faithful to the Gospel narrative evaporated in a scholasticism which was neither new nor true.

But Luther's appeal to the Scriptures is one that involved him in the greatest inconsistencies. Students of early Church history, if they study Luther, will be struck by the extraordinary resemblance between Luther and the great heretic of the second century, Marcion, in their arbitrary treatment of the New Testament. The old Catholic theory of the use of Scripture can be summed up in the maxim that the Church is to teach and the Bible to prove. Luther left the Bible to stand without the Church. He taught that Scripture is easy of interpretation.[1] He said, 'No part of Holy Scripture is dark', and once more, 'It belongs to each and every Christian to know and to judge of doctrine'. And he meant every German to judge and to know that he, Luther, was right. He proved his sincerity by translating the Bible into German, the simple spoken High German of his day, which he could write with a directness and force that none of his opponents could equal. The influence of this translation was enormous. In addition to its religious influence, it helped to reduce the Low German language to a provincial patois, and to unite the nation in such a way that Luther began what Bismarck completed. This opening of the Bible to the people had the inevitable result when there was no Church to say 'Understandest thou what thou readest?' and give a consistent interpretation of the written word. Novel views sprang up in every direction and Luther could not convince everybody that his doctrine was Bible truth. He was forced to discover some vindication of the canonical list of books, a list made by the early Church. Sometimes he comes near to the wise principle which guided the Church in separating the four Gospels from the forged Gospels. He accepts a book because it shows to us 'the Gospel concerning God's Son incarnate who suffered and was raised'. But his ultimate test is not witness to Christ, but witness to justification by faith as he conceived it. And therefore he not only called the Epistle of St. James when compared with other books 'a mere letter of straw', but also said 'St. Paul's Epistles are more a Gospel than Matthew, Mark, and Luke'.

Luther's depreciation of the Synoptic Gospels is surpassed by his contemptuous criticism of different parts of the Old

[1] *Werke*, ed. Walch, xviii. 1416.

Testament. Such criticism might be in part excused by his inability to recognize the gradual character of God's revelation to mankind. But it is in flagrant contrast to his uncompromising exaltation of blind faith above reason. Again and again he commends an irrational faith, which, he says 'wrings the neck of reason and strangles the beast.... But how? It holds to God's word: let it be right and true, no matter how foolish and impossible it sounds.'[1]

This antithesis between faith and reason is contrary both to the spirit and to the letter of the New Testament. And whereas modern German writers are wont to plead that Luther's Gospel will not prove antiquated if it be removed still farther from the New Testament, it would be wiser to say that its weakness is caused by a neglect of the very elements which the New Testament abundantly supplies.

We cannot be astonished to find that the sweeping victories of Lutheranism were soon checked by the recovery of Roman Catholicism, by the rise of antinomian sects, and by the penetration of Swiss Protestantism.

It is to the Protestantism of Switzerland, known on the Continent as the *Reformed* religion, that we must now turn our attention.

Huldreich Zwingli (1484-1531) was not like Luther a runaway friar who had passed through the pangs of spiritual trouble. He was a humanist who had studied at Vienna and Basel and had passed from the study of *Litterae Humaniores* to the study of Theology. In 1516 he was 'people's priest' at Einsiedeln, where the Benedictine monastery was, and still is, a famous place of pilgrimage, and a gorgeous rococo church now shelters the same dusky image of Our Lady that Zwingli knew. A man of

[1] *Werke*, ed. Walch, viii. 2043. Erklärung der Ep. an die Galater.

unchaste life, he was not unable to discern the motes and beams in the eyes of others, and even before his ordination was convinced that indulgences were 'a cheat and delusion'. So in 1519, when a friar named Samson arrived with pardons at Zürich, Zwingli preached against them. The Bishop of Constance approved, but was obliged to interfere when Zwingli assailed the observance of Lent. In 1522 he married, and debated with a Franciscan on the lawfulness of invoking the saints. Gradually he carried the clergy and the town council of Zürich with him and in 1525 the new order was set up. He was the first citizen in Zürich. The Church and the State were to be one body under different aspects and administered by the same persons, who were to make it a strong moral commonwealth.

Zwingli appealed to the Bible. He rightly gives to the word 'Gospel' a wider significance than Luther. A more cultivated man than Luther, he drew his teaching much less exclusively from St. Paul, indeed he actually omitted the Epistle to the Romans from his ordinary scheme of instruction. He is also more Catholic than Luther when he describes original sin as a disease (*morbus*) rather than as an offence (*peccatum*). And with this moderate view of original sin we also find in Zwingli the view held by certain early Fathers that the best ancient philosophers were instruments of God.

Zwingli's doctrine of predestination is similar to that of Luther. But the two men start from different points. Luther starts from his idea of fallen man, Zwingli from his idea of an omnipotent God. His God is absolutely powerful and active, causing sin and working evil as well as good. Everything happens through God and everything is in God. This God creates in the elect faith in His written word and the elect know that they are predestined. The visible Church exists for their sake. Nothing was to be allowed in worship unless it had the sanction of the Bible.

Therefore organs and bells were banished as well as images. Here he could contend that Spirit must act directly without a medium upon spirit. But if we deny that man can co-operate with God in the saving of his soul, and also deny that what is physical can be a vehicle of the grace of God, the sacraments cease to be for us sacraments in the Church's sense of that word. They are symbols of the work of Christ, but are not efficacious means of grace. And what Zwingli denied in doctrine he repudiated in practice. By an innovation of the most drastic kind the Eucharist was dethroned from its primitive position as the chief act of Sunday worship, and the Zwinglian communion service was reduced to an occasional feast at which cakes of unleavened bread were passed round in wooden platters together with wine in wooden beakers.

Zwingli's anti-sacramentalism was not an isolated phenomenon in his theology, but is connected with his conception of God, of Christ, and of grace. In opposition to Luther, who was willing to sacrifice everything to secure, as he supposed, the perfect revelation of divine love in Christ, Zwingli was unwilling to entertain the idea of the infinite communicating itself to the finite, and he sharply separated the divine and the human elements in Christ. We therefore reach the astonishing result that the two great religious revolutionaries of the sixteenth century had gone back to the errors of the fifth, Luther inclining to the heresy of the Monophysites of Alexandria, and Zwingli to the heresy of the rival school, the Nestorians of Antioch.

Zwingli's novel doctrine of the sacraments immediately exposed him to two dangerous attacks. If baptism be only a ceremony like circumcision, infants who are no longer under a ceremonial law like that of Moses need not be baptized, whereas adults may well receive baptism as an outward token of their adhesion to Christ. So argued the Anabaptists, and Zwingli, being unable to beat them in argument, had to use ridicule and persecution. Luther, on the other hand, with his strong belief in the real presence, passionately protested against Zwingli's treatment of the Eucharist and Zwinglian opinions made little progress in Germany. So when Zwingli died carrying a banner in the battle of Kappel in 1531, Protestantism was already rent in twain. It was shivered by the rock of Zwingli's anti-sacramentalism, the principle of which, if logically pursued, would make the Bible dumb and the manhood of our Lord merely an 'alien garment'.

John Calvin (1509–1564). It is not easy for Englishmen to think impartially of Calvin; and one reason for this is to be commended and another is to be deplored. The good reason is that an Englishman generally has a strong sense of justice, and he resents the notion of a God who refuses to a vast number of His creatures any chance of salvation. We ask with Abraham, 'Shall not the Judge of all the earth do right?' The bad reason is that we tend unconsciously to the oldest British heresy, Pelagianism. We like to be 'up and doing', active, practical, successful. We are apt to think that we are too vigorous, perhaps too virtuous, to need grace, the undeserved, unmerited help of God, in all that we do. We are slow to welcome that thought of absolute dependence upon God which gave strength and freedom to all His saints. And Calvin in spite of the monstrous nightmare which he himself admitted to be 'a horrible decree' of God, and accepted, although it was horrible, at least had the merit of teaching that we cannot reach God without God's help.

Calvin's great work, the *Institutes*, appeared only five years after Zwingli's death. It is a work of genius. It is an attempt to build an impregnable wall and it is not a mere monument of defiance protesting against mediaeval Rome and modern paganism. It is meant as a defence which no Italian intellect could take by storm, and which could not be undermined by Lutheran inconsistency, Zwinglian rationalism, and Anabaptist explosions. The foundation of Calvinism is the doctrine of double predestination. 'Predestination is the name that we give to God's eternal decree by which God has determined with himself what He wills to be done with every man . . . for some eternal life, for others eternal death is foreordained.'[1] And 'if we cannot give a reason why God has mercy on His own, except that so it pleases Him, so in the reprobation of others we have no cause but God's will'.[2] Calvin resolutely maintains that if man perishes in his corruption he only pays the penalty of a calamity into which by God's predestination Adam fell, and all his descendants with him. He ridicules the view of those who deny that God decreed that Adam should fall. 'I grant you', says Calvin, 'it is a horrible decree, yet no one can deny that God foreknew the end of man before He formed him, and foreknew it because by His own decree He had ordained it.'[3]

Calvin, a typical Frenchman of Northern France, but the patriarch of all Puritans, studied in Paris at the same time as George Buchanan and Francis Xavier. He could write admirably even at the age of ten, and was so censorious that when at school he was called 'the accusative case'. In clear eloquent Latin he writes down the dogmas which men ought to believe and the discipline which they ought to obey, attempting to undo the mischief caused by Luther's degradation of the ministry and Zwingli's degradation of the sacraments. Everything is in logical connexion with his view of predestination. His doctrine of baptism and the Lord's Supper is far nearer to that of St. Paul than was the doctrine of Zwingli, and it is not unlike that of Clement

---

[1] *Instit.* Lib. III, cap. xxi, sect. 5.   [2] *Ibid.*, cap. xxii, sect. 11.
[3] *Ibid.*, cap. xxiii, sect. 7.

of Alexandria and Origen, though it is mutilated by the theory that real grace is given only to the elect. It is taught that for the government of the Church Christ instituted four orders, first pastors, then doctors, then elders, and fourthly deacons, and that from the first every Church had its senate. The practice of voluntary private confession to a pastor is strongly defended by Calvin.[1] The true visible Church is upheld by doctrine, discipline, and sacraments.

To leave the external communion of this Church is absolutely without excuse. After quoting the promises made in the Old Testament concerning the everlasting privileges of Sion, Calvin upholds the duty of fidelity to the Church, saying, 'Of this Christ himself, the apostles and almost all the prophets have left us an example. Terrible are those passages in which Isaiah, Jeremiah, Habakkuk, and others deplore the maladies of the Church of Jerusalem. Among the people, the magistrates, the priests, everything had become so corrupt that Isaiah does not hesitate to compare Jerusalem with Sodom and Gomorrha. Religion was on the one side despised and on the other side defiled: everywhere there are recorded in descriptions of men's manners acts of theft, plunder, treachery, murder, and similar crimes. Nevertheless, the prophets did not for that reason erect new churches for themselves or build new altars on which they might have separate sacrifices; but whatever men might be, because they believed, in spite of all, that God had set His word among them, and had instituted the ceremonies by which He there was worshipped, in the midst of the throng of the wicked they lifted up to Him pure hands. Verily, if they had thought that they had thence contracted any contagion, they would have rather died a thousand times than have suffered themselves to be dragged into it. Nothing therefore restrained them from

[1] *Op. cit.*, Lib. III, cap. iv, sect. 12.

making a schism but their zeal for preserving unity.'[1] Then, after appealing to the example of Christ and His apostles, he quotes St. Cyprian to the effect that though there be unclean vessels in the Church it is not our duty to withdraw from it but to labour that we may be vases of gold and silver.

So then the Bible, as he truly argues, supports the authority of the Church. And why do we believe the Bible? We believe the books of the Bible because they were 'composed at the dictation of the Holy Spirit'; the writers of the New Testament were 'authentic amanuenses of the Holy Spirit', the prophets uttered the 'oracles' of God. The authority of the Bible rests upon two facts, the fact that it was dictated by the Holy Spirit and the corresponding fact that the same Holy Spirit witnesses to it and seals it in our hearts. It is worth noticing that this view of the authority of the Bible is the result of an endeavour to improve upon the views of Luther by a doctrine derived from mediaeval Catholic theology. If the result is not entirely successful, it does express a religious truth when it asserts that there is a concurrent witness of the Holy Spirit in the written word and in the soul of the Christian. God has made a personal revelation of himself in Christ to man. The Bible is a means of putting us in contact with that Christ. And from Calvin's own premisses it might well be maintained that the tradition of the Church guided by the Spirit, and always recalled to its original type by a reverent use of the Scriptures, is a third element coalescing with the witness of the Spirit in the written word and in the individual soul.

Earnest as were the disciples of Calvin, they could not exorcize the spectre that haunted the new Church which he founded. That spectre was Socinianism. Zwingli had imperilled the doctrine of the Incarnation by his shallow

[1] *Op. cit.*, Lib. IV, cap. i, sect. 18.

view of the sacraments, for it is in the sacraments that we find ' an extension of the Incarnation '. Yet he maintained a belief in the Holy Trinity and in the Deity of Jesus Christ. But Faustus Socinus (d. 1604), an Italian humanist, well born and well educated, the nephew of a priest of Siena, emphasized to the utmost the negative elements of Zwingli's teaching, so as to deny the doctrines of the Incarnation and the Trinity. He taught a reduced view of Christ's Person and His work, corresponding with an imperfect realization of human sin and guilt. According to Socinus, Christ did not exist before He was born of Mary. He may be worshipped because God delegated divine power to Him as to a viceroy. His moral teaching is to be followed, but His atoning work is limited to His example of obedience and to the forgiveness of God which He offers. This doctrine, nominally based upon the teaching of the Bible, was in its essence a revival of the heresy taught in the third century by Paul of Samosata who replaced the scriptural truth that the ' Word was made flesh ' by the theory that a divine character was infused into a human person. Its delusive modernism attracted a good many adherents, especially in Poland, and they proclaimed its victory in the lines,

> Tota iacet Babylon, destruxit tecta Lutherus,
> Calvinus muros, sed fundamenta Socinus.

Socinianism certainly did not destroy the foundations of the Church. But in one form or another it never ceased to attract men who imagined that in abandoning Calvinistic doctrines of predestination sin and atonement it is necessary to abandon the substantially orthodox doctrine of Christ's Person which the Calvinists retained.

For a time, however, Calvinism remained the only important Protestant rival of Lutheranism on the Continent. The differences between them are profound in theology, worship, and ethical temper, and the history of modern civilization cannot be understood unless these differences are in some degree appreciated. They had in common an appeal to the Bible, an assent to the doctrines of the Trinity and the Incarnation, a strenuous opposition to Rome, and a zeal for education. But they differed even in regard to their belief in God and predestination and good works. Luther and Calvin both wished to exclude the idea that man's works can secure his salvation. But Luther in so doing wished to preserve the believer's own subjective certainty of salvation. God is love and He means to save His elect, though they know that their works fall short of His demands. But to Calvin God is not primarily love, but infinite arbitrary power. He glorifies himself by revealing to man His sovereign freedom of action in the choice of His elect, and in their character as members of a community ruled by Christ. The first view tends to sentimentalism, the second to rigorism.

In Lutheranism organized ecclesiastical life was weak. In one German State after another Lutheranism formed a little patriarchal system. The prince became the absolute ruler of the Church, the noble patron became the tyrant of the pastor. Under this territorial system discipline became such a farce that a money payment was sometimes taken in lieu of penance, and Lutherans would throw down the fee, when they approached the confessional, and demand absolution from the pastor.[1] But soldiers were well drilled, workpeople were industrious, and there remained a sincerely pious remnant of people without much initiative, but witnessing to their faith and producing a devotional and even a mystical literature.

Calvinism, on the other hand, created a highly organized middle-class theocracy. God is represented by His elect who choose their ministers, elders, and synods, who learn

---

[1] For this and for other evidence of the almost inconceivable degradation into which Lutheranism fell, see Kerr D. Macmillan, *Protestantism in Germany* (Princeton University Press and Oxford University Press, 1917).

how to govern and exercise discipline. The quasi-Catholic doctrine of the Church developed a far greater sense of international life and common action than we find in Lutheranism. And at the same time the right to a share in Church government developed a power of initiative and a sense of individual responsibility. If Lutheranism produced good musicians, soldiers, and workmen, Calvinism produced good scholars and clever men of business. The modern capitalist is usually a child of the Ghetto or a grandchild of Geneva.

In the century and a half which followed the death of Luther, Calvinism, a first-class fighting religion, pushed itself through the midst of Germany. One by one Bremen, Anhalt, Hesse-Cassel, and Lippe deserted Luther for Calvin, and on Christmas Day, 1613, John Sigismund, Elector of Brandenburg, left Lutheranism for the Reformed Church. Modern Prussia has been built up by rulers trained in Calvinism moulding a people trained in Lutheranism.

In the meanwhile there flourished a Lutheran scholasticism devotèd to the defence and development of Luther's teaching. As a result of his teaching with regard to the Incarnation, the Lutheran schoolmen, like some of the schoolmen of the Middle Ages, disputed greatly concerning the conditions under which the divine attributes were exercised by our Lord Jesus Christ during His ministry on earth. We need not regard these disputes as a mere flood of sterilizing controversy. Similar problems were debated here early in the eighteenth century, and more recently within the memory of some who are in this church to-day. And it would be well if we could learn from the mistakes of Lutherans, Calvinists, and Socinians the moral and the intellectual dangers of departing from the Christ of the New Testament.

Lutheran Christology has not the high merit of the work of Richard Hooker. It sacrifices too much to *a priori* considerations. It leaves the Master less humility, less reality. But Biblical exegesis had some distinguished representatives in Germany, such as Erasmus Schmidt of Wittenberg, and Sebastian Schmidt of Strassburg; and any religious community, which through the Bible tries to keep in contact with Christ, has within it a grand corrective of academic errors.

Side by side with the Bible Lutheranism preserved some good ancient traditions in public worship. Corresponding with their different views of God and the sacraments, Calvinists and Lutherans manifested a wide difference in worship. The Calvinists kept alive the iconoclastic spirit of Zwingli. They denuded their churches of ornament, so that the omnipotent Spirit might be adored with less distraction. They wished for nothing in public worship which the New Testament does not obviously sanction. The Lutherans wished to retain ceremonies which the Bible does not forbid. They left their churches adorned with rich altars, tapers, and crucifixes, ready for the presence of Emmanuel. The people of Berlin rose in protest when John Sigismund tried to banish crucifixes and fonts. The Marienkirche at Danzig is still famous for its store of mediaeval vestments, and John Wesley, when he visited Meissen in 1738, was surprised to see a Lutheran minister in a chasuble of gold and scarlet, ' and a vast cross both behind and before '.[1] The Calvinists abolished Christmas and the whole cycle of old festivals. The Lutherans kept the more important. Their services kept part of the ancient liturgical outlines. Indeed, one of the most recent Lutheran

---

[1] *The Journal of the Rev. John Wesley*, vol. i, p. 113 (London, 1830). Wesley also notes that at Berthelsdorf, near the Moravian settlement of Herrnhut, there were two large lighted candles on the altar and a crucifix over the pulpit.

Prayer Books, that used by the large body of English-speaking Lutherans in the United States,[1] follows mediaeval German precedents. It perpetuates Luther's rejection of episcopacy, and also his omission of the old sacrificial language in the canon of the Mass which he misunderstood. But it contains forms for private confession and for confirmation, it teaches baptismal regeneration and a doctrine of the real presence, and gives careful directions as to the ornaments of the altar. It even contains a laudatory reference to our First Prayer Book of Edward VI, and though inferior to it in some important particulars, it is both directly and indirectly a real tribute to the value of some of our best liturgical traditions.

With the Lutheran liturgy went sacred song. Lutheran hymnology of the sixteenth and seventeenth centuries, going back through Luther himself to mediaeval hymns, is of a high quality, marked by a new devotion to the Holy Trinity, the Incarnation, and the work of the Holy Spirit. The terrible times of the Thirty Years' War were rich in sacred poetry. During and after that war wrote Paul Gerhardt (d. 1676), the greatest of German hymn writers. With him the older school of sacred poetry culminated. Later in the same century came Johann Franck, whose poetry is inspired by the idea of union with Christ through His mystical birth in our heart, and Johann Scheffler, better known as 'Angelus Silesius', who became a Roman Catholic priest. The art of hymn writing in the eighteenth century became disfigured by a weak emotionalism. The works of Gerhardt Tersteegen are a happy exception to that rule. We have in English John Wesley's fine translation of his hymn

<blockquote>Lo, God is here, let us adore,</blockquote>

[1] *Common Service Book of the Lutheran Church* (Philadelphia, The Board of Publication of the United Lutheran Church in America, 1919).

and Catherine Winkworth's[1] still more beautiful rendering of Scheffler's hymn with the refrain:

> O Love, I give myself to thee,
> Thine ever, only thine to be.

The doctrine of many German hymns reminds us that the tendency of official Lutheranism to favour scholasticism increased an opposite tendency in the direction of mysticism. And mysticism sometimes degenerated into theosophy. This theosophy is extremely complex. In it we can find Luther's strong antithesis between nature and grace, the mediaeval mysticism of Eckhart and Tauler, the speculation of the Lutheran pastor Weigel, and the method of Andreä, who founded the secret brotherhood known as the Rosicrucians. Nor must we entirely omit the influence of the Jewish Kabala, with the elaborate system of emanations from God by which the Jews, after rejecting the Messiah, tried to bring God into contact with the world. The prince of Lutheran mystics was Jacob Boehme (d. 1624), of whom Angelus said:

> God's Heart is Jacob Boehme's Element.

He would teach us that there is nothing nearer to each one of us than heaven, paradise, and hell, and that we may, if we will, be now in heaven and enjoy that unutterable joy which the Father has in the Son. But this is not gained by mere dreaming. We must go through Christ's whole progress from His incarnation to His ascension, enter into His process. Boehme is a prophet of the life that is in God, in spite of his obscurity, his serious errors, and his misunderstandings. In the time of King Charles I his works were translated into English,[2] and they exercised a dominant influence on William Law, the greatest English devotional

---

[1] See her *Lyra Germanica*, Hymns for the Sundays and chief Festivals of the Christian Year, translated from the German, new edition (Longman, London, 1859).

[2] By John Sparrow and John Ellistone, for whose works see *Dictionary*

writer of the eighteenth century. If we wonder how a man of the intellectual eminence of William Law could become in many things a disciple of this German visionary, it may be that we forget that a fisherman, a tent-maker, a cobbler, may understand some depths of the human heart which are not sounded by the ordinary philosophy of the schools.

George Calixtus, or Calissen (1586–1656), is a Lutheran theologian and Church historian who also should not be left unmentioned. He laboured for forty years to promote union between the Lutherans and the Reformed, suggesting as a basis for union the Holy Scriptures and, as a secondary authority, the consensus of the first five centuries. He was very learned, a clear writer, and a sincere peace-maker. By his example and by his instruction he promoted sounder methods of interpreting Scripture and a clearer recognition of the necessity of historical investigation in the domain of theology. He visited France, Belgium, and England, broadening his mind and sympathies. The fact that he was accused sometimes of being a Crypto-papist, and sometimes of being a Crypto-calvinist, gives us a good indication of his true position. But his own words throw light upon these accusations. For he always said that ' his tutors in Germany had not done as much in spurring him on to the study of ecclesiastical history as the English bishops and the well-stored libraries that he had seen among them '.[1]

John Ernest Grabe (1666–1711) was an actual convert from Lutheranism to the Church of England. A native of Königsberg and a member of the university of that place,

of *National Biography*, article ' Sparrow, John '. See also ' Pordage, John ', and ' Pordage, Samuel '.

[1] H. Ph. C. Henke, *Calixtus' Leben*, vol. i, p. 149. Calixtus was accused of Romanism, though the great Bossuet called him Rome's ablest antagonist. He was accused of Judaism for teaching that the doctrine of the Trinity was not revealed with equal clearness in the Old as in the New Testament, and suspected of undermining the doctrine of justification by faith because he taught that salvation might be endangered by sins of unchastity !

he became convinced that there could be no valid orders apart from an episcopate derived from the apostles. He therefore contemplated joining the Church of Rome, but resolved first to present a memorial of his difficulties to the ecclesiastical consistory of Sambia in Prussia. The reply which he received was unconvincing. But one of the divines who composed this reply was no less a person than Spener, the founder of German Pietism. Spener, while believing, as Luther and mediaeval writers had believed, that there is a priesthood common to all believers, also believed, unlike Luther, that the Christian ministry is of divine appointment. He generously advised Grabe to turn to England rather than Rome. He came to England and received a pension of £100 a year from William III. He was ordained deacon in 1700, and became a chaplain of Christ Church, Oxford. In 1706 he received the degree of Doctor of Divinity at the Encaenia.

Grabe devoted his time at Oxford partly to the study of the Fathers and the production of books which embodied the results of this study, and partly to an edition of the *Codex Alexandrinus*. By his numerous emendations he destroyed the value of this laborious edition of the famous Greek manuscript of the Bible. He also wrote in English in 1711 an Essay to oppose the learned Whiston's strange view that the 'Apostolical Constitutions', a work of the fourth century, was 'the most sacred of the canonical books of the New Testament'. On August the 22nd, 1711, Grabe wrote to the Lord Treasurer complaining of his broken health and the non-payment of his pension. His pension was paid together with a gift of £50. He died in the following November, the occasion of his death being a bruise near the liver caused by his last journey to Oxford in the stage coach. According to Robert Nelson, Grabe was a man of exemplary piety, humility, and patience. 'His learned Studies did not so engross his Mind, as to prevent his daily attending the

Hours of publick Prayer, to which purpose he always chose his Lodgings near a Church. He laid the chiefest Stress upon the constant Practice of the Virtues of the Christian Life, and was also a strict Observer of all the Rules of the Apostolical Times, and of the Catholick Usages of the first Christians '.[1] He frequently received absolution and holy communion with great devotion during his last illness, ' to fortify him in his Passage to Eternity '.

If we turn from the Lutherans to the Calvinists, we shall find additional reasons for believing that the Anglican position was well chosen.

Geneva was an intellectual as well as a geographical centre. Learning and Calvinism often grew side by side so that it is sometimes boldly claimed that the Reformed Church showed a clear pre-eminence in almost every branch of knowledge, Biblical, classical, Oriental, legal, and historical. And we need not surrender the claims of Ussher and Pearson, Walton and Pococke, if we grant that it is also an imposing list which includes the names of Justus Scaliger (1540–1609) the great scholar of Geneva, Claude Salmasius (1588–1653) the French scholar, Daniel Heinsius (1580–1655) of Leiden, the two Buxtorfs (d. 1629 and 1664), the Hebraists of Basel, and many others. But a close examination of the facts proves that among the greatest of the Reformed writers there was a decided tendency to modify or abandon the distinctive views of Calvin. Instance after instance can be quoted, and some of these are of special interest for British scholars. Among them are John Cameron, a notable Scotch professor at Montauban, Isaac Casaubon, and Gerhard Voss of Leiden.

John Cameron, born of poor parents in Glasgow about 1570, was a typical Scot, independent, brave, disputatious, generous, with a preference for living outside Scotland.

---

[1] Robert Nelson, *Life of Dr. George Bull*, 2nd edition, pp. 404–5 (London, 1714).

He became a pastor at Bordeaux, a professor at Montauban, and founder of the theological school of Saumur. He was a prudent innovator who tried to discover joints in the armour of Calvinism through which he could quietly inject a gentler and more wholesome spirit. He tried to modify the strict doctrine of predestination by teaching that God calls all men to salvation while He does not give to all the gift of faith, and his doctrine of the Church would not exclude an Anglican or even deny to a sincere Papist the possibility of salvation. After his death he was accused of heresy, but the French Huguenots as a body regarded Cameron with sincere esteem.[1]

Isaac Casaubon (1559–1614), one of the most learned men in France, is a man who should never be forgotten by the Church of England. The world has seldom known a more eager student, a more sincere seeker after truth, one more glad to be 'alone with God and with his books'. We who are surrounded by a knowledge of the antique world accumulated by the labour of more than four hundred years cannot realize the difficulties, but we can respect the toil, of one who at Geneva, Montpellier, and Paris sought diligently for truth and wisdom. Regretting every moment snatched from study, he could hold his own with the French king, Henry IV, with Cardinal Du Perron, or with the theologians of Holland. His religion was not confined to his study. When in Paris he would go ten miles to worship at a Protestant temple, even when he had to walk both ways in bad weather. And it was this man who by slowly formed convictions crossed over to the position of the Church of England. Writing to his friend Daniel Tilenus, professor at Sedan, he explains that he had read Bellarmin, and that on Scripture, the authority of the old interpreters, human traditions, on the power of the Pope, on images, on

---

[1] For Cameron, see G. Bonet-Maury, ' Jean Cameron ' in *Études de Théologie et d'Histoire* (Fischbacher, Paris, 1901).

indulgences, he could by certain reasons demonstrate all Bellarmin's positions to be false. But when he came to the chapter on the sacraments (though there were also some things which could no less be refuted) it was clear to him that on certain points the whole of antiquity with one consent was on the side of their opponents; 'for', he says, 'unless I am mistaken, I can most certainly prove that those of our writers who have attempted to show that the Fathers held our views have egregiously wasted their time and been blind in broad daylight'.[1]

After a transient wish to go to the Greek Church at Venice, he determined to see the Church of England. He came and he was convinced. He had to lose many old friends, both Calvinist and Roman Catholic. But he won good new friends, including the saintly Bishop Andrewes. His remarks on Oxford, and his comparison of our university with that of Paris, are judiciously in favour of Oxford, though he says 'we are occupied in perpetual feastings'. He was well received, and at Magdalen College he was splendidly entertained. He was not destined to live long in his new home. He had worked too hard, and he suffered from an excruciating disease which brought him to the grave in 1614, while still engaged in writing a reply to the Roman Catholic protagonist Baronius. On his death-bed he received the holy communion at the hands of Bishop Andrewes and asked that the *Nunc dimittis* should be read to him. He is a man in whom it is difficult to find a fault, except that he never took a holiday.

The tendency to break away from Calvinism is once more illustrated by the career of Gerhard Johann Voss (1577–1649), a scholar of Dutch family who was born at Heidelberg, but studied under Gomarus at Leiden, where he became the lifelong friend of the celebrated Grotius. From

---

[1] *Isaaci Casauboni Epistolae*, Ep. 1043 (Fritsch et Böhm, Roterodami, 1709).

1614 to 1619 he was director of the theological college at Leiden, and had already gained a high reputation as a scholar when he was compelled to escape expulsion by resignation. He had published a history of the Pelagian controversies, in which he maintained that absolute predestination was not a doctrine of the primitive Church, a view which modern writers regard as unassailable. The book excited keen interest in England, and Voss accepted from Archbishop Laud a prebend in Canterbury without residence, and was given a doctor's degree at Oxford. He died at Amsterdam, where he had been appointed professor of history in the Athenaeum.

In no country was the tendency to desert from Calvinism more pronounced than in Holland. Officially Holland became 'Reformed', that is, Calvinist, but it was in Holland that Calvinism had to fight against one of its most powerful opponents, Jacobus Arminius (1560–1609). He had been a student at the university of Geneva under Beza and became a professor at Leiden. He was widely travelled, open minded, and a faithful pastor. He taught that election and reprobation are conditional, and depend upon the perseverance, foreseen by God, of some men in good, of others in evil. He denied that grace is irresistible, and would not admit that the merits of Christ are only for the elect. He did not deny election, but would admit nothing as true if it made God the author of evil.

No doctrines could be more hateful to men who were convinced that their own election was a certainty. He was opposed by his colleague Francis Gomarus, and all Holland became involved in the dispute. In 1610 the followers of Arminius addressed to the Dutch Parliament a *Remonstrance* comprising five articles which protest against Calvinism and assert the universality of grace. Arminius, worn out by a controversy which he had not desired, had died in the previous year. The leader of the party was now Episcopius, who was supported by Oldenbarnevelt, the distinguished statesman, and Hugo Grotius, the celebrated jurist. Maurice, Prince of Orange, at first took their side, and then basely deserted them. Oldenbarnevelt was executed. Grotius was immured in the fortress of Loevesteyn, and would have remained there indefinitely if it had not been for the heroic ingenuity of his wife who smuggled him away in a box intended for books and dirty linen.

To settle the dispute once for all, the Synod of Dort was summoned to meet in 1618. It was meant to be international, but the French Calvinists were refused permission to attend, and the German delegates included no representatives from Brandenburg. The decisions of the synod were almost a foregone conclusion. They were not quite so extravagant as the doctrines of Gomarus, but they repeated the five shibboleths of the Swiss Reformation—unconditional election—a limited atonement—the total depravity of man—the irresistible nature of grace—and the final perseverance of the elect who will never be cast away. The sessions at Dort, the most imposing in the history of the ' Reformed ' religion, closed with a luxurious feast, and the Arminian teachers were banished from the greater part of Holland. The result was hailed with joy by the Calvinists of Great Britain, where, in the days of James I, to be called an Arminian was the equivalent of being called a ' Puseyite ' sixty years ago. The synod also attempted to establish a uniform system of Church government throughout Holland. The attempt failed, and the different States of the Republic continued to act separately in their relations with the Church. This division of the Church into different compartments facilitated its subjection to the Government, and at The Hague the House of Orange ruled both Church and State on political principles more Machiavellian than Calvinist. Political considerations secured freedom for Lutherans, Arminian Remonstrants, and other Protestants, and the Roman Catholics steadily multiplied.

The general temper of the Dutch nation, thoughtful, cautious, and resolute, was very favourable to liberty. They were a rich mercantile people, and as the Spanish proverb has it, ' Mr. Money is a good Catholic '. They liked comfort, good houses, and good pictures. The Protestant churches which they built were plain but dignified; even in their colonies such churches as those in Ceylon at Jaffna and Galle are far from being contemptible. Unlike so many of their Scottish co-religionists, who abhorred a ' kist of whistles ', the Dutch liked fine organs, and the famous organ which the Calvinists set up in the cathedral church at Haarlem is as sweet as the cathedral's mediaeval bells. Amsterdam has been called ' the Venice of the North ', and the resemblance is more than the mere outward resemblance of narrow streets and interlacing canals. Like Venice it was a home of art, though an art which was no more Catholic than it was Puritan. Like Venice it became a city of refuge. Hither came the Jews who fled from Spain and Portugal. Here they built their stately synagogue, printed their books, and for many generations spoke the antique Castilian dialect that may still be heard in Salonika.[1] Here they excommunicated the great philosopher Spinoza, whose Pantheism was destined to do more injury to Protestantism than to Judaism. Hither to Amsterdam came Descartes, who had learnt much and observed much, resolved to forget everything and to reconstruct for himself the edifice of knowledge. And the *élite* of the Protestants expelled from France, men of refinement and learning, came to Holland before the seventeenth century was gone.

[1] The existing ' Portuguese synagogue ' at Amsterdam was consecrated with much pomp, August the 2nd, 1675. It is a fine building in a Dutch version of the Palladian style. The sermons of the rabbis were not wanting in the imagination engendered by enthusiasm; one of these sages discovered the name of William of Nassau, Prince of Orange, in the Book of Isaiah. On the languages spoken by these Jews, see app. note 12, p. 266. The Jewish authorities promised Spinoza a yearly pension of 1,000 florins if he would outwardly conform to the rites of the synagogue. On his refusal he was excommunicated, 1656.

Out of this Dutch life, a life far more varied and less phlegmatic than we may sometimes think, there came two distinct tendencies. The first was the tendency for the State to tolerate deliberately side by side with an established Church other religious bodies, usually though not invariably Christian, and to tolerate the printing of any religious opinions not actually blasphemous. This represents the attitude of William III, and it is quite clearly opposed to the originally theocratic character of the Genevan polity. The second tendency found its expression in the Pietists. The word 'Pietist', which was at first used in German as a term of reproach, nearly corresponds with our word 'Evangelical', and not with the present German meaning of the word 'Evangelical'. It is wrong to identify Pietism at all exclusively with Germany, and it is also wrong to think that it began in Holland. It was international, and it was the outcome of the devotional books, mainly English, which appeared in the seventeenth century like springs in the desert. Behind it there is the *Pilgrim's Progress* of John Bunyan, the *Saint's Everlasting Rest* of Richard Baxter, the *Spiritual Guide* of the Spanish mystic Molinos, the book *Wahres Christentum* by John Arndt, a devout Lutheran, and especially the *Practice of Piety* by Lewis Bayly, Bishop of Bangor, which was translated into at least five Continental languages besides Welsh and the language of the Indians of Massachusetts.[1] Nevertheless, Holland may be said to have nursed this international Pietism. Gisbert Voet (d. 1676), one of the leading Dutch theologians of this period, a learned opponent of Labadie and Descartes, and a sturdy Calvinist, had a mystical element in his religion, and he hailed as a second Thomas

---

[1] The *Practice of Piety* was first published in or before 1613; the English editions are almost numberless. It is marred by occasional coarseness but is both vigorous and devout. It advocates fasting, monthly communion, and private confession. In the Epistle Dedicatory, addressed to Charles, Prince of Wales, mention is made of 'Tobacco pipes' in 'Bibbing houses'.

à Kempis his compatriot Teellinck, whose Calvinism was combined with a spirit of brotherly forbearance and a love of the divine Redeemer like the love manifested by St. Bernard. Teellinck had studied in England and lived with English Puritans. And Spener, the celebrated founder of German Pietism, is known to have been influenced by the work of Bayly.

The Pietists differed from the mystics principally by the greater stress which they laid upon the gravity of sin and man's need of the atoning death of Christ. They thought more of obtaining peace with God through the death of Christ than of gaining immediate union with God through the indwelling Word within our soul. They took for granted the Deity of Christ and revived the mediaeval devotion to His Person and His Passion. They read the Bible, reverenced it, and tried to obey it. In Holland their plain dress, strict observance of Sunday, and avoidance of plays and public games recalled the habits of the English Puritans. Spener himself was not a rigorist in doctrine like Voet, but he was a rigorist in morals. Humble and learned, he was the principal of a seminary at Frankfort-on-the-Main, and then was made head court preacher at Dresden (1686). He was expelled from Dresden on account of his religious zeal, but was given a position in Berlin and there used all his influence to secure good appointments being made to the theological faculty in the new university at Halle. His *Pia Desideria*, published in 1675, touched upon the corruption of Protestantism in Germany and expounded to the people the remedies which he proposed, foremost among which was the diffusion of the word of God. He was a man of faith and charity, and made the university of Halle a centre of religion.

Moved by the example of Spener three young graduates of Leipzig founded Bible classes, *collegia philobiblica*, for the practical study of the Bible. These classes were suppressed by the university. Leipzig treated the Pietists very much as Oxford treated the six Evangelical students at St. Edmund Hall in 1768 and the Tractarians at a later time. The three friends were obliged to go, but their work went on. One of them was August Hermann Francke (d. 1727), whose strongly practical theology, illustrated by his care for the poor, his orphanage and his hostel for students at Halle, spread his name far and wide, and that which he loved better than his name. It was Francke who rolled away from Lutheranism one of its greatest stones of reproach by persuading his co-religionists to begin missionary work among the heathen.

Pietism gradually deprived itself of the power of doing more effective work for the kingdom of God by its sentimentalism, by its neglect of learning, by its disapproval of innocent recreation, by its practice of fostering little associations which kept themselves to themselves, and by regarding as an impossible ideal the leavening of the whole body of society with a Christian spirit. Yet it left a mark upon many who had little sympathy with its hard discipline. The mistaken notion that religion is in essence a feeling, a longing, a sentiment, was strengthened by Pietism, and a long line of German writers from Lessing to Schleiermacher derived from it some impulse towards their conviction that there is an eternal Gospel free from dogma, a Gospel in which enthusiasm and morality have met together. A more genuine ' Practice of Piety ' which came from England returned to England. Through the German Moravians and the Methodists a testimony to Jesus Christ, a love of the Bible, and a zeal for souls were handed on. If these Christians were wrong in not believing that all secular things can be hallowed to the Christian man, and if we in some sense draw nearer to the world than they, let us yet seriously consider whether we are overcoming the world or the world is overcoming us, and whether in some things where we differ from the Pietists, we differ for the better or for the worse.

IV

THE ROMAN CATHOLIC CHURCH FROM 1700 TO 1854

Eph. iv. 4–6: There is one body, and one Spirit, even as also ye were called in one hope of your calling; One Lord, one faith, one baptism, One God and Father of all, who is over all, and through all, and in all.

AT the beginning of the eighteenth century the position of the Roman Catholic Church was still magnificent. It is true that the political prestige of the Papacy was waning, and the new thought which had begun to stir in Italy was not allied with zeal for Christianity but with the shallow poetry of the society known as the Arcadian Academy. In Great Britain the folly of the Jesuits had proved the ruin of King James II and blasted the hopes of their wiser co-religionists.[1] But in many countries victory seemed well assured. Great numbers of the German people had left Lutheranism for Rome. Most of the Poles who had favoured Calvinism or Socinianism had forsaken their new creed. Opposition had been quelled in Bohemia. Amsterdam was dotted with Roman Catholic churches, though they were built to look like private houses.[2] In Spain the last remnants of Mohammedanism and Judaism appeared to be nearly extirpated, after generations of persecution, almost simultaneously with the erection of the beautiful little Spanish synagogue that still remains like a forgotten stowaway in the city of London.[3] The new world of America promised to be almost wholly Roman Catholic. The Jesuit

---

[1] For this, see Ethelred L. Taunton, *The History of the Jesuits in England* (Methuen & Co., London, 1901); and for the method of governing the English Roman Catholics by Vicars Apostolic and not by Bishops, see another Roman Catholic authority, Joseph Berington, quoted below, p. 269.
[2] See app. note 13, p. 267. [3] See app. note 14, p. 267.

missionaries in Canada had been fearless pioneers of the Cross. There was already a cathedral church in Quebec and a shrine for Canadian pilgrims at St. Anne de Beaupré.[1] The Indians of Mexico revered Our Lady of Guadalupe, and the churches of Central and Southern America were buildings of massive grandeur. Louis XIV had expelled from France the Protestants of all ranks including members of the old nobility. It was believed in England that this expulsion of the Huguenots was contrary to the wishes of the Pope,[2] and Archbishop Fénelon refused to preach to them till Louis had withdrawn his troops, saying that if missionaries and soldiers worked side by side people would be willing even to accept the Koran. Be that as it may, Louis could boast that his kingdom, like himself, was outwardly most Catholic, though the moral and material resources of France were diminished, and London and The Hague gained what France had lost.

Not only was Roman Catholicism outwardly victorious over Protestantism and able to dispatch missionaries to China, India, and Ceylon, as well as to America; it was also skilfully undermining the ancient ramparts of Eastern Christendom. Among the Slavs the political power of Poland favoured the creation and extension of a great Uniat Church, acknowledging the supremacy of the Pope and the decrees of Trent, while permitted to retain almost unaltered the liturgies and the ceremonies of Eastern Orthodoxy.[3] For the masses of the people the transition was not difficult so long as they saw the same icons and the same

---

[1] This lecture was delivered on March the 19th, 1922: a few days later the beautiful modern church of St. Anne at Beaupré was destroyed by fire.

[2] See *Verney Memoirs*, vol. ii, p. 446 (Longmans, London, 1907).

[3] By the Union of Brest (1596), a great body of Russians within the kingdom of Poland (named later Ruthenians) submitted to Rome. Finally the archdiocese of Lemberg came into union with Rome May the 5th, 1700, and many more thousands of Ruthenians then became members of the Uniat Church. In recent times frequent efforts have been made, largely under Polish influence, to give a Western character to their services.

vestments and listened to the familiar sonorous chanting of the Old Slavonic. Farther south the same untiring propaganda was at work. The Jesuits were busy in the islands of the Aegean and were seconded by the Capuchins, who at the request of Colbert had founded a school of languages at Constantinople. In the distant patriarchate of Antioch, Cyril, one of two rival Orthodox patriarchs, submitted to the Pope in 1709 and sent a profession of his faith to Rome. The influence of France was in favour of these proselytizing activities in the Ottoman Empire just as the influence of Poland was in favour of similar activities among the Slavs. And there is good reason for supposing that the same influence will again be exercised in the same direction, for French statesmen who oppose religion in France usually value it as an export to Asia.

Now this wide extension of Roman Catholicism is connected with a religious question of grave importance, one which was by no means completely solved by the Council of Trent. It is, what is the proper relation of a national Church to the universal Church of which it claims to be a part? The genius of Christianity, or let us rather say the very mission of our Lord Jesus Christ, is adverse to the erection of barriers by which one nation endeavours to separate its religion from the religion of others. He took means to secure that His followers should form one visible body, and the acknowledgement of one Lord, one faith, one baptism, proved a potent corrective of the tendency to create exclusive religious societies. If St. Paul has truly interpreted the mind of Christ, there can no more be two separate bodies, two seeds of Abraham, two universal visible Churches, than there can be two Saviours, and so far as any local or national Church asserts a distinctive doctrine peculiar to itself, so far does it cease to be Christian and become a sect. The part must be subordinate to the whole and its independence must be limited by the life of the whole.

A fruitful diversity in practice and worship is quite compatible with these truths, and wherever Christianity embraces the most vital elements in a nation, it will be found to develop these elements in such a way that they enrich the international Catholicism which is represented in and by the national Church.

The outward unity of the primitive international Church was first secured by the authority of the apostles, and, after their decease, by the bishops, who succeeded to those functions of the apostles which were permanently requisite for the government of the Church. It was not necessarily a menace to this ecclesiastical constitution that one of these bishops should enjoy a primacy of honour, and such a primacy was attributed by the ancient Oecumenical Councils to the Bishop of Rome. The later doctrine that the Bishop of Rome is infallible, and the doctrine that he and he alone can give and take away the jurisdiction of all other bishops, are quite distinct from such a primacy. Now a conviction that the Pope is the chief of Christian bishops, even by divine right, was strongly held two hundred years ago in union with a denial of his absolute power and personal infallibility. And as this belief, which permitted to each national Church a large degree of ordered liberty and independence, was most forcibly advocated in France, it won the name of Gallicanism. If we may use a modern political phrase, Gallicanism means 'Dominion Home Rule' in ecclesiastical affairs.

The substance of Gallicanism had been expressed in the celebrated Four Articles drawn up by a General Assembly of the clergy of France in 1682. Louis XIV, making use of a power which had previously been exercised by kings of France, claimed, while a bishopric was vacant, the right of nominating to benefices in the diocese, and also the right of appropriating the revenues of the see. This authority was disputed, especially by two bishops who, though condemned by their own metropolitans, appealed to Pope Innocent XI. The quarrel then became a quarrel between France and the Pope, and many of the clergy considered that the Pope had attacked the liberties of the Gallican Church. The General Assembly, to defend these liberties, passed the Articles drafted by Bossuet, the great Bishop of Meaux. The first Article declared that the Pope has only a spiritual power, and that in temporal matters princes are subject to no ecclesiastical authority. The second affirmed with the Council of Constance that the fullness of 'Apostolical' (i.e. papal) power is limited by the authority of General Councils. The third asserted that the exercise of papal power is limited by the canons of the Church, and also upheld the usages of the Gallican Church. The fourth declared that the judgement of the Pope without the Church's consent 'is not irreformable'. These Articles agree in the main with the doctrines previously upheld by the Sorbonne, and they were re-affirmed by Louis XV, by Napoleon, and by Charles X.[1]

Did our Lord, in order to secure the unity of the Church, give first to St. Peter and then to each Pope in turn the authority which the Four Articles contested? During the whole of the eighteenth century, and a large part of the nineteenth, there was a struggle, a fight to the finish between the adherents of two views of the Papacy, the moderate and the modern, the Gallican and the Ultramontane. On the one side were marshalled the Gallicans, the Jansenists, and those who wished to conform to the Church of the ancient Fathers. On the other side were the Ultramontanes, the Jesuits, and

[1] A discussion of the different types of Gallicanism is given in the article 'Gallicanisme' in Vacant et Mangenot, *Dictionnaire de Théologie Catholique*, vol. vi (Letouzey, Paris, 1920). For the Declaration containing the Four Articles, see W. H. Jervis, *History of the Church of France*, vol. ii, p. 49 (Murray, London, 1872).

the advocates of new forms of devotion. Some men, like Bossuet, wisely occupied a central position, firmly maintaining the rights of a national Church, and loving antiquity, without falling into the narrowness of Jansenism. But such men were few, and the result was that when Jansenism fell it dragged with it other causes which have no necessary or logical connexion with the Jansenist doctrine of irresistible grace.

In the meantime the Gallicans, by their serious study of Christian antiquity, sought like the Anglicans for a common ground where the differences between all contending Christian parties might be honestly reduced. In France the result of this sympathetic study of the past became obvious. Two Roman Catholic writers have described it as ' an instinctive opposition to the developments which Catholicism had received during the mediaeval and the modern period, and a desire to return with regard to doctrine and practices to a Christianity that was more spiritual and more sober, more episcopal also and less papal, and such as was held to have been the Christianity of the Fathers and particularly St. Augustine '.[1] That is not an unfair summary of the case, and a collision between this spirit and the spirit of Ultramontanism was inevitable. It was not a matter of academic speculations, but of two different conceptions of truth, of history, and of worship.

Gradually Gallican priests began to reduce the speed at which mass was read. Invocations of the Blessed Virgin and the saints became more strictly requests for their prayers and not for such help as is given by God. Diocesan service books were revised, and in the revised versions there was more of the Bible and less of legend. For instance, in the Parisian breviary of 1680 Lazarus ceased to figure as a bishop, and Dionysius the Areopagite no longer appeared

---

[1] Brou and Rousselot, *Christus*, p. 915, edited by Joseph Huby (Beauchesne, Paris, 1912).

as the first Bishop of Paris. The Parisian breviary of 1736 went still farther. Its lectionary was derived exclusively from the Bible, it suppressed the festival in honour of St. Peter's chair at Antioch, and replaced an Invitatory addressed to 'the prince of the apostles' by another worshipping Christ as 'the Head of the body, even of the Church'.[1] It was a result of the renewed study of the Bible that the contending factions in the Church of France defined themselves sharply in 1713, when Pope Clement XI issued the Bull *Unigenitus*. This Bull condemned one hundred and one propositions extracted from a work called *The New Testament with Moral Reflections* written by the Oratorian priest Paschasius Quesnel. Of all these propositions only twelve were condemned as actually heretical.

Quesnel's book, which was intended to promote the devotional study of the New Testament, first appeared in 1694, and might have escaped censure at Rome, if a priest had not refused to absolve a penitent suspected of Jansenism. The priest's action raised anew the whole question as to whether it was lawful for a man who explicitly acknowledged the Pope's authority in regard of doctrine to observe simply a 'respectful silence' in regard of the Pope's authority as to fact. It was possible to hold the theory that the Pope had the right to declare this or that proposition to be heretical, but nevertheless had not the right to compel the faithful to say that this or that proposition accurately represents the opinion of the author from whose works it is professedly taken. The forty doctors of the Sorbonne held that such a theory was lawful. But the Pope absolutely condemned their view, ordered the destruction of the convent of Port-Royal as a centre of the Jansenism with which the Gallicans were often in sympathy, and appointed congregations of cardinals and theologians who pronounced

[1] Pierre Batiffol, *Histoire du Bréviaire Romain*, p. 273 (Picard, Paris, 1894).

against Quesnel's *Moral Reflections*. Clement XI therefore made a simultaneous attempt to weaken the revival of Augustinian doctrine and to fortify papal authority. The Church of France then found itself divided into two camps, the *Acceptants* who submitted to the Bull, and the *Appellants* who appealed against it. On the death of Louis XIV the opposition to Rome daily increased, about thirty bishops were in the ranks of the Appellants, and among them was Cardinal de Noailles, Archbishop of Paris.

It is at this point that there was made that remarkable effort to unite the Church of France with the Church of England that we associate with the name of William Wake,[1] a Student of Christ Church, Oxford, then chaplain to the English envoy in Paris, and in 1716 Archbishop of Canterbury. Wake had been previously blamed for advocating 'comprehension with Dissenters', and he was now scurrilously attacked for making 'concessions in favour of the grossest superstition and idolatry' for the sake of union with Rome. This was unjust, for he had done nothing of the kind. To a certain extent reunion was in the air. The English Nonjurors, warned by their experience of King James II, turned their hopes of reunion towards the Orthodox Eastern Church. But other men had other plans, and in 1704 there appeared a notable eirenicon under the name of a *Proposal for Catholic Communion by a Minister of the Church of England*,[2] suggesting the possibility of union with Rome. So long as Gallicanism was a living force the barriers might reasonably be considered not insuperable, and even as late as 1824 a Roman Catholic Irish bishop,

[1] J. H. Lupton, *Archbishop Wake and the Project of Union* (1717-1720) *between the Gallican and Anglican Churches* (George Bell & Sons, London, 1896).
[2] Reprinted by George Bonham, Dublin, 1781. New edition with Introduction, edited by H. N. Oxenham, *An Eirenicon of the Eighteenth Century* (Rivingtons, London, 1879).

Dr. Doyle of Kildare and Leighlin, held out an olive-branch to Anglicans.[1] In the case of Archbishop Wake, as in the case of Dr. Doyle, overtures did not first come from the Anglican side. The French theologian Du Pin, acting with the concurrence of Cardinal de Noailles, entered into communication with Archbishop Wake and came to the conclusion that the points of difference between England and Rome were capable of adjustment. In treating of the jurisdiction of the Roman Pontiff, Du Pin plainly declared that the Pope ' can do nothing in those things which relate to the government of a Bishop in his own Diocese ', and that his primacy ' does not give him a higher grade among Bishops : he is only their fellow-bishop, though first among Bishops '. Wake replied, ' The honour which you give to the Roman Pontiff differs so little, I deem, from that which our sounder Theologians readily give him, that, on this point, I think, it will not be difficult, on either side, either to agree altogether in the same opinion, or mutually to bear with a dissent of no moment '. Wake hoped for mutual acknowledgement of the two Churches and intercommunion between them without minute agreement, and many in Paris openly avowed that they wished for union.

Negotiations were broken off by the death of Du Pin (6 June 1719), by the vacillation of the Archbishop of Paris, by the revived energy of the Jesuits after the accession of Louis XV, and by the assistance given to the Ultramontane party by the infamous Archbishop Dubois, who had destroyed the register of his marriage in order to obtain an archbishopric and opposed the Gallicans in order to gain a cardinal's hat. Louis XV, in spite of the opposition of his Parliament, required that the Bull *Unigenitus* should be registered and obeyed as a law not only of the Church but

---

[1] Dr. John Doyle wrote under the signature of J. K. L. (John Kildare Leighlin) *Letters on the State of Education in Ireland* and other works, one being a reply to the charge of the Archbishop of Dublin, Dr. Magee.

also of the State. The Appellants were persecuted within the Church, harried by the police, and seriously injured by the unbalanced fanaticism of adherents who conducted themselves like the victims of a modern revival. In spite of grievances and the heart-burnings provoked by the despotic policy of Louis XV towards Jansenism, it was only in Holland that a little Jansenist remnant permanently continued under their own bishops and priests in their secluded churches, openly maintaining the Augustinian doctrine of grace and the severe manners of Port-Royal.[1]

Primitive austerity had indeed suffered a defeat. In the middle of the century a good and sensible pontiff, Benedict XIV, was on the papal throne (1740–1758), but a certain artificiality and decadence can be observed throughout the greater part of Roman Catholicism. The decadence of Continental Protestantism became far more serious. But within the Roman communion there was no defender of the faith like our Joseph Butler. Monasteries and bishops' houses were built to resemble palaces. Preaching declined even in France, and we approach the period when Louis XVI, after listening to a sermon of the type then popular, remarked, ' If the abbé had only said a little about Christianity there is no subject which he would have left untouched '. Church music became secular in character, and the increased use of stringed instruments in church made the liturgy a pretext for a concert. The superb church music of J. Sebastian Bach does indeed belong to this period. But Bach was a Lutheran who wrote a composition for a festival held in 1730 to commemorate the Confession of Augsburg. Neither his Cantatas nor his Masses are an index to the character of Roman Catholic ecclesiastical music. As for the churches, and

---

[1] See J. M. Neale, *History of the So-called Jansenist Church of Holland* (Parker, Oxford, 1858); and P. Buys, *Rome en Utrecht* (H. ten Oever, Amsterdam, 1864).

especially those of the German-speaking countries, let us hesitate to condemn outright the architects of the rococo style. Their labour may have been a labour of love when even in monastic churches like those of Einsiedeln, Steinhausen, and Zwiefalten, they combined the solemnity of a sanctuary with the decorations of a pavilion. Yet amid the peach-coloured marble, the gilded cornices, the floating cherubs, the columns twisting themselves in sympathy with the statues of saints who writhe in eloquence or ecstasy, St. Benedict and St. Bernard could only have come as visitors, ill at ease if not indignant.

But though worldliness was weakening the Church, Ultramontanism had as yet gained no universal triumph. It was opposed by Febronianism in Germany and Josephism in Austria, which closely correspond with the Gallicanism of France.

German Roman Catholics, strong in the south and west of Germany, had for a long time been dissatisfied with the Concordat which had been made with Rome in 1448 before the Reformation. Complaints against the Curia were made in 1522 and again in 1673 in a memorandum drawn up by the Archbishops-Electors. In the next century the call for reform took a more definite tone.

At the election of a new Emperor in 1742 the matter again came up for discussion, and Nikolaus von Hontheim, auxiliary bishop of Trier, determined to investigate the nature of these grievances, very similar to the grievances dealt with by our English Parliament in the time of Henry VIII. He embodied the result of his studies in a work published in 1763 under the pseudonym Justinus Febronius, and called *De statu ecclesiae et legitima potestate Romani pontificis liber singularis ad reuniendos dissidentes in religione Christiana compositus.* The book was far from asserting any Protestant theory with regard to the Church. The conclusions were in harmony with Gallican conclusions, and a modern Roman Catholic historian of unimpeachable authority says that in it 'the constitution of the Church is brought back to its condition in Christian antiquity'.[1] The Pope is acknowledged as head of the Church, on whom it devolves to supervise the observance of the canons, the preservation of the faith, and the proper administration of the sacraments. He is even to pronounce judgement when matters of faith or morals are in dispute, and his decision is to be respected unless the universal Church or a General Council be of a contrary opinion. On the other hand, the book urges that there should be withdrawn from the Pope all those privileges which were first conferred upon him during the Middle Ages, especially those which were granted as a result of the False Decretals. The right to confirm or to depose a bishop is to be restored to the bishops, and princes are advised to reform their national Churches with the advice of the episcopate.

The book was promptly put on the Index at Rome, but its circulation was enormous and it was translated into German, French, Italian, Spanish, and Portuguese. Deputies of the Archbishops-Electors met at Coblenz in 1769, and under the presidency of von Hontheim himself drew up thirty grievances against Rome in agreement with the offensive book. The author before his death deplored the tone but not the theology of his work. In 1785 Febronianism asserted itself once more. On the occasion of the establishment of a papal nunciature at Munich, the Archbishops of Mainz, Köln, Trier, and Salzburg made a final effort to make the German Church less dependent upon Rome. They deputed delegates to meet at Bad Ems in 1786 and draw up twenty-seven articles to be presented at Rome. Rome refused to accept these articles. And a good many bishops had no

[1] F. Xavier Funk, *Die Kultur der Gegenwart*, 'Die christliche Religion', p. 229 (Teubner, Berlin und Leipzig, 1905).

wish for them, astutely suspecting that subjection to a distant Pope might be less galling than subjection to a neighbouring metropolitan. Thus by a strange paradox it was the immense power of these princely metropolitans which frustrated the national and reforming movements which they fostered. Very soon the French revolution caused these visions of liberty to be forgotten.

Joseph II (1765-1790) had been associated during the later years of her reign with his mother the Empress Maria Theresa (1740-1780). She had introduced a number of ecclesiastical reforms genuinely intended for the good of her people. A limit was put on the increase of monasteries, it was most wisely enacted that monastic vows should not be taken under the age of twenty-five, public education was organized, several new bishoprics were founded, and the clergy were no longer dispensed from paying taxes. It was further enacted that papal briefs should have no force in the Austrian Empire until they received the imperial placet. This last enactment was not likely to be viewed with kindly eyes at Rome. But no great trouble was caused, for Maria Theresa was a good friend of her Church. Every inch a woman, tactful, wise, and with a loyal sense of duty, she was no hypocrite. She believed what she professed. Judged by the standard of her age, she was tolerant in religious matters, and her policy was not only fitted to protect the Church against revolutionary movements but also to increase its numbers by favouring secessions from Eastern Orthodoxy.[1]

Joseph II succeeded in marring what Maria Theresa had begun to make. He was the incarnation of autocratic liberalism, and though he had been associated with his mother for several years in the government of the empire

---

[1] For the benefit of the many Rumanians in Hungary who united with Rome, Maria Theresa erected the diocese of Gross-Wardein. This was in addition to an already existing Uniat see at Fogaras (Alba Julia).

he had not learned his mother's caution. His aims were sometimes excellent, but he tried to create results without making preparations. He granted a large measure of civil and religious liberty both to Protestants and to Eastern Orthodox Christians. He largely increased the number of parishes, suppressed six hundred and six out of two thousand convents and monasteries, and suppressed the small diocesan seminaries to replace them by great central institutions in Vienna, Buda-Pesth, Prague, and other cities. The professors for these institutions were to be chosen from men known to be in favour of his own principles. To sever as much as possible the connexion between the bishops and Rome, papal Bulls were put under civil control, and bishops were allowed to issue dispensations for marriages in cases of consanguinity in the third and the fourth degree, a process which appeared to be quite as moral as paying for papal faculties for dispensations in cases of the second degree. In vain Pope Pius VI came to Vienna in 1782 to make a protest: he was received with respect but not with subservience.

But if some of the reforms of Joseph II were desirable, he had a genius for doing the little things that irritate, and he pleased the people as little as he pleased the Pope. Febronianism had started within the Church. Gallicanism, though powerfully supported by the Church, was in its essence a protest of the State against a rival and aggressive power in the Church. Josephism, as it came to be called, was an attempt to turn an established Church into a State Church controlled by the Emperor. Hated by the Ultramontanes, Joseph II was ridiculed by the Freethinkers and dubbed ' my brother the sacristan ' by Frederick of Prussia. In the affairs of both State and Church he failed with the pathetic failure of a man who is determined to do good to people who simply wish to be left alone, and makes few of them happy and all of them ungrateful. He died brokenhearted in 1790.

Maria Theresa's zeal for Church reform was also shared by her second son Leopold II of Tuscany. He found a warm ally in Scipio de' Ricci, Bishop of Pistoia-Prato. A synod held by Ricci at Pistoia in 1786 passed a number of decrees according to Leopold's mind. The four Gallican Articles were accepted and the writings of Quesnel were recommended. As only three bishops of the grand duchy were at all favourable to the plans of Leopold, the only possibility of carrying them into execution lay in his own hands. He was called to the imperial throne in 1790 and therefore had to abandon the task. Ricci resigned his office and Pope Pius VI condemned eighty-five propositions of the Synod of Pistoia. Once more we see men involved in what appeared to be the endless conflict between one absolutism and another absolutism, that of the Pope and that of the monarch; between one servitude and another servitude, that of those who wish to be bound by the traditions of men and that of those who tremble before a God whose justice is not consistent with love.

The suppression of the Jesuits by Pope Clement XIV in 1773 is an event which coincided to some extent with the national movements within the Church. Jealousy of their immense wealth and power, together with the spread of the scepticism of the movement known as the enlightenment, and the absolutism of the reigning kings, contributed to the downfall of the Society of Jesus. But the story of their downfall is complicated with every kind of motive. In 1757 an attempt was made on the life of Louis XV by one Damiens who had been a menial in a Jesuit college. Popular fury raged against the Jesuits and Busenbaum's standard work on Moral Theology was burnt by the public executioner. The next year the King of Portugal was fired at when returning from a visit to his mistress, and the Jesuits were suspected of complicity in the attempted assassination.

It is to the credit of the Jesuits that Madame de Pompadour had an excellent reason for hating them; and Pombal, the powerful minister of the King of Portugal, hated them because they had opposed a scheme by which their Indian converts were to be moved from their homes in consequence of an exchange of provinces between Spain and Portugal. The Jesuits were dissolved as a corporation, but the dissolution proved to be futile. It was futile in spite of the solemn and emphatic language of the Bull *Dominus ac Redemptor*.[1] The Jesuits pretended to defer to the Pope's sentence, but they not only defied the Holy See by nominating a new Vicar-General, but circulated a forged papal Brief, dated June the 9th, 1774, expressing the Pope's joy at the position of the order in Russia, whither many Jesuits had gone for refuge. The suppression was also futile because the dogmatic and moral teaching with which the Society had so largely identified itself was not condemned. It was, as we shall see, revived by St. Alphonsus Liguori, and in the nineteenth century became the dominant theology of the Roman Catholic Church.

The success of the Jesuits in the mission field was one of the causes which led to their dissolution and their dissolution crippled that success. In particular their great work among the Indians in Paraguay was permanently ruined.

The Spaniards of the eighteenth century may be likened to an ancient family fleeced by foreign speculators and living in a fine mansion two hundred years old and slowly falling into decay. Yet in spite of some poverty of intellect they grew in a knowledge of history and science. They built the cathedral of Cadiz, they numbered among them a great painter, Goya, and a great missionary, Father Junipero Serra, the apostle of California. There still exists a picture

---

[1] For the medals which commemorate the suppression of the Jesuits, see app. note 15, p. 268.

of the Franciscan friar with a face of strange and eager hope. He with three friends was an inmate of a convent in Majorca, and from their student days they were made one by the desire of being missionaries in the Spain that lay on the other side of the Atlantic. They left Cadiz in 1749 in a small English coaster. The voyage took ninety-nine days. Father Palon, one of the four, tells us that the English captain, who knew no language but English and a smattering of Portuguese, greatly tormented them with theological arguments though Father Serra refuted him, quoting text for text. 'The captain would thereupon rummage his greasy old Bible, and when he could find no other escape would declare that the leaf was torn and that he couldn't find the text he wanted.'

Arrived in Mexico they were kept at work for nineteen years, founding missions and preaching. But when the Jesuits were dismissed from the Spanish dominions[1] in 1767 it was decided to send Franciscans to take charge of the Jesuit missions in California. Serra was chosen as president of all the Californian missions and put over a band of sixteen missionaries. When he received the appointment ' he was unable to speak a single word for tears '. He was now fifty-six years of age, and he had waited for that call some forty years.

The first mission founded was that of San Diego in 1769. Then came a time of hardship and hunger followed by the choice of Monterey as the centre of the work. The Indians burnt to the ground the buildings of San Diego and murdered one of the fathers; but both the Spanish military commander and the friars determined that the Indians should be treated

[1] Under Charles III, a king of Spain whose merits as a friend of his Church and of his country have been obscured by his unfortunate foreign policy and by the prejudice of historians. A comparison between Charles III of Spain and the first three Georges tells greatly in favour of the King of Spain. The question of the expulsion of the Jesuits is dealt with at length in Danvila y Collado, *Reinado de Carlos III*, vol. iii (Madrid, 1894).

with even greater kindness than before. The work went steadily forward. Before Serra died in 1784 he had founded nine separate missions; two years later there were more than five thousand Christian Indians in Upper California. In 1823 there were twenty-one missions with more than twenty thousand Christians, no longer savages, but busily engaged in agriculture, weaving, and metal work. There were handsome stone churches, surrounded by schoolrooms, workshops, and enormous tracts of land in a high state of cultivation. Almost the whole of this fine achievement has been annihilated. In 1834, after Mexico had become independent, the property of the missions was secularized and the fathers and the Indians alike were reduced to abject poverty. Among the pitiful stories of the time is that of the mission of Soledad, where Father Sarria, who had laboured there for thirty years, shared every morsel of his food with the Indians until while saying Mass one Sunday morning he fainted from starvation and fell dead in the arms of his people. In 1846 the American flag was raised in Monterey and the business of destruction still continued for about ten years when the churches and some fragments of property were returned to the Roman Catholic authorities. Thousands of Indians, beggared, homeless, unshepherded, were left to live as best they might on the confines of the new immigration, and the half-ruined churches remain to tell us that the first civilization of California, and perhaps the best, was built upon the love which a Spanish schoolboy had for Jesus Christ.[1]

In Great Britain during the eighteenth century Roman Catholicism passed through a period of deep depression. In London it was kept alive by the six chapels attached to the foreign embassies. It was still strong in Lancashire,

[1] 'Father Junipero and his Work', *The Century Magazine*, May and June, 1883 (The Century Co., New York; F. Warne, London).

in parts of Yorkshire, and in the western Highlands. Violent persecution had ceased, but the penal laws were harsh and adherents steadily declined in number. In Scotland they, like the Episcopalians, suffered from the fury of the Duke of Cumberland's soldiers, even the remote and humble seminary at Scalan being discovered and looted. In England, when the cause of the Stuarts was seen to be hopeless, one wealthy family after another conformed to the Church of England, and their retainers gradually followed their example. As for their religious belief there is evidence to show that there was a decided tendency to Jansenism in Scotland, derived not from Presbyterianism but from influences at work in Paris.

The English College at Douai fell under suspicion of fostering the same opinions, and in 1711 the Dean of the cathedral of Mechlin, who had written against Jansenism, was sent to examine the college ' from the President downwards '. The dean was no extremist, acted very justly, and entirely acquitted the college of any charge of heresy. Among the schoolboys who were then at Douai was Richard Challoner, the son of 'a rigid Dissenter', afterwards a Roman Catholic priest in London, then Bishop of Debra and Vicar Apostolic of the London district.[1] From the day of his consecration as bishop in 1740 in a sequestered convent in Hammersmith we have abundant records of his character and work. Throughout his life he rose at six and spent the time in prayer and meditation until he celebrated the holy mysteries at eight. He allowed himself sufficient time for his meals and for a walk in the afternoon, but gave every possible moment to spiritual reading, writing, and

---

[1] See Edwin H. Burton, *The Life and Times of Bishop Challoner* (Longmans, London, 1909). The first of the two volumes contains a good reproduction of a well-known plate of the good bishop in cope and mitre. Under the cope he wears a long linen rochet of the type usual among English Roman Catholic bishops before the introduction of Italian rochets and cottas in the nineteenth century.

receiving the persons who came to seek his help, paying also short visits to the members of his flock in the evening. He never had a house of his own and he gave to the relief of the poor every penny that he could spare. For forty years he worked in garrets, in cellars, in workhouses, and in prisons, making excursions to visit his flock scattered over several English counties. His care extended to the British colonies in America, and it is a singular fact that for some years the only Englishman who continued to exercise any authority in the United States was this now frail and aged bishop.

His death was hastened by the Gordon riots of 1780, when Roman Catholic chapels and houses were systematically wrecked, and the bishop just escaped from the clutches of a fanatic mob through the energy of a priest who with great difficulty persuaded him to leave his rooms near the Sardinian embassy. He died in London on January the 12th, 1781. The last word which he was heard to utter was the word 'charity'.

Of his numerous writings two at least should be mentioned. His *Meditations for Every Day in the Year* form a book of strict and sober piety which raises the author to the first rank of English devotional writers, and his *Garden of the Soul* is a little guide for Christians 'living in the world'. Since the death of Challoner the *Garden of the Soul* has been mutilated, expanded, and even deliberately falsified.[1] But in its original form it is still the proof, as it was once the model, of what was called 'the old religion'. The generations which it trained were separated by deep differences from the paths afterwards favoured by Cardinal Wiseman and Cardinal Manning. And we can judge of

[1] Among the latest editions is that published by the Anglican 'Society of SS. Peter and Paul'. In this edition there is added to the Litany of our Lady of Loretto the words 'Queen conceived without original sin' and 'Queen of the most holy Rosary', neither of which clauses appears even in the last edition, the tenth, issued by Bishop Challoner.

118 THE ROMAN CATHOLIC CHURCH

these old English Roman Catholics not only by the prayers which they recited but by the fact that all their bishops in their official Protestation to the Government in 1789 added their signatures to the words 'We acknowledge no infallibility in the Pope'.[1] What wonder is it that in the subsequent onrush of Ultramontanism the hereditary Roman Catholics of England were regarded as unprogressive, anti-Roman, and anti-Papal?[2]

It was into this quiet backwater of ancient piety that there came great ripples from the wreck in France.

At the outbreak of the Revolution the Church of France was in a condition of belated feudalism.[3] The bishops numbered one hundred and thirty, not counting the five bishops of Corsica. Their blood was of the bluest, and their names were historic. They united elegance with dignity, and they moved in universities, in parliaments, and in embassies. Many of them were benevolent and very few appear to have been bad. But they had no new Bossuet, or Pascal, or Fénelon. The whole of Christianity was insolently challenged, and all these bishops could not produce a David to defend it. And the monks, especially the ancient orders, were smitten with spiritual paralysis. The Benedictines of St. Maur had indeed continued their literary work; but as a rule the monasteries had kept the wealth and abandoned the industry of better days. And clinging to the Church, feeding on the Church, were the holders of 'simple benefices', sinecures, abbots, priors, chaplains, prebendaries, parasites who did nothing but

---

[1] For a fuller quotation from this remarkable 'Protestation', see app. note 16, p. 268.

[2] E. S. Purcell, *Life of Cardinal Manning*, vol. ii, p. 88 (Macmillan & Co., London, 1895).

[3] A luminous account of the state of the French Church immediately before and during this time of crisis is given by W. H. Jervis, *The Gallican Church and the Revolution* (Kegan Paul, Trench & Co., London, 1892).

amuse themselves. The scandals of the court of Louis XV and the luxury of noblemen and prelates made the Church a prey to the gibes of Voltaire, the hallucinations of Rousseau, and the contempt of the people. It is a striking proof of the goodness of many of the parochial clergy that in the next generation there remained so many Frenchmen who had not bowed the knee to Baal.

Blow after blow was aimed at the Church. In 1789 the Assembly began by confiscating all ecclesiastical property and reducing all the bishops and clergy to the position of ill-paid *salaried* servants of the State, and we imagine the thrill which passed through the ranks of these baronial prelates when the word fell from the lips of Mirabeau. Then in 1790 the religious orders were suppressed, and under the pretext of restoring the primitive Church the 'Civil Constitution of the Clergy' was made law. The number of bishops was reduced to eighty-three, the number of new departments in France, all chapters were suppressed, and the boundaries of parishes were altered. And that the Church might be absorbed by the State, the bishops and parish priests were henceforth to be elected by the people, not simply the faithful laity, but the persons of any religion or no religion who elected the civil officials. Incumbents were to be canonically instituted by their bishop, the bishop by his metropolitan, and the Pope's jurisdiction quietly eliminated. The law overstepped itself. All the bishops, except four, and the majority of the clergy, rallied to the side of the Pope and refused to take the required oath of obedience to the civil Constitution.[1]

[1] The most notable of the Constitutional bishops was Henri Grégoire, Bishop of Blois, who ruled his diocese with exemplary zeal from 1791 to 1801. He was a convinced Republican. His book, *Les Ruines de Port-Royal-des-Champs*, contains an interesting chapter dealing with the severe morality of the Dutch Jansenists and the laxity of their opponents in giving absolution to 'immondes créatures livrées au libertinage'. He was a man of fearless courage. During the Terror he not only said Mass daily but wore his episcopal dress in the streets.

In spite of this general resistance to the new law, it had the result of creating a schism. The clergy were divided into two parties, the non-juring or ' refractory ' party, and the ' Constitutional ' party which acquiesced in the action of the State. Before the end of 1791 the Legislative Assembly replaced the milder Constituent Assembly. It was largely composed of young freethinkers of an extreme revolutionary type, and it proceeded to suppress all religious corporations and societies, even those which were devoted exclusively to hospital service. Then in August 1792 all the non-juring clergy were sentenced to banishment, a measure which drove some forty thousand persons out of the country. In September massacres began in Paris, two hundred cut-throats led by tavern demagogues attacking the prisons where priests were confined, many of them the flower of the clergy of France. Of the twelve hundred persons who perished in that week about three hundred were priests, so that, in the words of Danton, a river of blood was put between Paris and the emigrants who had gone from France. Similar butcheries took place at Meaux, Châlons, and Rennes.[1]

The completion of the work of destruction was left to the Convention (1792-1795) which replaced the Legislative Assembly. Sundays and the Christian method of reckoning times were replaced by the observance of every tenth day as a day of rest and by a totally new calendar. And to inaugurate the triumph of unbelief a girl from the opera was enthroned as goddess of Reason on the altar of Notre-

[1] The emigrants who fled to England were so numerous that in London and its neighbourhood alone ten Roman Catholic chapels of the simplest character were built for their accommodation. In one of them, that in Little George Street, Portman Square, there were sometimes present sixteen French bishops and the highest aristocracy of France. See F.-X. Plasse, *Le Clergé français réfugié en Angleterre* (Société Générale de Librairie Catholique, Paris, 1886). Of these ten chapels there still remained in 1903 the chapel near Portman Square, St. Aloysius, Clarendon Street, Somers Town, and St. Mary's, Holly Place, Hampstead.

Dame of Paris amid the delirious homage of the revolutionaries. In the meanwhile even the Constitutional clergy, headed by Gobel, the Archbishop of Paris, were harried into apostasy while the non-juring clergy were tracked like wild beasts. The horror culminated in the Reign of Terror (1793–1794) when the revolutionary tribunals sentenced thousands to death, including one hundred and twenty priests at Lyons alone. Under the Directory (1795–1799) open hostility to Christianity still continued, but the failure of the worship of a prostituted Reason began to become evident. The Government tried to find a better rival to Christianity in a form of Deism known as Theophilanthropy, a return to an imaginary natural religion. The centre of this Deism was the church of St. Sulpice. Christian worship, first in private houses, then in churches, was once more tolerated. And though the refugee priests in England, among whom was the saintly writer, Father Grou,[1] won admiration by their heroic patience and gentle piety, France owes most to the priests who, close to the guillotine, ' endured, as seeing Him who is invisible ', and continued to minister in France, compelling the respect of their enemies.

Pope Pius VI, who had been compelled to cede important possessions to France, died in exile at Valence in Dauphiné in 1799. That year Napoleon Bonaparte was in name First Consul and in reality an autocratic despot. The Church of France was in a state of anarchy, and the Theophilanthropists, though weakening, were still disputing with the Christians the use of their churches. Bonaparte disliked

[1] Jean Nicolas Grou, S.J. He died in 1803 at Lulworth Castle, the seat of Mr. Thomas Weld. The chapel at Lulworth is a peculiar and interesting edifice. Mr. Weld was a personal friend of King George III, and asked of him permission to build a Roman Catholic chapel. This being against the law, the king suggested that Mr. Weld should build a family mausoleum which he might furnish as a chapel. The suggestion was followed.

anarchy, and he saw that the Revolution had not destroyed the Church and that the non-juring clergy were gaining the influence which they deserved. He was convinced that society cannot exist without morals and that morals cannot exist without religion. Therefore, in spite of the malevolent intolerance of some of his companions and colleagues, Bonaparte determined to raise up from the earth the religion which was that of the great majority of his people.

But, if religion was to be raised, it was necessary for her to be the servant of her protector. He would not imitate Henry VIII in openly quarrelling with the Pope, nor like the Emperor Joseph II try to limit the number of candles to be set upon the altar. He would make use of the new Pope, Pius VII, to control the Church, and he would infuse into the clergy a spirit adapted to the new state of society. That could only be done by the creation of a new hierarchy. In collecting the necessary elements of his future court he fell back upon the members of the old régime on the principle that 'they are the only people who know how to be servants'. But he knew that the old bishops would either refuse to be his servants, because they were royalists, or would be inefficient servants because their flocks suspected them of compromising with the atheists. Therefore all the old bishops must resign and be replaced by a new body; there then could be no more schism between the non-jurors and their opponents, and order would be restored under the aegis of the First Consul.

The Pope took no initiative in the direction of a Concordat; and he had some reason for suspecting the great general who had robbed Rome of some of her fairest provinces. But a Concordat was arranged in 1801 by which the Catholic Apostolic and Roman religion was to be freely practised in France. There were to be ten metropolitans and fifty bishops instituted by the Pope. They were to be nominated by the First Consul and in turn they were to nominate the parish priests, and all alike were to take an oath of fidelity to the Government. The Pope pledged himself to ask the former bishops to resign, and had to acquiesce in the alienation of Church property taken by the State during the Revolution. Lastly the First Consul was allowed certain special privileges granted to the kings of France by former Popes. It was found that eighty-one of the former bishops were living. Of these forty-five yielded to the Pope's exhortations and abdicated more or less voluntarily. Of the eighteen French bishops in England only five consented to resign. The others wrote to the Pope a respectful but strong protest, saying that they would have to answer to the supreme Judge for abandoning their flocks, words which implied their adhesion to the primitive doctrine of episcopacy.[1] All who refused to resign were then deposed by a papal Bull.[2] Of the total number thirteen refused to acquiesce in this deposition, and were supported in their resistance by a certain number of the faithful, especially in La Vendée and Poitou. This small community of Catholics maintained itself throughout the nineteenth century under the name of La Petite Église, and though without bishops and priests it was not wholly extinct in the first years of the present century.

Bonaparte had intended to make the new bishops his own creatures, and therefore wished to select many of them from among the Constitutional prelates. This was opposed

[1] The French prelates in England who refused to resign their sees were the Archbishop of Narbonne, the Bishops of Angoulême, Arras, Avranches, Léon, Lombez, Montpellier, Nantes, Noyon, Périgueux, Rodez, Vannes, Uzès, and the Bishop nominate of Moulins.

[2] By this Bull *Qui Christi Domini vices*, dated November the 29th, 1801, Pius VII 'suppressed, annulled, and for ever extinguished' all the French sees then existing, and deprived the bishops of all canonical jurisdiction. The Bull is therefore an important illustration of the doctrine of papal supremacy, and a testimony to the fact that the present Church of France is a modern creation.

by the papal legate Caprara, but Bonaparte insisted upon the appointment of fifteen. The remaining forty-five were selected from among the non-jurors, and were chosen well.

The Pope's temporal power was recognized by the Concordat. But he found, to his pardonable indignation, that when Bonaparte published the Concordat he had added certain *Organic Articles* which had never been submitted to him for his approval. By these Articles the decrees of the Pope and of foreign, even General Councils, were not to be enforced in France without the *placet* of the Government, no Church Councils were to be held in France without the authorization of the Government, and the four Gallican Articles of 1682 were imposed as obligatory on professors engaged in seminaries. By a remarkable anticipation of papal policy in the near future the adoption of a single liturgy throughout France was prescribed. The object of these Articles was to secure for Bonaparte all the supremacy, and more than the supremacy, which the kings of France had exercised in ecclesiastical causes. The Pope protested while courteously expressing the hope of 'change and amelioration'.

Bonaparte in 1804 was elected Emperor of the French and was crowned by the Pope in Paris. His subsequent conduct towards Pius VII was marked by alternate trickery and intimidation. His seizure of the Papal States, his excommunication by the Pope, and the Pope's imprisonment, are matters of secular history. At a National Council of the Church of France held in Paris in 1811 Napoleon induced the bishops to agree that metropolitans should have the right of confirming elections to bishoprics if the Pope had not given canonical institution to the bishop elect within six months. To this the Pope agreed on condition that the consecrating prelate should always act as the delegate of the Pope. But he refused to give to the Four Gallican Articles the approval which the Emperor demanded. The quarrel was not over when disaster after disaster befell Napoleon, and he had to sign his abdication while Pius VII entered Rome in triumph. Pius treated the rival who had bullied him with Christian generosity, interceding with England for a kindly treatment of Napoleon and offering a refuge in Rome to the members of the imperial family. After all, he had reason for being grateful to the tyrant. Bonaparte had indeed created a new Gallican Church, one in which the Pope was no longer regarded as a meddlesome primate but as a martyred patron.

The Congress of Vienna restored the Papal States to the Pope, and with the help of Cardinal Consalvi Pius reorganized Roman Catholicism in Germany and Switzerland. He died in 1823 after one of the most romantic careers in history. He had re-established the Jesuits throughout the world. He had also performed an act, the record of which falls outside the scope of the ordinary historical manual. He beatified (1816) Alphonsus Maria Liguori, who in the modern Roman Catholic Church occupies a place like that which St. Augustine occupied three hundred years ago. He is the special representative of that dogmatic theology and that moral theology which may be described as anti-Augustinian, anti-primitive, and hostile to all nationalism in religion except the nationalism of southern Italy.

The authority now ascribed to Alphonsus Liguori is hard to exaggerate. He was canonized in 1829, made a doctor of the Church in 1871, and forty years before he was elevated to this supreme rank it was decreed that a confessor is always free to follow his opinion without weighing it. By this decree the Church of Rome has indirectly sanctioned Probabilism, the doctrine that a man when in doubt may legitimately follow a course which is probably right even when the stricter course seems to him to be more probable.¹ Liguori himself, after holding a stricter view, became first an advocate of Probabilism, and then of Aequiprobabilism, which allows the more indulgent opinion to be followed if the authorities in its favour are as good as the authorities on the sterner side. The influence of Liguori, as a moral theologian and in other ways, has been prodigious. His life was prolonged over almost the whole of the eighteenth century, his abilities were good, his zeal untiring, his interest in the poor found a concrete expression in the religious order which he founded, and the circulation of his books was wide and rapid. They contain all the most distinctive features of modern Roman Catholicism.

Against Febronius he defended the doctrine of papal infallibility, arguing that Pope Honorius, who was notoriously anathematized by the Church for his pernicious error with regard to the Person of Christ, was not anathematized for heresy, and quoting in favour of papal jurisdiction forgeries which his own contemporary Pope Pius VI very properly said might be burned.² He made popular the practice, encouraged by the Jesuits, of rendering to the sacred human heart of Jesus the worship which the ancient Church rendered to His divine and eternal Person, a practice which he also linked with prayers addressed to the heart of Mary.³ His large devotional book, *The Glories of Mary*, is

---

¹ This is in substance admitted by the author of the important article 'Alphonsus' in the *Catholic Encyclopedia* (London, Caxton Publishing Company). He says, 'The Church herself might be held to have conceded something to pure probabilism by the unprecedented honours she paid to the Saint in her Decree of 22 July 1831, which allows confessors to follow any of St. Alphonsus's own opinions without weighing the reasons on which they were based'.

² For this, see the Second Letter of Father A. Gratry to Mgr. Dechamps. Authorized translations of Gratry's Four Letters made by T. J. Bailey were published in London by J. T. Hayes at the time of the Vatican Council of 1870.

³ For the cultus of the hearts of Jesus and Mary, see app. note 17, p. 270.

not content with those special prerogatives which the Evangelists and the Fathers recognize as the true glories of the Mother of God, but places her in a position like that of an Arian Christ, and in order to do so tells one puerile legend after another and quotes as from the Fathers sentences which the Fathers never wrote. St. Augustine, whose teaching directly excludes the view that the Blessed Virgin was conceived immaculate, is quoted as teaching the exactly opposite opinion.[1] Pope Pius IX, in declaring in 1854 that she was conceived without original sin, in promoting the worship of the Sacred Heart and the use of such prayers as ' Sweet heart of Mary, be my salvation ', and finally by proclaiming the doctrine of papal infallibility, acted as the faithful disciple of Alphonsus Liguori.

The standard of truthfulness upheld by Liguori has been a matter of vehement controversy, a controversy which in England is associated with the names of Mr. Kingsley and Dr. Newman, and is not likely to end until the Roman Church proscribes certain opinions which Liguori maintained. All moralists would probably grant that in certain special circumstances it is right to withhold the truth, and that there may even be a just cause for using words in which one sense is taken by the speaker and another sense intended by him for the hearer. The question of right or wrong depends upon the gravity of the cause. We may reasonably believe that the gravity of the cause can only be appreciated rightly by the man who is habitually truthful, and Newman, in spite of his defence of Liguori, in spite even of his own words that St. Alfonso ' was a lover of truth ', has summed

---

[1] *The Glories of Mary*, English translation, revised by the Right Rev. Robert A. Coffin, Bishop of Southwark, and approved by Cardinal Wiseman, p. 271 (Burns, Oates & Washbourne, Ltd., London). For the real teaching of St. Augustine on this subject as expounded by a learned and candid Roman Catholic theologian, see J. Tixeront, *Histoire des Dogmes*, vol. ii, p. 472 *n*. (Lecoffre, Paris, 1909).

up the whole matter by saying, ' I avow at once that in this department of morality, much as I admire the high points of the Italian character, I like the English character better '.[1]

Liguori, a man of the most austere life and eager for the conversion of souls, made the tragic mistake of supposing that opinions which appear to be edifying require no rigorous evidence, and that great leniency towards sin is a legitimate method of attracting sinners. At the epoch of the French Restoration (1814) his moral and dogmatic teaching made its appearance in France. It found advocates in spite of the protests of the older French priests, many of whom had suffered for the faith, and who, if sometimes too severe, had the wisdom to realize that ten serious conversions are better than fifty that are only superficial. The struggle took forty years. When it was over, Ultramontanism had completely triumphed and Gallican traditions, like Gallican service books, became a matter of past history.

In estimating the result of this transformation of the Church of France, it may be well to quote the words of a learned French ecclesiastic whose dislike of Jansenism doubles the value of his criticism. He says, ' In speaking of Jansenism and of the happy reaction which has delivered us from it, we have already hinted at a reproach which can be directed against contemporary devotion. Among a good number, among a great number, it is composed too exclusively of the very elements of which Jansenism had deprived it. In former times earnest Christians kept away from the sacraments: to-day, I shall carefully refrain from saying that many have recourse to them too often—there could be no such thing as excess in approaching the sources of divine life;—but people have recourse to them under a wrong impression as to the true character of the sacramental system, which is a means, not an end, a help to virtue

[1] *Apologia*, p. 417 (Longman, London, 1864).

and not a substitute. To be a Christian a man ought to go to confession and communion, but only to go to confession and communion is not to be a Christian: exactly as if one were to say: To live a man must eat, but to eat is not to live. . . . People believe that they are Christians because they keep in contact with the means of salvation. They count upon their last hour to confirm in goodness a feeble will that has fled from trial until the moment when trial is about to end. To suppose that this presumptuous calculation is not mistaken is to have a religion which at the best is useful for a good death: true Christianity is useful for a good life. What ought to have been sought from the sacraments is the courage to act: people have sought in them, on the contrary, a kind of dispensation from effort, an effort which they supposed to be rendered useless by the facility of obtaining forgiveness.'[1]

[1] Mgr. d'Hulst, Rector of the Catholic Institute of Paris, *La France chrétienne dans l'Histoire*, p. 634 (Firmin-Didot, Paris, 1896).

V

RELIGION IN GREAT BRITAIN AND AMERICA FROM 1689 TO 1815

Eph. ii. 18: For through Him we both have access in one Spirit unto the Father.

'WHAT I have done, I have done in the integrity of my heart.'[1] These words, repeated by Archbishop Sancroft on his death-bed, might be called the motto not only of his own life, but that of a great majority of the Nonjurors. They believed that they would have violated their oath of allegiance to James II if they had taken the oaths imposed by the Government of William III. Sancroft himself had been an exemplary bishop. And it is strange that a good man like Bishop Burnet should, even in the heat of political antagonism, have misunderstood him so culpably. For Sancroft was both learned and active in well-doing; he had firmly defended the liberties of the Church and the nation; a devout member of the school of Andrewes and Laud, he had written with wonderful delicacy of those whom he calls 'our brethren the Protestant Dissenters'; munificent in his liberality, he had himself lived in such frugal simplicity that when he was uncanonically deprived of his great position he could say, 'Well, I can live on fifty pounds a year'. If he and those who followed him were mistaken and quixotic, they have left to us the great example of men who preferred what they knew to be poverty to what they believed to be perjury, and consulted conscience, whether well or ill informed, rather than comfort. Nine English bishops and

---

[1] George D'Oyly, *Life of William Sancroft*, vol. ii, p. 62 (John Murray, London, 1821). D'Oyly effectually demolishes Burnet's caricature of Sancroft.

about four hundred priests retired from their posts quietly and with dignity.

For a time the Nonjurors had fifty chapels in London alone, and they made a vain attempt to secure union with the Eastern Orthodox Church. But their numbers steadily dwindled until they became extinct in the early years of the nineteenth century. The decline was inevitable. For whatever men might think of the House of Hanover, it was impossible for those who had not taken any oath of allegiance to the House of Stuart to feel exactly as the first Nonjurors felt towards the Prince of Orange, the author of the treacherous massacre of Glencoe, equally detested for his frigidity and his favouritism. But though they dwindled, the Nonjurors left behind them a long roll of names that ought not to perish. In addition to the holy and courageous Bishop Ken, there were John Kettlewell and Robert Nelson the devotional writers, Thomas Hearne the famous antiquary, Richard Rawlinson, the bishop who bequeathed to St. John's College his heart and his worldly treasure,[1] and William Law, the brilliant writer and practical mystic.

The secession of the Nonjurors weakened the intellect and the piety of the Church of England; but it was some fifty years before the effect of that secession could be measured. The Church was still able to rear such bishops as Thomas Wilson (1663–1755), a true father in God to the Manx people, and Joseph Butler, Bishop of Durham. Two great religious societies, that for the Propagation of the Gospel and that for Promoting Christian Knowledge, had recently been founded. Smaller societies for upholding a godly life existed in many parishes and drew numerous adherents

---

[1] Dr. Richard Rawlinson died in 1755. His heart reposes in a marble urn in a niche in the small chapel on the north side of the sanctuary of the college chapel. The words *Ubi thesaurus, ibi cor* are painted below the urn. As a singular instance of academic gratitude, it may be noted that in the next century (? in 1843) the top of the monument was badly broken and perforated with a gas pipe. It was not restored until 1919.

from the lower middle and the working classes. Imposing churches were still erected. Religious books were widely read. Fasts as well as festivals were by many strictly observed. Private confession to a priest, though voluntary, was often practised. And we might have been much impressed if we had entered one of the London churches in the time of Queen Anne, let us say on a Christmas morning, the church unheated and bitterly cold, but fragrant with rosemary and bay, thronged with people at seven o'clock in the morning or at twelve, all fasting except the sick or luxurious, the small altar with its marble top covered with choice velvet and the costliest silver candle-sticks and vessels, the citizens in fine brown cloth and ladies in blue brocade, in some cases not merely kneeling but prostrating themselves and smiting their breasts as they drew near to the richly carved altar rails, murmuring the Agnus Dei and placing their hands in the form of a cross to receive the body of the Lord.

It was not the weakness but the strength of the Church that provoked the hatred of anti-Christian writers and a keen criticism of traditional beliefs, a criticism which exercised itself even within the borders of the Church.

The quest for a new Gospel and a Christ different from the Christ of the creeds was no new adventure even in the time of Queen Anne and George I. But it was pursued with an eagerness and with a learning that would surprise many of the readers of our current ecclesiastical magazines. What were the limitations of our Lord's knowledge during His ministry, and do those limitations militate against the doctrine of His Deity; how, if at all, can we attribute to Him any pre-existence; did He work miracles; can a theory of the Atonement be constructed that will avoid the conception of a vicarious sacrifice; can the doctrine of the Trinity, if true at all, be so restated as to remove all mystery; is it quite right for a minister of religion to repeat in church, and subscribe out of church, the creeds which he does not believe?[1] Such were among the problems of two hundred years ago. And the two systems known as Deism and Arianism, though opposed to each other, united in answering these questions in a tone of revolt against the Christian faith.

The revolt of the Deists was open and aggressive. We cannot call it organized: both in England and on the Continent the Deists fought singly, and if they formed groups, they did not form a party. Their work was essentially destructive, whether directed against the truth of the Pentateuch or the truth that the prophecies of the Old Testament are fulfilled in Christ, or the truth of His miracles. They ignored or directly impugned the unique value of the Holy Scriptures and some questioned even the immortality of the human soul. But they held that there is a God, and that God and duty can be known by 'the Religion of Nature'. It was their belief that God has given a moral law to man, and that this law is simply a circumstance of our actual existence, plain to every man in the world alike, and that a natural religion is superior to any revealed in the Bible and the Church.

This belief was connected with another and less prejudiced movement of ideas.

In the first half of the eighteenth century men were gaining a crude but increasing knowledge of non-Christian religions. One proof of this can be found in the great work on 'Religious Ceremonies', with copper-plates by Picart,[2]

[1] For this, see Waterland's treatises on 'Arian Subscription' in W. Van Mildert's edition of his *Works*, vol. ii, pp. 281 ff. (Oxford, 1823). 'Those gentlemen make no scruple of subscribing to our Church's forms; it is their *avowed principle* that they may lawfully do it in their *own* sense agreeably to what they call *Scripture*.'

[2] *The Religious Ceremonies and Customs of the several Nations of the known World*, written originally in French, was published in a fuller form in English (Nicholas Prevost, London, 1731).

in which attempts are made to describe and illustrate all the religions of the world. The illustrations of the ceremonies of the Roman Catholics and of the Jews are peculiarly accurate and artistic, those of the Japanese and other distant races are at least the work of a very ingenious imagination. The tone of the book is more sceptical than religious, but it shows an awakening interest in the variety and unity of religious beliefs. More serious was the work of certain Jesuit authors who laid stress upon the natural good qualities of the heathen races among whom they laboured, not excluding even the American Indians. In spite of the hideous sufferings inflicted upon some members of their order by the Iroquois, we find them painting optimistic pictures of noble savages whose simple life they believed to be untainted by the corruption of civilization. In this way they quite unwittingly put an argument at the disposal of the enemies of Christianity. And so behind all the differences between Protestant and Catholic, Jew and Christian, the Bible and the Vedas, men were invited to recognize a natural religion, the happy mean between the coarseness of atheism and the artfulness of priestcraft.

Of the English Deists it is probable that the Platonic Earl of Shaftesbury and the licentious Viscount Bolingbroke did not greatly injure the religious life of their contemporaries. But the influence exercised by Toland's *Christianity not Mysterious* and Tindal's *Christianity as old as the Creation* was rapid and serious. Both these writers had been for part of their lives Roman Catholics and both assumed the mask of Christian language while denying all mystery in religion. Toland's own religion seems to have been a Pantheistic form of Unitarianism. He visited Hanover and sowed the seeds of unbelief in the soil of a decaying Lutheranism, seed which bore abundant fruit. Indeed the coincidences between English Deism and the modern Rationalism and Liberalism of Germany are highly significant. Toland and Morgan anticipated F. C. Baur in their views concerning the relations between St. Paul and the original apostles, and in asserting the right of the Unitarian Ebionites to a place in the Church. Woolston anticipated Strauss by trying to find inconsistencies in the Gospel record of the miracles, and by treating all miracles as no more than allegory. Chubb, by assailing the Deity of Christ in tracts of a popular character, anticipated the modern rationalistic press in England and Germany. The name rather than the nature of the controversy has been changed. For in retaining a belief in providence and claiming to be Christian while steadily denying all supernatural revelation and any special redemptive interposition of God in history, the Deists were not far removed from some theologians of a later time whose anti-dogmatic latitudinarianism can hardly be distinguished from dogmatic Deism.

The adversaries of the Deists were numerous and capable. Of William Law we must speak later. Another fervent Nonjuror who opposed the Deists was Charles Leslie (1650–1722), an Irish Scot, chairman of quarter sessions for County Monaghan. Burnet, after accusing him of being 'the first man that began the war in Ireland' by declaring that King James was unfit to reign, proceeds to attack him for changing sides and becoming 'the violentest Jacobite in the nation'.[1] His theological works, written in a lively style, were directed against Jews and Roman Catholics as well as Deists, and won from Dr. Johnson the opinion that Leslie was 'a reasoner, and a reasoner who was not to be reasoned against'. He wittily confronted the believers in 'natural religion' with the Hottentots at the Cape of Good Hope as a proof of what nature can accomplish when left to herself; he dealt with the alleged parallels between the story of

---

[1] *History of His Own Times*, vol. v, p. 436 (Oxford, 1833). Here again Burnet's representation of an opponent cannot be regarded as impartial. There seems to be no proof that Leslie was a turncoat.

Christ and the Siamese legends of the Buddha;[1] and his arguments in favour of the miracles of the Bible, though in themselves of little weight to-day, contain some acute and valuable suggestions.

Joseph Butler (1692–1752), Bishop of Durham, eclipsed all other contemporary defenders of Christianity. Anonymous writers, afterwards discovered to be men who, while holding views at variance with the creeds, retained preferment in the Church of England, accused him of favouring or even of embracing Romanism, and in later times his *Analogy* has been blamed as in essence sceptical. But the great majority of students no more doubt his attachment to the Church of England than they doubt the impressive and positive character of his argument. Butler displays an ascetic, even rugged reserve in language. This reserve is part of his profound reverence for truth, and we may justly say that he proves very much because he never attempts to prove too much. His *Analogy* has been criticized as a mere 'retort', but the retort formed a refutation, showing that from our experience of nature no argument can be brought against the possibility of revelation, and that the things to which the Deists objected are not incredible and can be proved by external evidence. It refuted men like Toland and Tindal who tried to banish mystery from religion by telling their readers to observe nature, and the incongruity of nature with alleged revelation. Butler himself was a philosopher of ardent faith. He refused to see a manifestation of the Holy Spirit in the hysteria which was sometimes produced by Wesley's preaching, but he had a deep thirst for the vision of God. The champion of reason, he believed no Christianity to be reasonable if it did not glow with the love of God. And if his *Analogy* was primarily

---

[1] 'Sommonocodom', evidently Sakyamuni, as is proved by the 'Letter about Sommonocodom': Charles Leslie, *Theological Works*, vol. i, p. 130 (London, 1721). This letter is one of the first accounts of the Buddhist religion written in the English language.

a book for his own day, it remains as a solemn warning against that common fearlessness with regard to what may be hereafter which nothing could ever logically justify except 'an universally acknowledged demonstration on the side of atheism'.[1]

Midway between Deism and orthodox Christianity was Arianism.[2] The English Dissenters—in the eighteenth century they were proud of that name—had profited by the advent of William III; their influence in the country was important and seemed likely to be increased by a closer union between the middle-class Presbyterians and the more democratic Independents. But a new division cut across the two communities with disastrous results. That division was caused by a revival of Arianism. There must be some attraction in Arianism, for it has attracted many people since it was first taught in Alexandria in the opening years of the fourth century. In its original form it professed not to destroy but to explain both the spirit and the letter of the Bible, and especially of those verses which proclaim the unity of God or show that Jesus Christ lived in filial submission to the Father. The lovers of cheap logic relished the argument that every father must be older than his son, and that therefore the Son of God cannot be eternal; and they did not pause to consider that a man is called his father's son, not because he is younger, but because he derives his life from his father. And to minds which were imperfectly weaned from the later forms of Greek philosophy, the notion of some great intermediate being between the Most High and this sordid world was an acceptable delusion, even though this exalted creature had not a perfect

---

[1] *Analogy of Religion*, Part I, ch. ii; *Works*, vol. i, p. 45 (Oxford, 1849).
[2] A valuable outline of the history of English Arianism and of its relation to Nonconformity is to be found in the works of Mr. J. Hay Colligan, *The Arian Movement in England* (Manchester University Press, 1913) and *Eighteenth Century Nonconformity* (Longmans, London, 1915).

knowledge of God, and mankind could not gain through Him an access to the Father. A demi-god can be neither the soul's guide nor the soul's rest.

The question whether such a creature as this Christ could properly be worshipped was answered in the affirmative by the ancient Arians, who for that reason were correctly accused by the orthodox of polytheism. In the sixteenth century the Socinians, who taught a similar Christology, were sharply divided on the subject, and in the eighteenth some English Socinians refused to worship Christ. Others, however, were reluctant to abandon the practice, and until the last decade of the eighteenth century there were Dissenters who, while denying His Deity, treated our Lord as God 'in the language of devotion', carrying spices to a shrine which the Lord had never occupied.

The causes which led the English Dissenters into Arianism were very complex. Knowing that they had left the Catholic Church of antiquity, they began to feel a dislike of the Catholic creeds which their forefathers had retained, and wanted to appeal to the Bible only. They had all been brought up in the Calvinism of either the Westminster Confession or the Savoy Declaration, and they rebelled against it. Calvinism had given them a bias against the doctrine of the Trinity by theories of grace and atonement which made the Father in His awful justice appear essentially different from the merciful Jesus. Those who had studied in Holland inclined to Arminianism and the Arminians were infected with Socinianism. The immoral Antinomianism taught by the more ignorant Calvinistic ministers in England as a direct result of Calvin's doctrine of election gave them an opportunity for appealing to men's reason, and the appeal was made to men whose conception of the Church and the Sacraments was lower than that of Calvin and who were therefore more prepared to accept a reduced Christology.

Such was the field which was rendered more completely

barren by the far-reaching work by Dr. Samuel Clarke (1675–1729), named *The Scripture Doctrine of the Trinity* and emphasizing the subordination of the Son to the Father. It has been thought that Clarke was not quite an Arian, and that he was more like the old-fashioned bishops who supported Arius because they wrongly suspected that the Nicene Creed was Sabellian, and because they did not understand what their own position implied. But, though his language sometimes wavered, he was really a buttress of Arian heresy. The nature of his views on the Trinity was adequately tested by a Roman Catholic named Dr. Hawarden, who was invited to meet Clarke by Queen Caroline. Clarke unfolded his theory, endeavouring to defend it as scriptural and orthodox. Hawarden listened patiently, and then said that he had just one question to ask, and would the reply be given in a monosyllable? Clarke agreed; 'Then I ask', said Hawarden, 'can God the Father annihilate the Son and the Holy Ghost? Answer me, "Yes or No".' Clarke continued for some time in deep thought, and then said it was a question which he had never considered. The conference then ended. Quite plainly he could not answer without either confessing that the Son and the Spirit are essential to the One divine Being, or pronouncing them to be creatures and unworthy of the adoration which they have always received from the Christian Church.[1]

During the generation which followed the publication of Clarke's book, Isaac Watts (1674–1748) and Philip Doddridge (1702–1751) maintained positions which combined a mitigated Calvinism with a somewhat eclectic doctrine of

---

[1] W. Van Mildert's Introduction to *The Works of the Rev. Daniel Waterland*, vol. i, part 1, p. 102 (Oxford, 1823). Clarke also mutilated a copy of the Book of Common Prayer, adapting it to an Arian standard. Editions of the *Book of Common Prayer reformed according to the plan of the late Dr. Samuel Clarke* were published by J. Johnson, St. Paul's Churchyard, London. The third edition was printed in 1785. It is strongly Arian in tone but goes beyond Arianism in excluding the worship of Christ.

Christ's Person, both accepting the theory of Origen that Christ's soul existed before He was born in this world. Their undoubted piety was of great service to the cause of religion and their hymns powerfully aided the revival of Christianity in English Dissent in the second half of the century. 'O God, our help in ages past' and 'My God, and is Thy table spread' are hymns not likely to be forgotten while English Christianity continues to exist. Doddridge, who at his birth had been actually thrown aside as dead, and became a cultivated and convincing preacher at the age of twenty, is one of the most attractive figures in the annals of English Nonconformity. His religion was thoroughly practical and his writings, his sermons, and the training that he gave to about one hundred and twenty candidates for the ministry won and deserved gratitude, affection, and respect.

At the date of the accession of George III Arianism, strictly so called, had done its worst. William Hogarth's picture of 'The Sleeping Congregation', dozing under the emblem of an inverted triangle, was a satire well deserved by the section of the Church which had been hypnotized by Samuel Clarke and his friend Dr. Hoadly, the prelate in whom George I had recognized a kindred spirit. But while the formularies of the Church prevented the wholesale inversion of Christian doctrine, the Dissenters had less protection against the Arianism of the ministers trained in their own academies. With the abandonment of the worship of Christ, prayer declined, the sacraments became more and more neglected, the sermon became a lecture unkindled by 'enthusiasm', and English Dissent, especially in its Presbyterian form, sank into a state of profound decay. One of the most influential Dissenters in the middle of the century was John Taylor (1694–1761) of Norwich, whose chapel was described by Wesley as 'too fine for the coarse old Gospel', a divine of somewhat Arian opinions, who criticized the

Calvinist doctrine of Original Sin and total depravity in a work which in America prepared the way for the religious revolution which we shall consider later. And it was to this man that John Wesley, himself an enemy of Calvinism, wrote, 'Either I or you mistake the whole of Christianity from the beginning to the end. Either my scheme or yours is as contrary to the Scriptural as the Koran is. Is it mine or yours?'

Those words were written in 1759. By that time Methodism and the general Evangelical movement were not only stemming the whole tide of Arian and Socinian opinions, but were ousting them from the meeting-houses of the Independents. The English Presbyterians showed less power of recovery than these Independents or Congregationalists. And the connecting links between English Presbyterianism and Unitarianism are all illustrated in the career of Priestley, the Birmingham scientist.

Joseph Priestley (1753–1804) was brought up in Calvinism, and became prejudiced against it because he was refused membership in a local meeting-house for not assenting to the Calvinist doctrine concerning the 'new birth'. He became first an Arminian, then an Arian, then a Socinian, and finally a Unitarian, teaching in Birmingham and in Philadelphia that Jesus was only an exalted prophet of supernatural powers and Messianic office. His book on *The Corruptions of Christianity* was criticized in 1783, the year following its publication, by Samuel Horsley, Archdeacon of St. Albans, afterwards Bishop of St. Davids, and then of St. Asaph. Horsley was a firm friend of religious freedom. As bishop he wrote a pamphlet on behalf of the Dissenters, his speech in the House of Lords to secure relief for the English Roman Catholics was so effective that it was believed to have turned the scale in their favour, and in 1792 he took an active part in securing more toleration for the Scottish Episcopal Church. But he was a drastic controversialist when controversy was necessary. And in spite of some blemishes in his own work, he was able to show that Priestley was neither enough of a scholar to translate the early Christian writers nor enough of a philosopher to understand them.[1]

By a strange coincidence the year after the accession of George III, 1761, was the year in which died not only John Taylor, the eminent Nonconformist author, but also William Law and Benjamin Hoadly, two of the most dexterous writers among Anglican divines.

Forty years earlier Dr. Hoadly, who during the six years that he was Bishop of Bangor had not paid his diocese a single visit, was promoted to the see of Hereford, and Hereford was only a stepping-stone to the still more important sees of Salisbury and Winchester. The secret of this promotion lay in the principles expressed in a sermon approved, if not instigated, by King George I. It was a calculated attack upon the authority of the Church, an attack in which the preacher was somewhat oblivious of the truth that if there be little need for the authority of a visible Church, there will remain still less need for the authority of a visible bishop. The sermon, not a great thing in itself, became historic. The king dismissed his chaplains because they disagreed with Hoadly, and strangled the Church by suppressing Convocation. And so there came into power a party which treated forms of Church government and worship, and even doctrine, as matters of indifference, Latitudinarians, who were described as 'believing the way to heaven is never the better for being strait'.

Hoadly's most brilliant opponent was William Law, a man who before he left the university had made it a rule to

---

[1] After Horsley's death a coloured print published by Deighton in 1806 popularized the bishop's features. It may still be met with and is a good illustration of the walking costume of a bishop of that period.

remember constantly the presence of God, to think humbly of himself, and to forbear from all evil speaking. His letters to Hoadly are lucid, logical, and courteous. The duty of being in full and external communion with the Church which Christ founded and commissioned is persuasively pleaded. As for Hoadly's arguments that it is absurd to believe in any apostolic succession in the ministry, they are cleverly shown from Hoadly's own premises to involve him in the admission that genuine bishops exist nowhere but within the Church of Rome. With equal skill Law cut through the fallacies which underlay Hoadly's work on the Lord's Supper, pointing out that his critical method was not only in itself mistaken, but would, if correct, do away with our need of a Saviour as completely as our need of a sacrament.

It is difficult to be an honest and accomplished controversialist. But it is more difficult to be a good Christian. And William Law was indeed a good Christian. The champion of the Church was also the prophet of an inwardly verified religion. As a student he was ardent and laborious. He was an ascetic, but no Manichaean. He allowed himself one glass of wine at dinner and one pipe of tobacco in the evening. He loved music and he loved children. A learned man and a reader of several languages, he had much in common with the Cambridge Platonists and assimilated the better teaching of the German mystic Boehme. No one since the days of Thomas à Kempis has written of Faith and Love with more glowing and convincing eloquence than William Law in his works called the *Spirit of Prayer* and the *Spirit of Love*. But his masterpiece is the *Call to a Devout and Serious Life*, a book that won the praise even of the cynical Gibbon and converted Dr. Johnson to a living Christianity. No other book in the English language combines such a fine delineation of human character with such an eager desire to show that the only road to happiness is the intention to please God in all that we do.

The characters in Law's book breathe the very air of England. There is the worthy merchant Negotius to whom the good of trade is the good of general life, honest, successful, generous, respected. He will subscribe to buy a plate for a racecourse or to rescue a prisoner from jail. But he has no higher inspiration than the wish to do more business than any other man. There is the shrewd Mundanus, old and judicious, who has exercised and improved his mind in everything except devotion, and in prayer can only repeat the little form of words that his mother taught him when he was six years old. There is Cognatus, the country clergyman who is a careful farmer and has saved up for a spoilt niece the money which really belonged to the Church. He is 'full of esteem of our English Liturgy, and if he has not prayers on Wednesdays and Fridays, it is because his Predecessor had not used the parish to any such custom'. There is Octavius, who seeing that the glass of life is nearly run, determines to furnish his cellar with a little of the very best of wine, and realizing the mistake of having too large a circle of acquaintances resolves to confine himself to three or four cheerful companions, and then dies before the wine has come. There is Classicus, the careful tutor who has a Bible in Greek, but thinks it 'a nobler talent to be able to write an epigram in the turn of Martial than to live, and think, and pray to God in the spirit of St. Austin'.

Law never gained and never sought what is called preferment, but he schooled himself to be almost incapable of hatred towards a single creature and was a true guide to the mystical treasure that is hidden in every human soul.

From William Law we may turn to the yet more famous John Wesley (1703–1791) and George Whitefield (1714–1770), both priests and evangelists who helped to give Oxford its unique place in the history of Christianity. We can profit by a knowledge of their mistakes as well as by a knowledge of their virtues.

It has often been debated whether the societies which owe their foundation to Whitefield and Wesley could have remained as auxiliary institutions in the Church of England, and it is sometimes suggested that if Wesley had been a member of the Church of Rome, Rome would have retained his allegiance and canonized him as a saint as she canonized Ignatius de Loyola. That is a fanciful suggestion. Very recently Rome has failed to deal by any other means than the method of excommunication with the leaders of the Mariaviten in Poland, a body of fervent Catholics who desired to introduce into Roman Catholicism far less serious innovations than Wesley would have introduced into the Church of England. Whitefield and Wesley drew apart, but it is hard to see how either the Calvinistic Methodism of the one, or the Arminian Methodism of the other, could continue to exist as an *imperium in imperio*. Both Methodist societies are skilfully constructed and signally complete. The class meetings, the leaders, the preachers, the assistants, the stewards, were soon part of a vast structure. Wesley himself probably believed that Methodism could form a kind of central hall of piety within the Church. But when he became convinced that a presbyter is a bishop and ordained ministers for the American Methodists, few but himself can have doubted that such ordination meant separation. The American Methodists were under no illusion in this matter. One of them, Watters, wrote, 'We became instead of a religious society, a separate Church. This gave great satisfaction through all our societies.'[1]

Wesley was openly impatient of authority, as he showed by his attitude, not only towards Bishop Butler but also towards the Moravian Zinzendorf, and especially Gibson, the kindly Bishop of London. His genius for organization

[1] See app. note 18, p. 272.

made everything in Methodism begin and end in his own supremacy. He wielded that supremacy for the promotion of holiness with untiring activity, with extreme self-denial, with tact, with dignity, with the courage that would always look a mob in the face. But these eminent gifts, used in the service of the Master, must not blind us to the dangers of his teaching. If in the latter part of his career he openly violated the constitution of the Church, he threatened the doctrine of the Church far earlier. His triumphant sermon on Free Grace directed against the Calvinism taught by Whitefield probably did more than any other sermon to bring English Calvinism to the grave. But Whitefield, and not Wesley, was with the Church when Wesley taught the possibility of sinless perfection being attained by man in his present state of existence.

Still greater danger attended the doctrine of the necessity of a sensible instantaneous conversion which Wesley had derived from the Moravians. In his old age he affirmed that he had not 'for many years thought consciousness of acceptance to be essential to justifying faith'. Yet that was the view which he had held with regard to his own conversion. That a conversion may be instantaneous, we can have no desire to dispute. A man who has doubted Christ, or has denied Christ, may begin at some time to believe, and he may well remember the day and the hour when he gained peace with God, the discourse, the prayer, the sight, the sorrow, that led him to his new conviction of the truth. But to confine the work of the Holy Spirit to one single method of operation, and to treat as insufficient that sanctification of the mind and heart whereby the seed which is sown in baptism grows through the silent influence of grace, is presumptuous and false. It leads men to judge the condition of their souls by the condition of their feelings.

Here Whitefield should be preferred to Wesley. As preachers they both possessed extraordinary talents. Whitefield was less cultivated than Wesley, but his superb voice, the perfect grace of his movements, and his earnest simplicity, riveted the attention of his hearers. The world has seldom seen such congregations as gathered on Boston Common to hear young Whitefield in 1740 ; and when Benjamin Franklin tells us how he emptied his pockets in response to Whitefield's appeal for charity, we understand that it was not only the uneducated whose hearts were melted. But only in one instance do we read of a sermon by Whitefield being followed by an outbreak of wild hysteria. It was otherwise when Wesley preached. In his eagerness to produce an instantaneous change of heart, and an immediate assurance of God's favour, he excited and terrified his ignorant hearers to such an extent that loud ravings, frightful convulsions, and blasphemous outcries were blended with shouts of 'Glory!' These disorders, which were attributed too frequently to supernatural causes, could not fail to prejudice many Christians against the whole Methodist system, and encourage the Antinomianism which Wesley himself abhorred and disclaimed.

Wesley had never been in charge of a parish and he undervalued calm, steady, parochial work. He undervalued it even in places where the clergy were his friends and were as eager as himself for the conversion of sinners. Among such men are to be reckoned John Fletcher (1729–1785) of Madeley, Samuel Walker (1714–1761) of Truro, and Henry Venn (1725–1797) of Huddersfield. To these men there became attached, before the close of the century, the name 'Evangelical' with something of a party significance, though it had been used by Bishop Berkeley simply of an inward and spiritual religion as opposed to the lip service or the will service of hypocrisy or superstition. While Wesley looked upon the world as his parish, these Evangelicals looked upon their parish as their world. Not that they exercised no influence outside their parishes. The romantic career of John Fletcher, the clever son of Swiss Protestants who chose the army for his profession, became tutor to an English family, and was converted by a poor old woman on the road near St. Albans, was rich in interest and influence. His mastery of two languages was so perfect that he could both move a French audience to tears and subdue the rough and brutalized colliers in Shropshire. He was a theologian of no mean ability. He wrote in opposition to Dr. Priestley, paying an honest tribute to his merits, but giving no quarter to the theory that the Church had made an idol of her Founder or to the belief that Socinianism was safe in appealing to the New Testament. He was alive to the Antinomianism and the fatalism which dogged the heels of Methodism, and he was indignant when he saw a merely emotional persuasion that our salvation was finished on the Cross made into a dispensation from holiness. He would have nothing to do with a religion which makes a merit of having no merits; and in spite of his ardent faith, or rather in consequence of that faith, he lays down what he names 'this just principle, that religion may improve but can never oppose good sense and good morals'.

The general effect of the Evangelical movement upon the religion of England was a great quickening of spiritual life and a magnificent impetus to missionary work among the heathen. It was, however, attended by a change which is thus described by Dr. Dale, the most eminent English Congregationalist in the nineteenth century. He says, 'The Evangelical movement contributed to the extinction among Congregationalists, and, I think, among Baptists and Presbyterians, of that solicitude for an ideal Church organization which had so large a place in the original revolt of the Nonconformists. . . . It demanded as the basis of fellowship a common religious life and common religious beliefs, but was satisfied with fellowship of an accidental and precarious kind. It cared nothing for the idea of the Church as the august Society of saints. It was the ally of Individualism.'[1]

Dr. Dale's opinion is correct. And although the best Evangelicals in the Church of England like Venn were strongly opposed to Dissent, the ordinary people tended to lose that conception of the Church which is presented to us in the New Testament and to make their choice of a religion depend entirely upon their approval of a preacher.

While we must lament the divisions which resulted from a neglect to consider the origin, the authority, and the grace of the visible continuous body of Christ, we can thank God that the Methodists and the Evangelicals called men back to the divine Head of that body. The waves of Arian and Socinian misbelief were gradually reducing the worship of Him whom St. John describes as 'The true God and eternal life', to admiration for the best man who gave to other men some good advice. Fletcher and Venn, to mention no other names, not only wrote to defend the Deity of Christ. They enabled others to know His power to save, to experience His Deity, to obey His commands, and to follow in His steps. That is to know the historic Christ, the Christ of the Gospels and the Creeds.

The effect of the fall of the Stuarts upon English religion was serious, but in Scotland and America it was profound and permanent.

In 1689 after the arrival of the Prince of Orange in London, Dr. Compton, Bishop of London, introduced to him at Whitehall, Dr. Rose, Bishop of Edinburgh. William addressed him, 'My lord, are you going to Scotland?' 'Yes, sir,' said Rose, 'if you have any commands for me.'

[1] *The Old Evangelicalism and the New*, pp. 16, 17 (Hodder & Stoughton, London, 1889).

The Prince replied, 'I hope you will be kind to me, and follow the example of England.' Then said the bishop, 'Sir, I will serve you so far as law, reason, or conscience shall allow me.' William knew what that answer foreboded. He would certainly have left Episcopacy alone if it had not been obvious that all the bishops, like the majority of the people of Scotland, were Jacobites, and in no mood to obey a Dutch Calvinist. Episcopacy was disestablished in July 1689 and entered upon its journey of a hundred years in the wilderness. Some relief was experienced as a result of the Toleration Act of Queen Anne in 1712, and in her reign the University of Oxford sent to Scotland thousands of copies of the Book of Common Prayer: one may still occasionally be found in a remote Scottish district.

Recent researches have very strongly confirmed both contemporary writings and lingering traditions as to the strength of the religious parties existing at the time of the revolution and the beginning of the eighteenth century. The 'Episcopals', as they began to be called, were in a large majority. In the south-west of Scotland a rigid Presbyterianism was dominant, in the south-east a somewhat more moderate Presbyterianism existed side by side with Episcopacy. In Edinburgh hundreds of persons were turned away on Sundays from the place where the Church service was read by Dr. Monro, the principal of the university, and even in 1716 the Episcopalian clergy in Edinburgh were more numerous than the ministers of the Established Church. In a few districts of the north of Scotland, the majority of the people were, as they still are, Roman Catholics,[1] and certain clans like the Campbells were divided in their religion. But as a rule Episcopacy was supreme from the country districts of Aberdeenshire to the western islands of Tiree and Coll, to Ardnamurchan where, we are

[1] These districts are near the Caledonian Canal, and eastward towards Braemar, and on the west include the islands of Barra and South Uist.

told, the people idolized the non-juring clergy, and Glencoe.[1] From the north not a single delegate appeared at the Presbyterian General Assembly of 1690. The diocese of Ross at the revolution included thirty-two parishes. In only two of these parishes was there any considerable number of Presbyterians, and of the thirty-one incumbents only one submitted to the new ecclesiastical government. In the whole of Perthshire only three accepted the change, and in the diocese of Moray out of fifty-nine clergymen only one. The people resisted the change by every means at their disposal; from parish to parish we find the same story with a dramatic variation of details. Sometimes they used actual violence, sometimes they locked the church or simply boycotted the new minister, and at Glenorchy they led him to the bounds of the parish while the local piper played the march of death, and then made him swear on the Bible that he would return no more.

In 1712 the magistrates of Elgin confirmed the right of the Episcopalians to use the chancel of the parish church of St. Giles. In Inverness Bishop Hay continued to reside until his death in 1707, and in spite of extreme bodily weakness did all in his power to help his fallen Church, extending his care as far as the Orkney Isles. One of his clergy, Mr. Hector Mackenzie, remained in possession of his living, officiating in English at the parish church and in Gaelic at the adjacent church until his death in 1719. The other charge in Inverness was not filled up until 1703, having been vacant for twelve years before it was possible for it to be taken by a Presbyterian. In a city where ecclesiastical antiquities are few, it is pleasant to behold

---

[1] For the history of the Church in these districts, see J. B. Craven, *Records of the Diocese of Argyll and the Isles*, 1560–1860 (William Peace & Son, Kirkwall, 1907). The author records that in Morven early in the nineteenth century there were still forty heads of families who were Episcopalians. There was neither bishop nor priest to visit them, and when they died all their families conformed to Presbyterianism.

the elaborately beautiful wooden pulpit once occupied by Mr. Hector Mackenzie,[1] and the simple white monument of Bishop Hay, which was rescued from a rubbish shop to be erected in the new cathedral.

Gradually the Episcopalians were caught in a complete network of penal laws. George I was not content to punish individual clergymen who were implicated in the rising of 1715, but ordered all the Episcopal chapels in Edinburgh to be closed.[2] In Edinburgh this command could not be carried into execution, but in other places magistrates shut the chapels, or soldiers were employed to eject the clergy from those parish churches which they still retained. Thirty years later, both before and after the battle of Culloden, the persecution became far more severe, and the chapels were systematically destroyed by the Duke of Cumberland's troops who behaved with savage barbarity. At Inverness General Hawley, a cruel and profligate braggart, ordered 'that the meeting house, with the seditious Preacher in the midst of it, should be burnt'. It was not burnt but pulled down, and the good 'preacher', Mr. Hay, escaped and before long was officiating in the loft of a house in a neighbouring lane. New and more stringent laws were passed and spies were employed by the presbyteries to see whether the laws were obeyed. Every place in which five or more persons assembled for worship was declared to be a meeting house, and no clergyman was allowed to officiate unless he presented his letters of orders and took the oath of allegiance to the Government. Then, in spite

---

[1] The pulpit, dated 1668 and somewhat resembling the best English Renaissance work of fifty years earlier, is in the present 'Gaelic church' connected with the Established Presbyterian Church. It is called 'the Irish church pulpit' in a Kirk session record of 1689. In 1921 I was told that the congregation was reduced to 'two or three dozen'. The Gaelic language has rapidly decayed in Inverness and its neighbourhood during the last fifty years, and the only considerable Gaelic congregation is to be found at the 11 a.m. service at the large Free Church.

[2] For the politics of the Episcopalians, see app. note 19, p. 273.

of the protest of the English bishops, the native clergy were totally disqualified, the registration of their orders, although already made, being declared null and void. Therefore no Scottish clergyman, whatever his political opinions might be, could even read prayers before a congregation of more than five persons, the penalty for the first offence being six months' imprisonment, and for the second offence transportation for life.

After a time the persecution lessened. In a quiet corner of a town house or in a low thatched cottage hidden among the trees, a congregation would gather round men 'unskilled in every art but the art of suffering for conscience' sake'. At long intervals a bishop would arrive. 'The bishops', says a sympathetic writer on Scottish life in the eighteenth century, 'form an interesting though dim feature in the social and religious life of those days. Little seen, little heard of in the Lowlands, where Presbytery was supreme, in the northern parts they are seen flitting in primitive apostolic fashion and penury from district to district, visiting the diminutive congregations in Ross or Moray, in the wilds of Sutherland or the bleak Orkneys. The worthy bishop, with his deacon, journeys on ponyback, wrapped in his check plaid and attired in quite unepiscopal habiliments, or travels on foot carrying a meagre wardrobe on his shoulders. Hard-working, hard-faring men, strong in the divine right of Prelacy, these simple-souled prelates in homespun maintained with a quaint dignity the honour of their office and poverty of their lot.'[1]

There is one word in that picturesque paragraph that requires modification. It is the word 'diminutive'. The Journal of Bishop Robert Forbes, with its delightful sidelights on the Scotland of the early years of George III,

[1] H. G. Graham, *Social Life of Scotland in the Eighteenth Century*, vol. ii, p. 125 (Adam & George Black, London, 1899).

tells us the size of some of these congregations whose devotion, he says, 'was admirable and past all Description'. At Brin he had an audience of a thousand people and in two days confirmed four hundred and eighty people, and in two 'country chapels' near Inverness he confirmed five hundred and twenty.[1] There knelt before him people of all conditions from a dainty little lady of seven to a gigantic Highlander who had been wounded, stripped naked, and then stabbed again and left for dead on the field of Culloden. The devotion of the Highlanders to their older forms of faith was such that nothing could have killed it but the impossibility of supplying them with clergy. Even when political barriers were removed by the death of Prince Charles Edward, the English Church did almost nothing to supply the need, and the few remaining priests were left to watch the grey shadows on the hills and on the sea and accept the inevitable bitterness.

During the latter part of the eighteenth and at the beginning of the nineteenth century great numbers of Highlanders migrated to eastern Canada, where many have retained their language, and others, especially the Roman Catholics, have become mingled with the French Canadian population.[2] Emigration thus completed the work which persecution had begun, and so Presbyterianism became solidly representative of the great majority of the

[1] These two chapels were at Arpafeelie and Muir of Ord. The present church at Arpafeelie, built about 1811, is very near the site of the old chapel. The chapel at Muir of Ord, now a dwelling-house, is probably the only country chapel dating from the time of the penal laws which now remains in Scotland. It is a thatched building, long, low, and picturesque. In the midst of one side is a kind of small transept where the altar and pulpit were probably placed. It was disused after the erection of the present church at Highfield.

[2] A most intelligent Highland soldier, who left Canada during the great war to fight in France, told me that he went into the cathedral of Notre-Dame at Montreal to read the names commemorated in the roll of honour. In a long list he found more Highland names than French. In the Canadian Roman Catholic dioceses of Antigonish and Charlottetown Scottish Roman Catholics abound.

nation. Little indeed could the remnant guess that, few as they were, they would exercise an incalculable influence upon the future. For it was in an upper room in a back street in Aberdeen on November the 14th, 1784 that three Scottish bishops did what the English bishops had never had the courage to do, consecrating Samuel Seabury a bishop for the Church in America. And it was in sight of

the distant Cheviots blue

that Sir Walter Scott, loving the Church 'whose system of government and discipline he believed to be the fairest copy of the primitive polity',[1] enlarged the minds of thousands to understand the past and to discover the reality that is latent in romance. Thus he prepared the way for the Oxford movement. No one can ignore what Seabury and Scott were able to contribute to the future; but behind both those men were others, obscure and forgotten, who 'against hope, believed in hope', the men who could bear to seem to fail, but could not bear to be disloyal to the truth.

Bishop Seabury arrived in America at a critical moment. Let us try to survey the situation. The Church of England had been established from the first in Virginia and in other parts of the south, where the white population was very scanty. It was also established in New York when New York became an English colony. No doubt the old Anglican churches in New York, Philadelphia, and Charleston, admirable specimens of the art of the Georgian period,[2] had large and generous congregations. But the whole work of the Church was crippled, and crippled deliberately, by the refusal of the British Government to send any bishops

---

[1] J. G. Lockhart, *Memoirs of the Life of Sir Walter Scott*, vol. vii, p. 414 (Robert Cadell, Edinburgh, 1838).

[2] For the architecture of these and other American churches, see app. note 20, p. 274.

to America in spite of the rapid increase in population and the entreaties of some of the best men in the Church of England. If it had not been for the Society for the Propagation of the Gospel the Church could hardly have survived. Farther east than New York, in Massachusetts, Connecticut, and New Hampshire, the Puritan colonists had erected Congregationalism as the established religion. It was completely in the ascendant, its connexion with the State was peculiarly close and was not severed till the nineteenth century had far advanced. In Connecticut especially the Church of England was non-existent until 1722, when Dr. Cutler the rector of Yale College and several of his colleagues became convinced that Congregationalist orders are invalid and the position of the Church of England scriptural. In order to be ordained, Cutler and two others sailed to England, which then involved a journey of about six weeks. Cutler and one of his friends caught the smallpox. The latter died. The two survivors went back to America, Cutler settling in Boston, and Johnson in Connecticut, the one and only clergyman in the colony. A few years later Mr. Beach, another devout Congregationalist minister educated at Yale, also became convinced that his ordination was invalid, and that the Church of England is, in his own words, 'Apostolic in her ministry and discipline, orthodox in her doctrine and primitive in her worship'. He too went to England, was ordained, and returned to America.

Johnson and Beach exercised a deep influence upon the religion of their country. They met with strong opposition, measures being taken even to hinder Beach's missionary work among the Indians. But the Church was joined by numbers of serious people who were wearied by Calvinist and Antinomian controversies, new English missionaries arrived, and at the time of the Revolution the Church of England in Connecticut was in a healthier condition than in any other part of America. During the Revolution it suffered far less than the Church farther south. In the south many church buildings were wrecked, especially in Virginia where also some years later the property of the Church was mercilessly confiscated, and a righteous judge who intended to restore it died the very night before his judgement was to be pronounced.[1] But more serious than these material losses was the spirit of frigid scepticism and rationalism which was affecting the better educated classes in America, a spirit which is the reverse of the wild revivalism of the camp meetings which came to be a feature of American frontier life.

This rationalistic spirit, hostile to the Christian doctrines concerning God and the sacraments, had infected the Church in certain districts and found expression in a now almost forgotten abridgement of the Prayer Book published in 1773. It omitted the Nicene and Athanasian Creeds, mutilated the *Te Deum*, and entirely erased the prayer of consecration in the communion service. This book undoubtedly influenced a 'proposed' Arianizing and anti-sacramental Prayer Book which was published with ecclesiastical authority in 1786 soon after Seabury reached America. The gravity of the danger can only be understood when it is remembered that only a few days before his arrival in Connecticut an anti-Trinitarian liturgy had been adopted by the most important church in New England,[2] the congregation of King's Chapel, Boston, a fine classical building which still keeps the altar plate given by the generosity of English monarchs. Seabury was unable to prevent some

[1] For the Church in Virginia at this period, see S. Wilberforce, *History of the Protestant Episcopal Church in America*, pp. 177 ff. and 274 ff. (James Burns, London, 1844). The Baptists seem to have displayed a peculiar hatred for the Church, and it was largely owing to their action that in 1802 the glebes, churches, and even the altar plate of the churches, were confiscated.

[2] The new liturgy was adopted June the 19th, 1785. Seabury was in Connecticut by the 'latter end of June'.

needless alterations in the Prayer Book,[1] but he took the lead in rescuing the Church from a position which two generations later was seen to be logically impossible and theologically profane. He died in 1796, but he had done his part in defending his brethren from what was soon to be known as 'the Boston religion'.

By 1800 the religion of Boston was in the hands of a group of so-called 'Liberal' Christians, in reality somewhat aggressive Arians.[2] They were Congregationalists who had deserted Calvinism. And so far as these men protested that God is beneficent, that Christ is imitable, and that men should be reminded of their dignity rather than of their depravity, they certainly deserve our sympathy. Their success was rapid. In a few years they had on their side wealth and fashion, culture, and legislation. They captured the University of Harvard, and whereas not a single Anglican congregation followed the example of King's Chapel, belief in the Holy Trinity was abandoned definitely in no less than one hundred and twenty-six Congregationalist churches. It has been truly said that no religious denomination ever started with such advantages as American Unitarianism. Yet it failed, and even the simplicity, earnestness, and lofty eloquence of its great advocate, Dr. Channing, could not prevent its decline. The Unitarians failed spiritually, because the Christian life is a product of the Incarnation and is not the acceptance of good rules. No Unitarian can say with St. Paul, 'I live, yet not I, but Christ liveth in me'. They failed morally, because while claiming to be liberal, they were intolerant, using their social and even their political power to ostracize their former co-religionists. They failed intellectually, because they began by claiming to be intensely scriptural, like the English Unitarians who

---

[1] On the other hand, Seabury insisted upon and secured a form for the consecration of the Eucharist more in harmony with antiquity and with the First Prayer Book of Edward VI and the Scottish Communion Office.

[2] See app. note 21, p. 275.

published a careful mistranslation of the New Testament to support their claim.[1] And then one of themselves, a prophet of their own, Theodore Parker, turned upon them saying that 'if the Athanasian Creed could be proved the work of an apostle, Unitarianism would deny it taught the doctrine of the Trinity'.

The controversy raised by Theodore Parker left the older Unitarianism under sentence of death. Arianism was no longer possible, Socinianism was no longer possible. It only remained to be determined whether our Lord should be considered as a perfect or as an imperfect man, and then to choose the latter alternative and to support it with rationalistic German criticism.

In the meantime the Church, first in Connecticut and then beyond it, served as a refuge for Christians who desired a religion both reasonable and devout. Its influence extended even to those who remained separated from its unity. It is a remarkable fact that the two kindred anti-Trinitarian sects, the Unitarian and the Universalist, that wrought havoc in Massachusetts, almost totally failed to gain a footing in Connecticut. In New York, where the Church was well represented, Unitarianism had no better success. As we look back upon these movements we cannot fail to notice how the divine providence made the Church's doctrine as to the necessity of episcopal ordinations a means of preserving and reviving the Christian faith. In the Church of ancient times the Fathers regarded the apostolical succession of their bishops both as a channel by which there is transmitted under the power of the Holy Spirit the grace appropriate for the divers orders in the Church, and also as a means of preserving the apostolic faith. This doctrine is ancient, primitive, and linked in no obscure fashion with the teaching of St. Paul, and in the first four

[1] *The New Testament in an improved version*, published by the Unitarian Society for Promoting Christian Knowledge and the Practice of Virtue (R. & A. Taylor, London, 1808; fourth edition, 'with corrections', 1817).

centuries of the Christian era it did much to preserve Christianity from being absorbed in an ocean of frothy and fruitless speculation. A threefold cord which could not be broken was formed by a defence of the Gospels, maintenance of the rule of faith, and loyalty to the bishops, who, as St. Hippolytus wrote, 'share in the same grace and high priesthood and teaching office' as the apostles.

So in America it was not by some blind chance that the doctrine of the Trinity in Unity was preserved from being dissipated and denied. We realize the importance of the means as we understand the importance of the result, and in both we see the hand of God. For the doctrine of the Holy Trinity is no figment of the speculative imagination, but a true description of what we as Christians know concerning God. Like the doctrine of the Incarnation it became clothed in the language of Greek philosophy, but it nevertheless corresponds with the deepest elements in Christian experience. The truth that the Man of Sorrows is indeed the eternal Son and Word of God, as well as our elder brother, throws an entirely new light upon the Fatherhood of God and the destiny of man. And the life of a new sonship, a life granted to those who believe in Christ's Name, is perpetuated in us by the fellowship of the Holy Spirit. The first Christians were deeply conscious of a Power that came to dwell within them and guided mind and heart, who revealed their weakness and removed it, and they knew that this Giver of life must himself be Lord. We return to the Father, through the Son, in the Spirit. Each is divine, the End, the Way, the Power. That is the centre of our creed, and it should be the centre of our life. The more firmly we believe it, the more sincerely we shall maintain the dignity of our human nature, the more earnestly we shall struggle to keep the purity, the integrity, the largeness of this life of ours, which was taken by the Son of God, to be eternally His own, and to be included by us in every thought of Him.

VI
ASPECTS OF LUTHERANISM AND CALVINISM SINCE 1700

Col. ii. 8: Beware lest any man spoil you through philosophy and vain deceit, after the tradition of men, after the rudiments of the world, and not after Christ.

THERE is in Pennsylvania a borough named Bethlehem, and there is another place named Ephrata. Those two names are memorials of two remarkable offshoots of the German Protestant Pietism which flourished at the beginning of the eighteenth century. For though Bethlehem is now famous for its iron and its steel, and lies in a district that has long since been invaded by railroads and furnaces, it is there that in 1741 the Moravian bishop Nitschmann, with his niece and Count Nikolaus Ludwig Zinzendorf, kept their first Christmas in America in a stable which they called Bethlehem. They had come to begin missionary work among the Indians, and their work was one of great adventures and considerable success. Some notable Red Indian braves sleep at Bethlehem.[1] And Ephrata was even before Zinzendorf's arrival the home of Protestant monks and nuns and hermits, whose austerity seems to us like a breath wafted from an Oriental desert. The Pietists had striven to form societies inside larger communities, and Zinzendorf had created such a society, more intensive and at the same time more oecumenical than the Pietist conventicles formed sporadically in German cities. The Pietists had also

[1] Among them is Tschoop, a Mohican, said to be the father of Uncas. He reappeared in the novels of Fenimore Cooper as 'Chingachgook'. Also 'Brother Michael', a ferocious warrior of the Munsey tribe, who became an exemplary Christian. Every quarter of an inch from his under-lip to the top of his forehead was adorned with a round dot to indicate the number of scalps which he had taken. He died in 1758.

encouraged individualism, and, in certain conditions hostile to pristine simplicity of life, religious individualism leads men to renounce all that is human in the effort to attain union with God. Thus the organized sect and the lonely hermit were both a protest against a Protestantism which was too stagnant and too secular.

Zinzendorf (1700-1760) himself must be put side by side with his younger contemporary John Wesley, though not upon so eminent a level. A godson of Spener he was reared in the strongest aroma of Pietism. He studied in Wittenberg, improved his studies in Holland and France, and in 1721 bought an estate at Berthelsdorf in Upper Lusatia, a district where the German language was encroaching upon that of the Slavonic Sorbs. There and in Dresden he tried to promote a 'religion of the heart' by means of private Church societies; but his religion took a new direction on the arrival of some German Moravian emigrants at Berthelsdorf, which with his help became the cradle of a neighbouring settlement which was called Herrnhut.[1]

These Moravians preserved some of the traditions of the Slavonic sect known as the *Unitas Fratrum* or Union of Brethren, a sect retaining an episcopal succession but vehemently opposed to the Papacy. In the fifteenth century it made numerous converts in Bohemia and Moravia, and spread into Poland in the middle of the sixteenth century. In 1620, after the outbreak of the Thirty Years' War, these Czech Protestants were crushed: some fled to Germany, and the Polish branch of the Union was absorbed in the Reformed (Calvinist) Church, retaining the episcopal succession in the person of John Amos Comenius (1592-1672) who published their *System of Discipline*, and consecrated as bishop his son-in-law Peter Jablonsky who

---

[1] Herrnhut lies 18 miles south-east of Bautzen on the Löbau-Zittau railway. Löbau was still Sorbish at the beginning of the twentieth century. For this interesting Slavonic region, see Franz Tetzner, *Die Slawen in Deutschland* (F. Vieweg, Braunschweig, 1902).

was court preacher in Memel. The latter, who was consecrated in 1662, handed on the episcopal succession in 1699 to his son David Ernest Jablonsky, who was court preacher in Berlin and consecrated Nitschmann as missionary bishop for the West Indies in 1735 and Zinzendorf himself in 1737.

Zinzendorf was a convinced Lutheran [1] of a strongly subjective temperament, delighting in the composition of somewhat sensuous hymns in which he allowed the worship of the Father to be obscured by the worship of Jesus, the Lamb of God and Brother of the Christian. He even spoke of the Holy Spirit as Mother in the life of the Trinity. When the *Unitas Fratrum* was fully reconstituted in 1747 it was a compromise. On the one hand it included Zinzendorf's sentimental German theology and his method of creating societies into which he tried to divert every stream of fervour which he could find in other sects. And on the other hand the careful rules of discipline and semi-Catholic ministry recall the great skill in organization which the Czechs always manifest whether in politics or in religion. Zinzendorf was pursued by the hostility of the Lutheran pastors and the Government until the whole community adopted the Augsburg Confession as its form of faith. Its right to exist was then formally recognized in Saxony in 1749. But it was before that date, and when he was banished from Saxony, that Zinzendorf had started the missionary work in Greenland, in Surinam, Georgia, Pennsylvania, and Santa Cruz, which became the real glory of the Moravian Church. He received John Wesley at Herrnhut, and though Wesley did not join the Moravians, he was deeply influenced by their example. The fervour of Zinzendorf in the service of Christ was as deep as Wesley's own. He had a true zeal

---

[1] The distinctive creed of the Moravians is stated in their so-called 'Easter Litany'. It was translated into English and slightly modified in 1749. See Ph. Schaff, *The Creeds of Christendom*, vol. iii, 'The Creeds of the Evangelical Churches', p. 799 (Harper, New York, 1877).

for the salvation of souls and he was one of the first of Protestants to recognize that missionary work is not a mere matter of colonial policy but the duty of every Christian as a Christian.

And then there is Ephrata.[1] Ephrata in the eighteenth century was a centre of the two different types of monasticism which we find in Egypt as early as the fourth century. There was the hermit life, and there was the ' common life ' of monks, and also nuns, living under the direction of a superior. About 1674 one John Kelpius, a native of Transylvania and a Master of Arts of the University of Altorf, went to America, withdrew from the world with several companions, some of whom were also men of learning, and lived in a cave near the Wissahickon, awaiting the return of Christ, the heavenly Bridegroom. He died in 1708 and most of his followers went back to the world. But his advocacy of the virgin life, his asceticism, and his mysticism produced a great effect on one Conrad Beissel. Beissel, who was a native of Ehrbach, had been by trade a baker, and in the days of his apprenticeship was devoted to music and dancing until he came under the influence of some extreme revivalists and migrated to America in 1720. He was a Baptist, and he adopted the view that Christians ought to observe the seventh day as holy. He selected a spot on the river Cocalico previously occupied by another hermit, and he was gradually joined by a considerable number of converts. The first coenobitic building, called ' Kedar ', was erected in 1735. In a few years' time it was necessary to add three others, not including the so-called ' Saal ' or chapel. The ascetics called themselves ' The Order of the Solitary '. Their religion was in accord with that of the German mystics of the period. It was marked by a craving after direct union with God, a sinking of self,

[1] For the monasticism at Ephrata, see *The Century Illustrated Magazine*, December 1881 (The Century Co., New York; F. Warne, London).

and an extinction of the individual will in the hope of obtaining the ecstasy of a divinely given intoxication. In order to express this ecstatic union with God in Christ the language of human love was ransacked; Christ the 'Bridegroom' and the 'Sophia' is addressed in the language of passionate affection, and in the hymns of Beissel the Church is the lonely and forsaken 'Dove' longing for His embrace. The earliest book of German poetry printed in America was a volume of his hymns printed by Benjamin Franklin in 1730.[1] The monasteries had no place for idlers. Every one was put to work, at the farm, the mills, the printing press; and the honesty of the monks did much to remove the prejudice of their less mystical neighbours. Their dress, which was intended to conceal as much as possible 'the body of our humiliation', resembled that of the Dominicans.

Beissel died in 1768 and the office of superior then devolved upon Peter Miller, a good scholar and a blameless man. But though he fled from the world, the world, or rather civilization, came nearer and nearer to Ephrata. Pennsylvania ceased to be a forest, the 'Solitary' ceased to be alone, and in 1814 the few remaining monks were already curiosities. But tradition handed on a tale of Peter Miller which is worth preserving. During the Revolution an innkeeper named Widman, a Calvinist who bitterly detested Miller and once spat in his face without provoking him to resentment, took the British side, and was said to have acted as a spy to the British. He was caught and sentenced to be hanged. Miller went to General Washington and begged him to remit the death penalty. Washington replied that the times needed the severest measures against spies and traitors; 'otherwise', he added, 'I should cheer-

[1] The first book of prayers printed in the country now known as the United States was Anglican. It consists of selections from the Book of Common Prayer translated into the Mohawk language, and was printed in 1715 by William Bradford, of New York City.

fully release your friend '. ' Friend!' replied Miller, ' he is the only enemy I have.' Washington was so deeply impressed that he signed a pardon, and Miller arrived at the gallows just in time to save his enemy.

Zinzendorf had been trained among the Pietists of Halle who had struggled against official Lutheranism for the right to live. Soon there were others who disputed with the Pietists for the same right. Among the first was the mathematician and philosopher Christian Wolff (d. 1754). He methodized and vulgarized the philosophy of Leibniz and came into conflict with the Pietists of Halle by professing to base theological truths on evidence of mathematical certitude. Open strife broke out in 1721 when Wolff delivered an oration ' On the Practical Philosophy of the Chinese ',[1] in which he praised—and to a great extent he was justified in praising—the moral philosophy of Confucius, pointing to it as evidence of the power of human reason to attain to moral truth by its own effort. He was banished from Prussia by King Frederick William I at forty-eight hours' notice, not for Confucianism but for determinism, the king being persuaded that if Wolff's fatalistic principles were accepted, no soldier could any longer be punished for desertion, his desertion being predetermined.

One of the first acts by which Frederick the Great (1740–1786) signalized his reign was to recall Wolff to Halle. He entered the town in triumph, and his teaching was propagated in other towns by philosophic clubs. It gave a stimulus to the rationalistic theology which had been introduced into Germany by the English Deist Toland and by English deistic books. These books were widely studied in Germany, and influenced both the middle classes and the universities. Their essence was presented to the public in the writings

[1] *De sapientia Sinensium oratio* (Trevoltii, 1725).

of Edelmann,[1] a facile and scurrilous writer, who wandered like a gipsy from sect to sect, praising the virtues of Christ and advocating the emancipation of the world from Christianity. The Pietists had not sufficient learning to stem the tide of unbelief, the old school of Lutheran theologians was extinct, and the newer freer school represented by Mosheim and Baumgarten (d. 1757) had to fight simultaneously against a subjective scepticism and a subjective Christianity. Baumgarten's influence was great; hundreds of students attended his lectures. But his too exclusively scientific treatment of theology led others to a merely intellectual conception of Christianity and to a lowering of Christian ideas which corresponded with the prevalent lack of moral earnestness. Whereas in England Deism prepared for the reaction of Methodism, itself half German in its origin; in Germany Pietism prepared for the reaction of a dogmatic Deism which was half English. And French culture, fashionable and frivolous, came to act with Deism as a creator of the so-called ' Illumination '.

Many of us have read Walter Pater's charming *Imaginary Portrait* of Duke Carl of Rosenmold. It is as charming, as enchanted and as unreal, as some dainty picture by Fragonard; it clothes in a golden haze the beginning of this movement and introduces at the end a beautiful description of young Goethe by Goethe himself. It may be unpleasant, but it is not unprofitable, to recall the real facts. Goethe (1749–1832) as a youth was already as debauched as he was conceited. Even before this pretty episode, when he went skating in his mother's cloak of red velvet and sables, and before he reached the age of nineteen, he was half exhausted by his follies, and characteristically declared that he had nothing specially to reproach himself with.[2] But he was repelled from Christianity by

[1] He began to publish in 1735.
[2] *Dichtung und Wahrheit*, Book VIII, vol. xi, p. 331 (Stuttgart, 1866). The skating incident is in Book XVI, vol. xii, p. 228.

the Lutheran doctrine of the total depravity of man, and by the dryness of the Protestantism in which he was reared, a religion which appealed neither to the understanding nor to the heart. And there is a touch of reality and pathos in his description of the private altar which he made as a child, an altar made of a red lacquer music stand, on which he burnt fragrant pastilles at the rising of the sun. English children do things like that. It was while Goethe was in his cradle that the 'Illumination' appeared at Potsdam.

Frederick the Great, who had studied and renounced the teaching of Wolff, mocked at Christianity though he sometimes respected a good Christian. Despising the German language, he liked to air his knowledge of French, and he persuaded a number of French writers to settle in Berlin, including Lamettrie, an avowed materialist. Voltaire also loved to make the Bible and the Church the targets of his satire, and if both he and Frederick had not been inordinately vain, they might have been joined in a permanent friendship. Invited by his royal patron, Voltaire arrived in Berlin late in 1751. And it is from this year that we can most fitly date the real beginning of the movement that swayed German thought so greatly and lasted until the early years of the nineteenth century, the *Aufklärung*.

The quarrel between Frederick and Voltaire forms a chapter in the history of kings and their philosophers. Voltaire shook the dust of Potsdam from off his feet, but his influence remained. The king treated the Church as a mere department of the State.[1] The art of pedagogy was remodelled after the style of Rousseau. A popular

[1] Dr. Pusey has preserved the interesting story related to him 'by one likely to be accurately informed', that Frederick shortly before his death, in expressing his regret at the decay of religion in his dominions, 'professed that he would gladly sacrifice his best battle, could they but be restored to the state in belief and in practice in which he had found them'. E. B. Pusey, *An Historical Inquiry into the probable causes of the Rationalistic Character lately predominant in the Theology of Germany*, vol. i, p. 123 (Rivington, London, 1828).

philosophy, bombastic and self-satisfied, arose on deistic lines, and a ' Universal German Library ' was published in Berlin, assailing all faith in revelation. The peculiar mark of this German Illumination, as distinguished from the systems of Toland and Voltaire, is that it sheltered itself within the organization of a Christian Church, and in so doing gradually made it possible for a man to call himself a Protestant when he had ceased to be a Christian. In religion the Illumination was in essence Rationalism, that is, a mode of thought which makes the acceptance of the supernatural truths of Christianity subject to man's faculty of reasoning divorced from the other faculties which are included with reasoning in faith.

Lessing (1728–1781), the brilliant precursor of the new humanism, shows points of contact and of conflict with this mode of thought. He spoke of the contending theological parties of his day in language too filthy to be quoted, but he slightly preferred the more orthodox, his vigorous mind regarding the newer school as shallow and hopelessly inconsistent. But when he was librarian at Wolfenbüttel [1] he stooped to the work of editing the so-called Wolfenbüttel Fragments (1774–1778), a series of deistic tracts written by Hermann Samuel Reimarus (d. 1768). These tracts denied that the Old Testament revealed a religion, treated the resurrection as an impudent fraud, and represented St. Paul as a trickster and Christ as a deluded eschatologist. The tracts set German Protestantism on fire, and the Illumination was at its height. Lessing's own belief was in close sympathy with that of the Jewish Pantheist Spinoza, and his philosophic drama, *Nathan the Wise*, shows his dislike of

[1] The Duke of Brunswick's library at Wolfenbüttel contained priceless but neglected rarities, among them three copies of a translation of the Bible in Low German printed at Köln before Luther. Lessing brought to light several of the treasures of the library, including a treatise of Berengar of Tours. By writing a tract on this work of Berengar, Lessing aroused an interest which anticipated the sensation which he created in 1774.

a positive religion, his love of an abstract religiousness, and his revolt against the distant Deity of popular religion. The position of the generous liberal Jew, Nathan, is nearly his own position. He was not unconscious of the necessity of faith, nor even of the value of tradition in the interpretation of the Scriptures, believing that the word of God cannot be confined to a book. In his heart he valued much of Christian truth. But he was not satisfied with the historical evidences for Christianity, and by treating it as a revelation for the youth rather than for the manhood of the world, he furthered the Rationalism which he really disliked.

With Lessing we may mention the three principal Lutheran theologians of this period, J. A. Ernesti (d. 1781), J. David Michaelis (d. 1791), and J. S. Semler (d. 1791). All three have been sharply blamed and warmly praised, and a nice judgement is required in balancing their merits and defects. Ernesti is chiefly remarkable for his treatment of the New Testament, and the great pains which he devoted to the discovery of its philological and grammatical meaning. He did good work by promoting the principle that the sense of Scripture must be determined by the science of language and not by preconceived dogmatic opinions. But he was imperfectly conscious of the fact that Christianity as a new religion modified the significance of words which had been employed previously to its advent. Michaelis was an eminent Orientalist, anxious to enrich biblical studies with analogies discovered in the languages akin to Hebrew. Unhappily, although he was a convinced, he was not a converted Christian. He did not abandon the creed of his good Pietist father, but his habits were disfigured by intemperance and his lectures were spiced with obscenity. These two scholars were not strictly rationalistic. Their desire was to be scientific, introducing into Germany that zeal for biblical history and textual criticism which existed in England and Holland before it existed in Germany. Their learning was extensive, but it would have been put to a better purpose if they had more often remembered that to be a theologian it is necessary to have a heart as well as a head, and that the teachers who insist that the Bible ought to be criticized like any other book are likely to have pupils who will criticize it like no other book.

Semler, who was the ablest of the three, is indeed an instance of the truth that the theologian who sows the wind may live to reap the whirlwind. A good man, who like Michaelis had been trained in Pietism, he was an exceptionally learned scholar, and became a professor at Halle where he succeeded Baumgarten. He rightly held that dogma to be studied fruitfully must be studied historically. And so long as he, a professor of Christian theology, freely criticized the New Testament, treated the history of the Church as a series of aberrations, and taught that every man ought to have a 'private' religion of his own and make his own system of belief, his popularity was impregnable. But this popularity melted like a cloud when Semler disclosed his conviction that private judgement might run wild, set himself to criticize the English Deists and the Wolfenbüttel Fragments, and opposed the infamous preacher Karl F. Bahrdt, a libertine alike in theology and in morals. He died broken-hearted when he saw that he had failed to stop the hurricane of unbelief and opposition, and by a cruel irony he became branded with the title of 'the father of Rationalism'.[1]

In a great degree these three theologians were the victims of their predecessors. A stiff and barren Lutheranism, posing as orthodox, had provoked the feeling that liberty

[1] It may be noted that the word *liberalis* occurs thrice, and *liberaliter* once, among the Latin titles of his works. The first instance is in his *Institutio brevior ad liberalem eruditionem theologicam*, 1765. Semler by 'liberal' meant 'candid', 'open-minded'. The sense of 'anti-orthodox' is a later use of the word.

could only be gained by departing as far as possible from a system which had kept the Christian student in the fetters of a new legalism. An understanding of the Bible was stifled by a mechanical theory of inspiration which taught that even the variant readings of the Old Testament were inspired, maintained the pre-eminent sanctity of the Hebrew language, and asserted that the books of Ruth and Esther were as indispensable as those comprised in the New Testament. The same school had also professed to find in the Bible all later developments of religious speculation accepted in Lutheran theology. And when it was shown that these developments had been subsequently evolved, there came a tendency to accumulate and emphasize their differences rather than to seek ' the higher unity in which much of this discordance would have harmonized '.[1]

The influence of Immanuel Kant (1724–1804) upon religion has been so variously estimated by his compatriots that an Englishman may well be cautious in giving his opinion. On the one hand he has been called ' the philosopher of Protestantism ', and on the other hand it has been replied that, if that be the case, Protestantism is ' the grave-digger of Christianity '.[2] He put the philosophy of criticism in the place which had been occupied by rationalistic dogmatism. The soil was the same, but he dug the foundations deeper, teaching men to see what they are and what they want. His insight into evil and his exaltation of the categorical imperative of the moral law were well fitted to help men to distrust themselves, to rid themselves of conceit, and even to feel conscious of a desire which only Christ can satisfy. But he was not a ' schoolmaster to Christ '. He

[1] E. B. Pusey, *op. cit.*, p. 145. The whole passage in Pusey is informing and judicious.
[2] So, as against Paulsen and Bousset, Dr. Albert Ehrhard, *Der Katholizismus und das zwanzigste Jahrhundert*, p. 185 (Jos. Roth'sche Verlagsbuchhandlung, Stuttgart und Wien, 1902).

gave the word religion a new meaning and one essentially opposed to Christianity. Historically religion has meant a personal relation between man and God, however God may be conceived by the worshipper, and God is above each man and all mankind. Kant's religion is not that relation. With him the ideas of God, freedom, and immortality are postulates of the practical reason; they are requisite for the moral life, and the fundamental principle of the moral life is esteem for man for his own sake. However majestic the categorical imperative appears, it cannot in religion act as an adequate substitute for that personal Word who came among us 'full of grace and truth'; and the moral and religious results of his philosophy are, as Dr. Friedrich Loofs observes, 'in essential agreement with the ideas of the Illumination'.[1] He was the chief of eighteenth-century rationalists, and in 1793 he defined a Rationalist as ' one who simply holds natural religion as morally necessary, that is, as a duty', while the Supernaturalist 'believes a supernatural revelation necessary for a universal religion'.

The distinction between the Rationalist and the Supernaturalist thus clearly made was widely acknowledged, and an effort was made by the Supernaturalists to maintain the truth of the revelation contained in the Bible. The State had already taken alarm, and various edicts were passed to suppress the growth of Rationalism. They failed, and by the beginning of the nineteenth century the battle was already lost. In England Deism and Arianism, after seriously threatening Christianity, had been overcome. In Scandinavia the kindred movements also failed. But in Holland, Switzerland, and Germany the Illumination was supreme. In Prussia especially the individual had been glorified and the Church divided into local societies. The liturgies were mutilated, the Church music was debased, the hymns

[1] *Grundlinien der Kirchengeschichte*, p. 285 (Niemeyer, Halle a. S., 1910).

which had been the glory of Lutheranism were transformed,[1] and pastors preached on moral improvement and natural science.

Among the Calvinists of Switzerland the decay of Christianity came even earlier than among the Lutherans of Germany. In 1763 Rousseau, who was himself a sentimental Deist with Protestant sympathies, wrote a scathing description of the ministers of Geneva and challenged them to show what difference existed between their belief and his own. ' You ask them if Jesus Christ is God, they dare not reply; you ask them what mysteries they acknowledge, they dare not reply. To what question then will they reply, and what will be the fundamental articles, different from mine, on which they are willing that a decision should be made, if the above articles are excluded? A philosopher casts a rapid glance at them: he sees through them, he sees in them Arians, Socinians. . . . They are really extraordinary gentlemen, your ministers; one does not know what they believe, or what they do not believe, one does not even know what they pretend to believe; their only way of proving their faith is by attacking that of others. . . . From all this I conclude that it is not easy to say in what the holy reformation at Geneva now consists.' [2]

The history of Dutch Protestantism during the eighteenth century is not easy to unravel. We can, however, detect certain forces which were making for the destruction of an orthodox Calvinism no less than the marked Socinian tendencies of the sect of Remonstrants. This Socinianism infected many of the English Nonconformists who studied in Holland. Within the State Church of Holland itself

[1] The common people sometimes resisted successfully the introduction of deistic hymns.
[2] J.-J. Rousseau, *Lettres de la Montagne*, pp. 231 sqq. (Paris, Dalibon, 1826). Rousseau is probably the first to use the word 'moderniste' in a quasi-theological sense. He addresses a materialist as a 'moderniste'. Lettre à M. De***, January the 15th, 1769.

there was a struggle between the strict Calvinists and the theologians who adopted the philosophy of Descartes. This struggle was further complicated by the differences between the rigid Pietists who followed G. Voet (d. 1676) and the disciples of J. Cocceius (d. 1669) who pushed to bizarre results the theory that the Old Testament is typical of the New and repudiated the almost Judaic sabbatarianism of the Pietists. The controversy between the Voetians and the Cocceians broke out anew early in the eighteenth century. It was gradually appeased; but the fact that both parties, while not repudiating Calvinistic orthodoxy, were indifferent towards its distinctive dogmas, prepared for the latitudinarianism which blotted out the distinctions between all the leading Protestant bodies in Holland. The close of the eighteenth century is the low-water mark of Dutch Protestantism and Dutch literature. Then came a reaction of some importance.

In the early years of the nineteenth century the most commanding figure in the Protestantism of Holland was not a professional theologian but the learned and original poet, Willem Bilderdijk (d. 1831). He was narrow in his art and in his patriotism; he scorned Shakespeare as well as the new Romantic poets; but he possessed great force of character and exercised it on the side of Christianity. He was supported by two cultured Jewish converts, Isaak de Costa, a poet and apologist, and Cappadose, a physician. The clerical mouthpiece of the party was a young minister, Hendrik de Cock, who was deposed from the ministry of the State Church in 1834. His followers were persecuted as separatists; but in 1839 they were recognized by the State as a Christian Reformed Church. It stands for the principles of the Calvinistic Reformation in special opposition to the rationalistic teaching of the so-called 'Modern' party in the State Church.[1]

[1] Some interesting remarks on the religion of the Dutch in South Africa

After Lessing the attitude of the heroes of German culture towards Rationalism was on the whole unfavourable. The men of the Illumination had not inherited the historic sense of Leibniz, nor had they been influenced by Kant's opposition to deistic dogmatism. And to the leaders of the new humanism their theories appeared to be stupid and inartistic. A brilliant group of these men of letters existed at the beginning of the nineteenth century. Lessing was dead. But there survived Klopstock, Herder, Wieland, Schiller, and Goethe. Klopstock, the author of the once popular 'Messiah', had tried to weave together lofty old German ideals with Christian poetry. Herder, who marks the transition from the Illumination to the classical German epoch, had found the soul of humanity expressed in the Christian religion. He appreciated the early German painters, saw the value of Gothic art, and protested against the current practice of making classical art a model for all times and all peoples. He had a real sense of historical evolution. He had a poetic insight into the beauty of the Old Testament, and for the ethical character of Christianity a sincere respect. But he thought that the Pantheism of Spinoza satisfied both the feelings and the intellect, and it is never quite clear whether he believed that the culture of the future would merely enrich or actually supersede the Christian religion.

Wieland wrote at a time when the higher classes were in their sentiments French, and French of a bad type. He pandered to their taste by using his great skill in composing attractive and graceful romances essentially frivolous and inspired by a cultured materialism. He was only severe when he wrote against severity, and gratified a public that relished his warnings against asceticism. Schiller was an

can be found in F. Th. Schonken, *De Oorsprong der Kaapsch-Hollandsche Volksoverleveringen* (Swets & Zeitlingen, Amsterdam, 1914). Two ideas of God are in conflict: one Calvinistic and almost purely of Old Testament origin, the other more Evangelical and Methodist.

artist of a very different mould. Idealist and optimist, dramatist and philosopher, his enthusiastic admiration for everything beautiful and good exercised a great influence in Germany, though that influence began to wane with the new growth of materialism in the second half of the nineteenth century. It has been said that he introduced to the people Kant's rationalism and Kant's ethics clothed in the raiment of fine poetry. But his own words are that Kant ' has made the law of duty repulsive, on account of its extreme severity ' and ' Sense and reason; conscience and sentiment; duty and inclination—these antithetical words denote discords that should be harmonized; and they are so harmonized in the mind of a true Christian, when he finds his delight in the fulfilment of the law. Hence Christianity must be called the only aesthetic religion.' This harmony of will and morals he elsewhere identifies with liberty, and maintains that we can be led to a sense of this liberty by the study of art.[1] His religion suffered from the icy breath of Rationalism, but it was not love of fame that led him to choose Christian themes for his works and to utter Christian convictions. And not long before his death he wrote these words: 'In the dark time of superstition Berlin first kindled the torch of rational religious liberty. That was then a necessity, and the act was one worthy of renown. Now, in this age of unbelief, there is another kind of renown that might be won, and without any forfeiture of the honour already gained. Let Berlin now add warmth to the light, and thus ennoble the Protestantism of which this city is destined some day to be the capital. The spirit of the present age demands this: that in France Catholicism should constitute itself anew, that also in Protestantism there

---

[1] Schiller's letters to Goethe dated December the 22nd, 1798, and August the 2nd, 1799 further show that he was dissatisfied with Kant's teaching, because, like that of Luther, it savoured of an escaped monk—a shrewd criticism.

should be some thought of religion, and that philosophy itself should follow in the same direction.'[1]

Schiller died in 1805. Under the influence of the French revolution Rationalism had begun to lay aside its Christian ornaments and to take the form of Atheism. The Illumination lost its power of enchantment. The gas flares were blown out, but the poisonous vapours had penetrated so deeply that Schiller might well speak of the need of 'some thought of religion'. Religion and the Church were regarded, when they were regarded at all, as utilitarian means of maintaining order. A strong current of fresh air was needed. At least a breath was coming, and it touched some chords in Goethe's essentially 'classic' nature. Goethe, who spoke of the 'solace and hope' expressed in the paintings of the mediaeval masters, and dilated upon the exquisite adaptability of the sacramental system to the needs of human life,[2] came in his old age to the conviction that Christianity is the highest principle of feeling and action and 'far above all philosophy'. The great receptivity of his mind and the wide range of his wisdom combine with his genius for reflective poetry to make him the most imposing figure in German literature. That receptivity enabled him to value the mediaeval as well as the modern and the antique, and that wisdom prompted him to praise the power of 'self-restoration' which Christianity has manifested. But no man can believe in Christ who does not love what Christ loves. And Goethe's subtle egotism and shabby sensuality kept him nearer to Pantheism in creed and the pagan Renaissance in practice than to a religion that preaches self-renunciation and self-control.[3] But we must

---

[1] From a letter to Zelter, dated July the 16th, 1804. *Schillers Briefe*, vol. vii, p. 166 (Fritz Jonas's edition). [2] See app. note 22, p. 276.

[3] Professor J. G. Robertson, in his article on Goethe in the *Encyclopaedia Britannica*, speaks of him as inheriting a '"holy earnestness" and stability of character which brought him unscathed through temptations and passions' (vol. xii, p. 182). The falsehood of this statement is shown by

not forget that the brilliant period of German literature which we have noticed came at a time when neither Protestantism nor Roman Catholicism in Germany were represented in such a way as to attract men of intellectual ability, and that these writers in particular were surrounded by a Protestantism that was ashamed of the Gospel and afraid to appear supernatural. It did not guide men to ' see Jesus '. Herder, Schiller, and even Goethe reverenced some of the moral as well as the aesthetic achievements of Christianity. But those achievements were not inspired by a belief in a great teacher such as even Spinoza fully acknowledged Jesus Christ to be. They were inspired by a belief in the infinite charity of the Redeemer, a charity which is infinite because the Redeemer is in the truest sense divine.

For thirty years after the death of Schiller Germany experienced the fascination of the Romantic movement. That movement was far more than a mere reaction against the massacres of the French Revolution and the mockery of Voltaire. In its genesis philosophy had played an important part. The system of Spinoza, which had appealed so strongly to Lessing and to Goethe, was denounced as atheism by the philosopher Jacobi, who in his turn was denounced as a Pietist and a Jesuit for maintaining that the keystone of all human knowledge and activity is belief. Idealism, the philosophy which teaches that ' subject and object stand in a relation of entire interdependence on each other as warp and woof ', began to gain many converts, especially in the University of Jena. However much they might differ from each other, Fichte, Schelling, Hegel, and Fries marked a new era. Religion is recognized as involving a real presence of the divine in man; union with God is

---

an allusion to Goethe's 'new mistress' (p. 184). Goethe was a snob as well as a sensualist. He felt an awe-struck reverence for King Ludwig of Bavaria, the dilettante who became a slave to the singer Lola Montez.

conceived of in different ways, sometimes practical, sometimes metaphysical, sometimes sensible; redemption is represented as an inward fact, and man's knowledge of God and the conversion of his will are shown to depend upon a knowledge of the great leaders of religion, of whom Christ is the chief. Fichte, who taught that the world is nothing without spirit, and Schelling, who taught that the world-soul is God, were the philosophers who most attracted the literary circle in which German Romanticism was cradled.

The word Romantic had already been used to describe the literature which appeals to a cultivated imagination, and it was now applied to an art which was distinct from, and even opposed to, the classical and antique. The beginning of the movement was marked by an interest in mediaeval poetry, especially that of the Romance nations, a poetry which includes a mythology which was external to the formulated belief of the mediaeval Church. Romanticism was not strictly a Catholic movement. But it gradually kindled an admiration for the social and religious institutions of the Middle Ages as well as the art of the Middle Ages, and in so doing it quickened and hallowed that historical sense in spiritual things which the subjectivism and individualism of both Pietism and Rationalism had brought to the verge of annihilation. It was instinctively opposed to Rationalism and to the spirit which begins to criticize before it has learned to appreciate. So the literary and aesthetic movement gradually became a religious movement, exciting a thirst for a faith that could satisfy both mind and heart. The result was twofold. It led a stream of distinguished converts, such as Stolberg, Friedrich von Schlegel, and Werner, into a reviving Roman Catholicism which possessed for them all the charm of novelty and the grace of antiquity. This Roman Catholicism was of a moderate type, disliking the Ultramontane view of the Papacy and convinced that Christianity can be combined with modern learning and modern liberty. Such a religion would have been an inestimable blessing to Germany if it had not been crushed by Rome at the moment when it was most sorely needed.

The second result of Romanticism was to give some life to the union made by King Frederick William III of Prussia between the Lutheran and the Reformed, that is, Calvinist, Church, a union effected by his order in 1817. The king, though a Calvinist, had been impressed by the beauty and dignity of the services which he had witnessed in Vienna, and believed that he could render Protestant worship more attractive by the universal introduction of certain forms and ceremonies, which, while compatible with the older Lutheranism, were distasteful to the Rationalist and the Calvinist. As a general he perceived the possible advantage of presenting a united front to irreligion and to Rome, and as a general he ordered the union to take place and his Prayer Book to be adopted. The difficulty was not very serious because most of the Calvinists had given up the doctrine of absolute predestination and most of the Lutherans had given up the doctrine of the real presence in the Eucharist, and both communities were deeply infected with unbelief. In the reception of the sacraments every individual was allowed to think as he pleased. The signs were kept as essential, but what was conveyed by those signs was left uncertain. The new community was given the name of the *Evangelical Church*. In spite of the good Pietists whom it included, its creation proved to be not only the token but also the instrument of the decay of definite religion, and sixty years later another King of Prussia had personally to intervene in order to prevent the Apostles' Creed from being struck out of the ' Evangelical ' liturgy. The genuine Lutherans who rejected the union were harshly persecuted. Many of them migrated to Australia and America. In this way German Protestantism was deprived of some of its best members, and the Christian world was left with a very impressive warning against methods of reunion which are not based upon spiritual convictions.

Among the sincerest promoters of this ecclesiastical union was Frederick Daniel Ernest Schleiermacher (1768–1834), the most imposing figure in German Protestantism since Luther.[1] In the year 1800 he became preacher at the church of the Trinity in Berlin. His father was a Calvinist minister, but he was sent to a Moravian school, a fact which greatly influenced his whole religion; for his very conception of religion as a feeling of dependence upon God is derived from Moravian Pietism. His learning, his scholarship, his eloquence, and his intercourse with the leaders of the Romantic movement in Berlin, all contributed to his efficiency as a lecturer and a preacher, and he quickly initiated a great attempt to reconcile and to mediate. All founders of religion, he taught, had a new intuition of the universe, and Christ had, above all others, such an intuition. He beheld everywhere the divine element and everywhere the irreligious and the unspiritual, and the need and the means of overcoming the unspiritual by the spiritual. And the clearness with which Christ saw the need and the means constitute what is specific in Christ. Salvation can be sought only in redemption, in the gaining of union with Deity. Christ was conscious of a unique knowledge of God, and of being in God, and He knew that this knowledge could communicate itself and kindle religion in others. He is the cause of the new life, the ideal type of humanity, and His perfection is proved on the one hand by the existence of the Church and on the other hand by the fact that His religious consciousness cannot be explained by merely natural causes.

[1] For Schleiermacher, see W. B. Selbie, *Schleiermacher* (Chapman & Hall, London, 1913); also the account in J. H. Kurtz, *Lehrbuch der Kirchengeschichte*, 14th edition (Neumann, Leipzig, 1906). The last division of this book gives a somewhat full outline of Continental Protestantism since

On the historical side Schleiermacher's system is weak, and this weakness is far-reaching. He under-estimated the connexion between Judaism and Christianity. Deeply attached to the Gospel of St. John he depreciated the Synoptic Gospels and agreed with the Rationalists in rejecting the virgin birth of Christ; a birth congruous with that essential sinlessness of Christ in which be believed. Imbued with the importance of the close relation between Christ and the fellowship of believers, he gave far too little weight to the fact that this fellowship was created, and could only have been created, by one who rose from the dead in the sense which the Gospels maintain. Hoping for a new unity of even the visible Church, he did not realize how the polity of the ancient Church depended upon unity and can once more become its safeguard. Mindful of the truth that the life of the Church proceeds from Christ, he did not recognize how admirably the ancient creeds and definitions of the faith serve to keep intact the witness of the Church to Christ, and in 1819 he not only advocated the view that Protestants cannot be bound by any dogmatic decisions of the past, but even urged that the only thing to which the Protestant clergy ought to be bound is a repudiation of Roman Catholicism.

His real work and his great work was to teach, and to teach from the heart, that the Christian religion was and is created by the impression which the Person of Christ produced and still produces in and through the Christian community. He returns to St. Paul when he emphasizes the reality of the Christian experience that Christ is our Redeemer as well as our Teacher and Example, and he returns to St. Paul in urging that at least the ideal is that there should be one Church to manifest belief in the one Redeemer.

1800. An English translation of an earlier edition of this part of Kurtz's work was published by Hodder & Stoughton in 1890.

The mantle of Schleiermacher fell upon Albrecht Ritschl (1822–1887). Like his predecessor, Ritschl exercised a great influence upon German thought by the thoroughness with which he emphasized the value of religious experience, and also of the regulative use of the idea of religious fellowship. He emancipated himself from the Rationalism of the Tübingen school and adhered closely to what he believed to be the fundamental principles of the Lutheran confessions of faith. He laid great stress upon the truthfulness of the New Testament as an authentic witness of the primitive Church to the teaching and the Person of Christ. Religion he treated as essentially practical and social, a thing not of emotion but of ethical power. A knowledge of Christ is revealed in the community which has believed in Christ. Christ's position is unique; through Him we know that God is love, and the love of God is His will as directed towards the realization of His purpose in His kingdom. Ritschl argues back from the experience of Christians to the Person of Christ, in whom we find all the great determining ideas by the aid of which God and man, sin and redemption, are to be interpreted. The immediate object of theological knowledge is the faith of the community and on that positive religious fact theology has to build. As a philosopher he may be said to have been baptized into Kant, and even more definitely than Schleiermacher, he banishes all philosophy from the realm of theology. He not only depreciates 'metaphysic' and 'mysticism' in the realm of theology, but limits theological knowledge to what he himself conceives to be the bounds of human need and experience. His insistence on the relative character of this knowledge and its sharp difference from theoretical knowledge lead him into serious ambiguities and inconsistencies with regard to some of the vital truths of Christianity.[1]

---

[1] Ritschl's most important work was *Die christliche Lehre von der Rechtfertigung u. Versöhnung*, of which an English translation by John S.

We may thus sum up the work of Schleiermacher and Ritschl. They asserted powerfully and persuasively the truth that Christ is to be regarded as the centre and focus of religion—that His life and death were a supernatural interposition on the part of God, who is love—that we need redemption and that Christ is essential for that redemption—that no confession that we make of His dignity is of any value unless it is the outcome of experience—that His work in us teaches us who He is—and that in any estimate of Him we must take into account the experience of the society which has manifested Him to the world; though with Schleiermacher the individual is primary and the community is secondary, while with Ritschl the whole religious community founded by Christ is primary and the individual is secondary.

But even according to the most generous criticism the message of them both falls short of the glory of the message of the New Testament. The religious importance of Christ's pre-existence, of His eternal reciprocal relationship with the Father and His exaltation and present life in heaven, is put aside. St. Paul draws the richest moral lessons from the thought that He who existed in the form of God humbled himself and was found in fashion as a man. The whole history of Christian worship and of Christian conduct has been moulded by a recollection of the intercession of our ascended and glorified High Priest, and by the belief that He will come to be our Judge. Neither Schleiermacher nor Ritschl adequately understood the religious value of the doctrine of the Incarnation. For the one Christ was a man who had a unique consciousness of God, for the other Christ had the value of God. But, as the Church had to maintain in the third century, it is one thing to confess that

Black was published in 1872 (Edmonston & Douglas, Edinburgh) under the title *A Critical History of the Christian Doctrine of Justification and Reconciliation*. Ritschl's *Unterricht in der christlichen Religion* and *Geschichte des Pietismus* are also important.

Christ was conscious of a unique indwelling of God, and quite a different thing to confess that in Him was the fullness of the Godhead. And, as the Church had to maintain in the fourth century, no one who is not veritably God can possibly have the value of God.

And, we may indeed ask, what profit was it to blame the Pietists and the Mystics and the Rationalists for their individualism and subjectivism and unregulated private judgement, and to appeal to the experience of believers in Christ, and then to disregard the most important confessions of their faith? A man is not a Christian because he claims the right to believe, but because he does believe. And an association of those who believe must sooner or later compose some definition of their faith. A church which declined to confess its faith would rapidly become a mere society for the promotion of good works, and thus involve itself not only in a repudiation of Catholicism but also in a reversal of the teaching of Luther.

The unfortunate concessions made by Schleiermacher to unbelief were of small avail. The very year after his death Strauss published the notorious *Life of Jesus*, and he, together with F. C. Baur, the head of the Tübingen school, drove the ploughshares of their criticism diagonally across the New Testament. Strauss criticized the Gospels as unintentional mythology, Baur criticized them as deliberate forgeries. The theories of these two writers have been largely abandoned, but that of Baur had at least one merit. He saw clearly that if the rationalistic view of Christ is correct and the Church is wrong, then we must explain how the Church came to be wrong. That is the problem, and for the solution of the problem it is necessary to discover the true position of St. Paul. We must return to this question in our last lecture. In the meantime we may notice that though a slow but certain destruction of Baur's theory was in progress, German Protestantism continued to struggle under hopeless difficulties. The middle of the nineteenth century was marked by a more definite organization of Rationalism under the name first of Free Protestantism, then of Liberal Protestantism, and more recently of Modern Protestantism. Parties were sharply divided and only united by a common hatred of Rome and by the occasional action of the law.

While it would be beside my purpose to speak at length of any living theologian, it seems right to mention Professor Harnack as a representative of German Protestantism. The fertility of his mind, his wide learning, his compact and lucid style, have won for him a very wide circle of readers outside Germany. His tribute to the moral value of Christianity is sincere and impressive. But he is not free from some of the worst defects of Luther, of Ritschl, and even of the Tübingen school whose opinions he has demolished. Like Luther he extols the 'Gospel'; but by the 'Gospel' he means his own mutilated version of certain parts of the New Testament. Like Ritschl he lays stress upon the facts of present religious experience; but he is far too ready to regard the philosophic formulation of Christian doctrine as a mere incubus. Like the Tübingen school he disparages evidence which conflicts with his own belief, and even goes to the length of accusing of deliberate dishonesty the Christians who first circulated the Gospel according to St. John. He has again and again come to the conclusion that Christian tradition was right in much that concerns the date and the authority of primitive Christian literature; and yet he tries to persuade us that Christian tradition is thoroughly wrong in regard to the doctrines of the Person of Christ, the Holy Trinity, the Atonement, and the Church, doctrines which inspired and united the authors of these venerable books.

In Germany the idea of liberty and the idea of authority

have never been reconciled, and the spirit of faith and the spirit of criticism are engaged in an endless duel. Protestantism is still able to produce some men who are personalities; but these very men by the force of their individuality tend to separate themselves from their fellows, to form a religion of their own, and to make their Christianity a mere apprenticeship in religious speculation. They can neither agree among themselves, nor can they like a true aristocracy of souls keep close to ordinary people on the ground of a common Catholic faith and practice. German Protestantism began by telling the plain man to open and to read the Gospels and go to Christ. It has come to shrouding the Gospels in a winding-sheet of sceptical scholasticism and erasing the grandest features of the Redeemer.

In Germany we find laborious and learned theologians, untroubled by wholesome misgivings, bent upon following one clue and disregarding others, and revelling in false antitheses. Since the days of Reimarus they have manufactured Christs which threaten to become as numerous as the idols of a Tibetan temple, and so different that it is hard to suppose that all are intended as representations of the same Being. The well-known works of Heinrich Weinel, Albert Schweitzer, and Dr. Sanday quickly put us in contact with the ideas of these writers.[1] We may perhaps lay aside the more extravagant theories which depict Christ as a myth, a madman, or a Buddhist. But we still find such deep divergences as that which separates those who believe that Jesus did, or did not, claim to be the

[1] Heinrich Weinel, *Jesus im neunzehnten Jahrhundert* (J. C. B. Mohr, Tübingen und Leipzig, 1903); translated and enlarged by Alban G. Widgery, *Jesus in the Nineteenth Century and after* (T. & T. Clark, Edinburgh, 1914). A. Schweitzer, *Von Reimarus zu Wrede* (J. C. B. Mohr, Tübingen, 1906); translated by W. Montgomery under the title of *The Quest of the Historical Jesus* (A. & C. Black, London, 2nd edition, 1911). W. Sanday, *The Life of Christ in Recent Research* (Clarendon Press, Oxford, 1907).

Messiah. There is an equally serious divergence between those who represent Him as the preacher of an inward kingdom of God which was to be realized peacefully through love, or as the passionate prophet whose every idea was swayed by the false conviction that this kingdom will be brought into the world by a sudden and terrible catastrophe. At the same time we can be grateful that these critics have added to the number of facts upon which we can, unlike them, put a fully Christian interpretation, and we can also be grateful for the thoroughness with which they have criticized one another's opinions.[1]

Quite recently a ray of hope has made its appearance in Berlin. A Christian reaction, openly called by its leaders 'High Church' (*Hochkirchlich*), and not dissimilar to the Oxford Movement of the last century, is influencing a considerable number of Protestants who desire a definite belief and a reverent worship.[2] But, broadly speaking, the Protestantism of Germany, Switzerland, France, and Holland is in a state of complete disintegration. For the more radical German pastors, 'Liberal' theology is not liberal enough. Their instructors said that it was right to reveal in the pulpit the results of criticism and science. They claim the same right as their masters, the right to say sincerely what they think sincerely, and they regard the ordinary 'Liberal' as a theological Tartuffe. They dislike ministers who call Christ the Son of God and the only mediator, when they deny His Deity and His perfect manhood. They know that the people are leaving churches

---

[1] As for the tone in which most of the books of this school are written, it may be noted that Dr. Sanday, in spite of his readiness to praise much of their contents, says, 'Every now and then one is pulled up sharp by passages like those of which I have been speaking, which I confess move me to indignation': *op. cit.*, p. 170. This was written with special reference to Jülicher, who in Germany would be regarded as by no means extreme. And Dr. Sanday adds, 'I am afraid there is too much of this in the school to which Jülicher belongs'.

[2] For this, see the *Guardian*, March the 24th, 1921.

which are 'spiritual cemeteries', and they wish to return to sincerity by departing from Christianity openly, while retaining their pastoral office in the Evangelical Church. In Germany the diminution of candidates for the Protestant ministry has been enormous, in Holland it has for some time been necessary to supplement the ranks of the ministers from the Dutch in South Africa. Other points also deserve our serious attention. One is that during the earlier years of this century statistics abundantly proved that throughout Germany the proportion both of illegitimate births and of suicides was higher in the Protestant districts than in the Roman Catholic districts.[1] The sense of moral obligation is weaker where the sense of submission to divine truth is weaker, and 'Modern Protestantism' has pulverized what Luther broke. As a spiritual force Protestantism on the Continent is quite ineffective in opposing Rome.[2] That is not merely because bands of irregular troops are no match for a highly disciplined army. The reason lies far deeper. It is that there are everywhere considerable numbers of people who realize that a Church keeping the original Gospels, even with an Italian Pope, provides us with an infinitely better religion than a school which offers us selections from a New Testament expurgated by mutually hostile professors. I have ventured to speak strongly about some existing corruptions in the Church of Rome. But, having so spoken, I say that the meanest Roman chapel in England is nearer to God than the finest temple where they preach any sham German Jesus.

And this is closely connected with something to which I would finally draw your attention. We have in England

[1] Arthur Shadwell, *Industrial Efficiency*, vol. i, p. 241 (Longmans, London, 1906).
[2] The weakness of Protestantism in Holland as a political and social force is shown by the Dutch Parliamentary elections of July 1922. Roman Catholics had 30 per cent. of the votes cast and secured thirty-two of the one hundred seats in the Second Chamber, thereby gaining political supremacy.

been repeatedly told by those who have lately introduced into this country the precise arguments which Germans have employed in undermining the faith of their fellow countrymen in various articles of the creed and in Christ himself, that their work is one of restatement and reconstruction, the clearing away of temporary misinterpretations, the strengthening of conviction as to the real message of our Lord. In view of these repeated assertions, whatever degree of sincerity they possess, it will not be amiss to quote the words of a German professor who cannot with propriety be treated as a nobody in the intellectual world, Professor Ernst Troeltsch. He sees quite clearly that the crucial thing in the difference between the Old and the New Protestantism is the question of Christology. What is now left of Christ is said to be His 'originality and spiritual creative power'. The rest is gone. With a candour which leaves nothing to be desired Troeltsch says, ' From this alteration in the central point of the system the most profound results issue, the old Christological dogma and myth are set aside, the doctrine of the Trinity and vicarious satisfaction are destroyed or rendered uncertain, the roots of the idea of the sacraments and the Church are plucked up, and direct communion with the Bible rendered difficult '.[1]

That is ' Modern Protestantism '.

Is there anything harsh or illiberal in our saying that to describe such an alteration as a ' restatement ' or ' reconstruction ', or even as a ' readjustment ' in theology, is a grave misuse of language, and that such a religion is ' after the tradition of men, after the rudiments of the world, and not after Christ ' ?

---

[1] *Die Kultur der Gegenwart*, ' Die christliche Religion ', pp. 446, 447 (Teubner, Berlin und Leipzig, 1905).

VII

THE EASTERN ORTHODOX CHURCH

Rev. ii. 13: I know thy works, and where thou dwellest, even where Satan's seat is: and thou holdest fast my name, and hast not denied my faith.

ON July the 16th, 1054, three papal legates walked through the congregation assembled in the great church of the Holy Wisdom at Constantinople, past the columns of porphyry under the domes of gold mosaic and the great wings and faces of the angels, through the jewelled screen, and placed upon the altar a bull excommunicating Michael Caerularius, Patriarch of Constantinople. If on the one hand the bull contained statements which were both abusive and false, yet on the other the conduct of the Patriarch had been arrogant and provocative.

During the darkest times of the Papacy the eastern Emperors with singular skill had strengthened their hold upon the provinces of Southern Italy. It was their policy to make the country once again a Magna Graecia. In Calabria eight bishops were made dependent upon the Greek Archbishop of Santa Severina, and five sees were placed under the Greek metropolitan of Otranto. Large numbers of eastern monks settled in the country, also acting as the apostles of Hellenism. The Greek language was widespread, and the Greek rite took such deep root that in some parishes it survived until the fifteenth century and even to the end of the sixteenth.[1] Rome did not prohibit, and does not now prohibit, the Byzantine rite, and in the monastery of Grottaferrata within sight of Rome it has lasted until the present day. But Michael Caerularius

[1] See app. note 23, p. 277.

would show no tolerance to the churches of the Latin rite in Constantinople.

The question of doctrine was entirely in the background. The points at issue were matters of ceremonial, not so very different from the matters that caused bitter controversies and even imprisonments in England in the nineteenth century. Michael, who observed the Eastern custom of consecrating leavened bread for the Eucharist, had a strong dislike of the Western custom, alluded to in England by the Venerable Bede, of consecrating bread that was unleavened. Both customs are very ancient, both are possibly apostolic, and in the ninth century Photius, the learned Eastern protagonist and opponent of Rome, wisely left the matter in silence. Michael also disliked the old Roman custom of fasting on a Saturday, an innocent practice which probably arose in imitation of the fast before the Easter communion, and was a means of preparing for the weekly communion which Bede also mentions as surviving in Rome in his day. It is difficult to avoid the conclusion that Michael intended to provoke a crisis in order to show that he repudiated the Roman claim to primacy. The Pope, Leo IX, who died before the legates excommunicated Michael, made that claim, a claim which the Oecumenical Councils allowed. But in stating it he put Constantinople, no doubt of set purpose, lowest in the list of patriarchates, in spite of the Second Oecumenical Council having placed it second only to 'Old Rome'. If we may lawfully pass judgement on the rivals, we can hardly hesitate to call the malice of Michael more culpable than the pride of Leo.

The papal legates had not excommunicated the Eastern Church as a whole, and some time elapsed before the width and the permanence of the schism were understood. But all subsequent attempts at union failed and the doctrine of papal infallibility has now made the vision of unity seem only a mirage in the desert. The schism between the East and the West brought its punishment in limiting the knowledge and the sympathies of both parties. In the West all intercourse with the Greeks, and a knowledge of the atmosphere in which early Christianity had developed, became delayed until the fifteenth century. The isolation of the Pope from the other patriarchs of the Church prepared for his autocracy and in the end for the dogma of his infallibility; and this autocracy led to that explosion of individualism and failure to recognize the corporate life of the whole Church which have been so common in Protestant Christianity. In fact it is hard to deny that there is considerable truth in the Russian view that Rome and Protestantism represent different aspects of one and the same fundamental error, the exaltation of the individual at the expense of the body of which he is a member. Nor can we fail to regret that the conviction that the Eastern Church is schismatical and heretical has caused Latin Christendom lavishly to spend men and money in making proselytes from Orthodoxy, when the same resources might have been devoted to the conversion of the enemies of the Cross.

Isolation from the West has in turn affected the East. The great stores of western theological and devotional literature remained almost unknown. Little was done to develop the more active side of monastic life, or, in modern times, of parochial life. Wherever possible a dignified worship and the strict observance of fasts and festivals were maintained; but the schism having originated with small outward things, a strange importance was attached to such matters as the kind of bread used in the Eucharist or the precise manner of making the sign of the Cross. Conservatism prevented the use of instrumental music in church, and the introduction of images as distinguished from sacred pictures. The short and simple service of low mass, apparently introduced in the West as early

THE EASTERN ORTHODOX CHURCH 195

as the sixth century, remained unknown. To this day the liturgy is never celebrated in the Eastern Church without incense and singing, and the length of the rite and difficulty of providing the necessary ceremonial render the celebration far less frequent than in the West. The custom of observing a very rigid fast [1] for a week before receiving the Holy Communion, a custom which originated in Lent and Advent, reduced the primitive weekly communion to a communion four times a year among the Slavs, and to once a year among the Rumanians. Such comparatively modern rites as Exposition and Benediction of the blessed Sacrament remain unknown, and though the Sacrament is reserved upon the altar hidden behind the curtain in the iconostasis, the devotion of the worshipper is quickened more by the sacred pictures than by a recollection of the adorable presence.

This Conservatism in worship and practice has sometimes tempted western Christians to speak of Eastern Orthodox Christianity as fossilized, or to describe its dogmas as ' flies in amber '. That is an unwise and hasty judgement. Eastern Orthodoxy has never ceased to be moulded by the central doctrine of Christianity, the Incarnation of the Son of God, and by the truth that we are made partakers of Christ, the God-Man. A deep reverence is felt for the Gospels. And we shall not find it hard to sympathize with the Eastern who thinks that western worship appeals either too much to the eyes or too much to the head, while his own liturgy, mysterious and half concealed, with its frequent pathetic supplications, appeals to the heart. His devotion to dogmatism is by no means excessive. It is true that the Oriental cannot conceive of a full Christian intercommunion in the sacraments which is not cemented by an agreement in doctrine; but the Oriental mind is averse from a minute

[1] Among Orthodox Easterns fasting implies abstinence from meat, eggs, butter, oil, cheese, all kinds of fish among the Slavs, and nearly all kinds among the Greeks.

definiteness in dogma. This aversion is most marked in the case of the Russians. An acute French writer observes, 'The Latin defines and catalogues the divine as he defines and catalogues himself; it is a physiological necessity ... accustom the Russian to definitions of which the Latin cannot have enough, and you will only arrive at making him doubt a truth which he can only grasp with his heart. The Latin has such a horror of human mysteries that he is obliged to penetrate into the mysteries of God as far as reason can take him; the Russian is so at ease in mysteries of every kind that to explain them makes them less real to him.' [1] And we who are not French or Latin need to come into contact with eastern Christians if we wish to understand how deeply our national and religious temperament has been influenced by a civilization which is essentially Roman.

The capture of Constantinople by the Turks in 1453 left Moscow as the great centre of eastern Christianity. The patriarchates of Alexandria, Jerusalem, and Antioch, though they survive to this day, had long been trodden under the feet of the Moslem. Serbia was to fall a few years later than Constantinople. Most of us, unless we are historians by profession, have forgotten the fear of the Turks, as we have forgotten the earlier fear of the Tartars. It would have been an ever-present fear to us if we had been alive when Luther rebelled against Rome. For in the year when Luther burnt the Pope's bull Suleiman the Magnificent ascended the throne of Turkey, and he reigned from Bagdad to Algiers and from Cairo to Belgrad and Buda-Pesth. The hapless eastern Christians might indeed ask themselves whether God was not on the side of the victorious sultan, and of the false prophet, whose religion is only

[1] J. Wilbois, *L'Avenir de l'Église Russe*, English translation by C. R. Davey Biggs, *Russia and Reunion*, pp. 126, 127 (A. R. Mowbray & Co., London, 1908)

a parody, though a serious parody, of the Christian faith. Apostasy was well rewarded. In Bosnia, after the wholesale massacres which established Turkish rule, the Slavonic aristocracy, who had been for the most part members of the strange semi-Christian sect of the Bogomili, accepted Islam, and their descendants have remained rich and undisturbed. In Constantinople, when a Christian of good position became a proselyte, he was led on horseback through the streets as one whom the king delighted to honour, and provision was made for his support, whether he were priest or layman. The policy of exterminating Christians has only been systematically followed by the Turks during the last forty years. During the decadence of the Church which inevitably followed the establishment of Turkish rule the number of renegades was considerable. But it is a matter for legitimate surprise that it was not infinitely greater and that in European Turkey the crescent never broke the Cross.

The sultans soon saw the advantage of having the highest ranks of the clergy on their side and under their hand. They could afford to treat the Patriarch with every honour if through him they could both tax and tame the whole Orthodox community and keep alive a jealous dislike of western Christendom. At the first, therefore, the Patriarch of Constantinople, as the head of a great community, enjoyed more power than he enjoyed under a Christian sovereign, and he began to wear on his brow a jewelled crown similar to that of the departed emperors. He was nevertheless an instrument of slavery and extortion. The Turks lived by fighting, and their intention was to maintain a warrior class on the basis of a subject population. This enslaved population had to fulfil three primary duties. First, they had to till the land for feudal landowners, the fiefs not being hereditary, but held directly from the sultan. Secondly, they had to pay taxes, especially a capitation tax paid by every non-Moslem. Thirdly, they had to pay the tribute of boys. Every four years the officers of the sultan made a selection of the male Christian children in Turkey between the ages of six and nine. These children were then circumcised, taught the faith of Islam, and in most cases enrolled in the corps of Janissaries. This inhuman practice sometimes turned to the advantage of the Christians, for the renegades occasionally dealt kindly with the people of their own race. A notable instance is the Serbian boy who was taken to Constantinople, became Grand Vizier, and was known by the name of Mechmed Sokolović. He was a strict Moslem, and in Constantinople he turned the church of St. Anastasia into a mosque. But he never lost his love for Serbia, and under his protection his brother, the Serbian Patriarch Makarije I (1557–1574), was able to restore several of the exquisite churches and monasteries of Serbia, some of which had been built when the Turks were at the very gates of Prince Lazar's dominions.

But, as a rule, in the latter part of the sixteenth century and during the greater part of the seventeenth, the position of the Church was desperate both in the cities and in the rural districts. Enormous sums were extorted from each Patriarch-elect at Constantinople, sums which had to be collected from the people by demanding fees for the offices of religion. Only by huge donations to the sultans were a few of the churches saved from being converted into mosques.[1] Even so, they were only rescued for a time, for the Greeks lost every ancient church in Constantinople except one small building, the Panagia Muchliotissa, built by the Greek princess Mary, daughter of Manuel Palaeologus, who became the bride of a Mongol Khan. In Serbia and

[1] The Christians were not allowed to build any new churches. After some great fires in 1660 when many churches in Galata and Constantinople were burned, the churches were rebuilt by the Christians but immediately destroyed by the Turks. See Paul Rycaut, *State of the Ottoman Empire*, p. 103 (London, 1670).

Macedonia, when the Moslem law against building new churches was enforced, the Christians tried to conceal them by building them partly underground, and the practice of making semi-subterranean churches survived until the beginning of this century. In one point the example of the Turks may be commended. They appreciated the beauty of the churches of Constantinople and the skill of the native Greek and Armenian architects. And for mosque after mosque, from that of Mohammed the Conqueror in Constantinople to that built in the nineteenth century in the citadel of Cairo, they employed architects of Christian race to design buildings wholly different from the primitive temples of Islam and almost purely Byzantine in their plan. Greatest among these mosques is that designed by the Armenian Sinan for Suleiman that it might surpass Justinian's church of Saint Sophia, and the other mosque erected by Sinan for the Sultan Selim at Adrianople. Why, we may ask, have we Christians built in India churches inartistic, exotic, and unsuited to the climate, when Indian art would lend itself to a style as delicate and appropriate as that of the churches of eastern Europe?

The Eastern Church was quickly affected by the Reformation. As early as 1559 Melanchthon opened a correspondence with the Patriarch Joasaph II with a view to promoting union between the Lutherans and the Orthodox, and between 1573 and 1581 there was a correspondence between the theologians of Tübingen and the Patriarch Jeremiah II. These theologians, like Melanchthon, desired an approximation as well as information. A controversy began which Jeremiah saw to be futile, and he finally asked them to write about friendship and not about dogma. More strange and pitiful is the story of Cyril Lucaris, Patriarch of Alexandria and afterwards of Constantinople (d. 1637). Living at the very darkest period of his Church's history, when the

Christians had at least twice been threatened with extermination, and had been deprived of no less than four churches to which the patriarchal throne had been successively removed,[1] he studied at Geneva and became infected with Calvinist principles. He corresponded with Calvinist divines in Holland and also with Archbishop Laud. He presented King James I with the famous manuscript known as *Codex Alexandrinus*, and one of his Alexandrine clergy, Metrophanes Kritopulos, came to Balliol College in 1617. Anxious for a union between the Greek Church and the Calvinists, he sent to Geneva in 1629 a Confession of a distinctly Calvinistic character. He met with bitter opposition not only from the Greeks but also from the Jesuits, who, backed by France, were extending their influence in the Levant. The Jesuits incited the Turks to close the printing press which had been opened under his patronage, and Cyril himself was thrown into the prison of the Seven Towers. He was accused of a design of stirring the Cossacks to fight the Turks, and Sultan Murad had him killed by the Janissaries. His body was thrown into the sea but recovered and buried by his friends.

The *Confession* of Lucaris, which in one year appeared in two Latin editions, four French, one German, and one English, must be regarded as authentic, as it was never repudiated by the Patriarch himself. Unlike the more moderate and orthodox Confession previously composed by Kritopulos, it had the almost inevitable effect of causing a reaction in the Romeward direction. It was not only in Constantinople that the Orthodox Church was threatened, nor only by the Jesuits. Kiev, the old holy city of Russia, was at this time attached with Lithuania to Poland. Protes-

---

[1] After the loss of St. Sophia, the church of the Holy Apostles was used as the pro-cathedral, then St. Mary Pammakaristos (made later into the Rose Mosque), then the church of Vlach Serai, then St. Demetrius. Finally, in 1601, the Patriarch was obliged to move to St. George of the Phanar on the site of the present church of that name.

tant churches had been built there and in other places of White Russia, and Calvinistic catechisms were translated into Slavonic.[1] The same thing was happening in Wallachia. And in the meantime Polish Roman Catholicism had driven a deep wedge into Russian Orthodoxy. In 1570 a Jesuit college was founded in Wilna, and at the close of the century no fewer than nine Russian bishops, including Michael, the metropolitan of Kiev, were received with their flocks into union with Rome at Brest (1596). On condition of their accepting Roman doctrine they were allowed to retain the Eastern liturgy and other rites. They were henceforth 'Uniats', and the ancient mosaics in the unique Byzantine cathedral of Kiev were covered with whitewash. Vast numbers of the descendants of these proselytes were brought back into the Orthodox fold early in the nineteenth century under Russian pressure, and many thousands returned to Rome early in the twentieth, when the Russian Government proclaimed religious toleration.

It was under Polish rule that a new standard of Eastern Orthodoxy was set up. In 1640 Peter Mogila, a Moldavian, the Orthodox metropolitan of Kiev, submitted to his synod an 'Orthodox Confession'. It was written in scholastic Latin, and its biblical quotations were from the Vulgate. It was approved by a synod at Jassi in Moldavia the next year, translated into Greek and approved by the four Orthodox patriarchs in 1643. This important Eastern document was first printed in Calvinistic Holland, and its strongly anti-Calvinistic tone caused Pope Urban VIII to send his congratulations to the author. In the meantime a dispute was in progress between the French Calvinists

---

[1] The Jesuit Skaga says that the Protestants secured three thousand churches in the kingdom of Poland. The Jesuits won back large numbers of these Protestants and then turned their attention to the Orthodox. They tried in vain to win Prince Constantine of Ostrog, who was the patron of nearly a thousand churches, and then they turned to the Ruthenian or Little Russian bishops.

and French Roman Catholics of Jansenist proclivities with regard to the doctrine of the Eucharist. Both sides claimed that the Greek Church supported their views, and the Marquis De Nointel, the French ambassador at the Porte, asked in writing what was the Eastern Orthodox doctrine of the Eucharist. After certain preliminaries a clear reply was given. Dositheos, Patriarch of Jerusalem, summoned a Council at Jerusalem in 1672. The result was a full repudiation of Calvinism, and the adoption of certain phrases of Latin theology, including those used in defining the doctrine of transubstantiation. This Council, which represents the high-water mark of Roman influence on Greek doctrine, gave its sanction to both the Confession of Peter Mogila and a clearly written and systematic Confession of Dositheos. The official theology of the Eastern Orthodox Church remains in substance that of this Council of Jerusalem. But the acts of this Council are not of supreme authority, though regarded as worthy of very high respect. In authority the Bible is placed first, then the acts of the Seven Oecumenical Councils, then the acts of the Council of Jerusalem including the Confession of Dositheos, and then the Confession of Peter Mogila.[1] Below these Confessions come the ordinary catechisms which have only the direct approval of the national churches from which they have issued.

A serious knowledge of the theology of the Eastern Church has become for us not a luxury but a duty. In the British colonies and in the United States, members of the churches of the Eastern communion and members of the churches of the Anglican communion live and work side by side. Christian charity demands that if there cannot as yet be a full ungrudging intercommunion between the two

[1] For these, see E. J. Kimmel, *Libri Symbolici Ecclesiae Orientalis* (Jenae, 1843).

bodies, there should at least be such a concordat as will absolutely prevent scandal and heart-burning with regard to baptism, confirmation, ordination, and mixed marriages. Such a concordat is being gradually reached.[1] And while we bear in mind that Eastern Christians regard Orthodoxy as a unity of life and not as a collection of dogmas, we should be prepared to consider whether the divergences in doctrine are such as to make a closer co-operation impracticable. The differences which would occur to the minds of most of us are four.

There is the old and lamentable dispute concerning the procession of the Holy Spirit, the dispute in which the Patriarch Photius took a leading part and which was revived after the schism had taken place in the eleventh century. The Easterns have simply kept in the creed the original phrase to the effect that the Holy Ghost proceedeth from the Father; the West has added the phrase *Filioque*, ' and the Son', inserting something that has not Oecumenical authority into a creed which had Oecumenical authority. The phrase ' and the Son ' is not false. It could only be false if it were spoken not by monotheists but by ditheists who imagined that the Son was a second god, separable from God the Father. And this doctrine of the procession of the Holy Spirit came as a natural development after the prolonged struggle of the Church with Arianism. From the age of the apostles the Holy Spirit had been to the Christian Church that Spirit who had wrought the miraculous conception of the Son of Mary and had spoken by the prophets of His advent. Yet the supreme necessity of concentrating attention upon the Person of Jesus Christ did for a time cause the doctrine of the Third Person of the Holy Trinity to remain

---

[1] Hopes of a closer union have been greatly strengthened by the pronouncement made by the Patriarch Meletios and the Holy Synod of Constantinople in favour of the validity of Anglican orders. For the Patriarch's letter on this subject to other Orthodox Churches, see app. note 24, p. 279.

somewhat immature and ambiguous. When, however, the fundamental Christian conviction that the Redeemer of the world can be neither a demi-god nor a human personality had found its definite expression, it was more clearly seen that the relation of the Spirit to the Son concerns Their essential life and not a mere temporal operation. The Holy Spirit, the Giver of Life, is not a creature nor a transient phase of God's self-manifestation. The one indivisible Godhead is self-conscious in three eternal modes. And the term ' from the Son ' was meant to suggest such a dependence of the Third Person of the Trinity upon the Second as is compatible with the divine Unity and a full recognition of the Deity of both the Son and the Spirit. In the East St. Gregory of Nyssa and St. Cyril of Alexandria were almost on the verge of stating it, and St. Augustine in stating it explicitly taught nothing that contradicted the deeper Eastern teaching.[1] If in East and West we are in complete agreement as to the Spirit's presence in the Church and His gracious work in human souls, let us witness to this agreement. We must not seek peace by saying that *Filioque* is false. It is a most valuable safeguard against low views of Jesus Christ. But could we not say that there is higher ecclesiastical authority for the older form of the creed, and even that we desire on certain solemn occasions to use that older form?

Another difference between the Anglican and the Eastern Churches has been suggested by the Greek definition of the real presence in the Eucharist. We have already noticed that the Council of Jerusalem adopted certain phrases of Latin theology in order to shut the door in the face of Calvinism. Among these phrases were the words μετουσίωσις and συμβεβηκότα, the equivalents of 'transubstantiation'

[1] For this, see H. B. Swete, D.D., *The Holy Spirit in the Ancient Church* (Macmillan & Co., London, 1912).

and 'accidents'. This is in harmony with the teaching of the Council of Trent, and the cursory reader would at once conclude that the Roman Catholic Church and the Eastern Church are here completely united. Such an opinion must be carefully qualified. The word μετουσίωσις was first used, and used three times, by George Scholarios, who had attended the reunion Council of Florence, then repudiated his own action, and became Patriarch of Constantinople immediately after it was captured by the Turks. It occurs also in three writers of the next century.[1] It is identical in meaning with transubstantiation, and is treated as such by the eminent Russian theologian N. Malinovsky, and an exact equivalent of the word is used in Russian.[2] But both before and after the Council of Jerusalem the terms used by the Greek Fathers to describe the operation of the Holy Spirit in the Sacrament were usually preferred even by the Greeks. Not only does Kritopulos in his Confession avoid the words transubstantiation and accidents, but even the Synod held at Constantinople in 1638 with the special purpose of counteracting the Confession of Cyril Lucaris also avoids both words. The attitude of the Slavs towards the question is even more significant. The acts of the Synod of Jerusalem were finally sanctioned for Russia by the Russian Holy Synod in 1838, but only after a revision which brought their phraseology in several points of doctrine into closer conformity with the old Oriental type. The change goes beyond mere wording. Thus the canon of Scripture is that of certain Fathers followed by the Church of England, not that of Trent. The word δουλεία as applied to the veneration of the saints, and ὑπερδουλεία as applied to

---

[1] Meletios Pegas, Gabriel Severos, Maximos Margunios. The question is discussed in the Orthodox Greek periodical Νέα Σιών, January 1907, p. 125 (Jerusalem, Press of the Holy Community of the Holy Sepulchre)

[2] *Pravoslavnoe Dogmatitcheskoe Bogoslovye*, vol. iv, p. 177, foot note 1. The Russians use *prelozhenie* to correspond with the Greek μεταβολή, and *presushchestvlenie* to correspond with μετουσίωσις.

the veneration of the Mother of God, are eliminated. Whereas the penitent is to undergo discipline, he is not said to perform works of satisfaction, nor are the souls of the faithful departed said to pay a penalty. Finally the section on the Eucharist omits the crucial words ' transubstantiated' and 'accidents', and modifies a phrase suggesting a material and sensible presence.[1]

To sum up. The whole Eastern Church has adopted words equivalent to transubstantiation, while not investing them with the highest authority and while repudiating a material or, as the Greeks say, ' physico-chemical ' sense of the word. And the Slavs, not the Greeks, decline to employ the word 'accidents' in connexion with their doctrine of transubstantiation. All the Eastern Orthodox declare that the mystery passes human understanding, and that to explain perfectly the manner of the change is impossible. And all would probably refuse to accept the sharpened Tridentine doctrine which was laid down by Rome in 1875, and apparently intended to exclude one view of the mystery for which strong support can be found in ancient writers.[2]

If the question of intercommunion were to be seriously considered, it is quite unlikely that Anglicans would be asked to accept the acts of the Council of Jerusalem in their original form. They would certainly be asked to signify their adhesion to the patristic doctrine implied in the Eastern liturgies and in the Anglican liturgies used in Scotland and America.

It seems fitting to say a little about the use of the icons or sacred pictures which are so conspicuous in Eastern worship and in Russia are almost ubiquitous. The scientific study of

---

[1] See a paper by W. J. Birkbeck in the *Guardian*, March the 31st, 1907.
[2] Darwell Stone, *A History of the Doctrine of the Holy Eucharist*, vol. ii, p. 416 (Longmans, London, 1909).

THE EASTERN ORTHODOX CHURCH

Russian icons as works of art may almost be said to date from 1903, when the Russian sect of Old Believers began to collect antique pictures to adorn the churches which were sanctioned by the edict of toleration. That icons had some religious and theological significance had long been recognized, and the history of the Iconoclastic controversy showed that serious political consequences attended both the veneration and the destruction of the sacred icons. But the actual teaching of the Eastern Church on the subject is not much better known in the West than the history of the art with which they are associated. There has been a vague idea that the veneration paid to them in church is idolatrous, and that in private they are employed as a kind of fetish. And that the credulity of the vulgar has sometimes combined with the avarice of blind guides to further superstition in this regard, no one will question. But if we know what grossly pagan superstitions have existed in Great Britain until our own time, we shall be very slow indeed to condemn the Russian peasant or Greek sailor who puts his trust in his picture of St. Nicholas or St. George. The official teaching of the Eastern Church is everywhere that of the Seventh Oecumenical Council, the Second of Nicaea.[1] The Council affirmed that the tradition of 'making pictorial representations is perfectly agreeable to the history contained in the Evangelic message for a confirmation of the real and not a phantastic incarnation of God the Word'. As Professor Bury has said, ' the material representation of the Saviour was clung to by the Greeks as a visible warrant and surety of His human nature'.[2] The whole history of Eastern heresies, ancient and modern, shows a tendency to

[1] For the history of the Council, see Dom H. Leclercq's *Histoire des Conciles*, a revised and augmented translation of the German work of Bishop Joseph Hefele, vol. iii, part ii, pp. 758 ff. (Letouzey, Paris, 1910). For a short account of the doctrine in question, see *The Seventh General Council and the Doctrine of Icons* (Society for Promoting Christian Knowledge, London, 1919) and Bréhier, *La Querelle des Images* (Paris, 1904).

[2] *The Pilot*, November the 3rd, 1900.

a false type of mysticism which in its eagerness for direct communion with God starves the senses, and neglects the means by which God has willed that we should apprehend Him, even the Incarnation itself. To keep the true balance, such a mentality requires what is material for its thought and in its worship. Accordingly, while the Council expressly denies that λατρεία, divine worship or adoration, may be paid to the icons, it upholds the salutation of them and τιμητική προσκύνησις, the reverence of honour. The salutation includes kissing, a tribute paid in England to the New Testament, and indeed the Council itself puts the respect paid to the pictures on the same level as that paid to the Holy Gospels. And the honour includes bowing such as in England is paid to the throne of the sovereign, and the use of incense and lights as a sign of respect to the sacred persons represented.

It would be easy to multiply quotations to show how strictly this teaching is guarded. Thus Kritopulos says this reverence is not λατρευτική, ἡ δουλική; the Synod of Constantinople says it is given οὐ λατρευτικῶς, ἀλλὰ σχετικῶς; Macarius, a conservative Russian theologian, compares it with the respect that we pay to the portraits of our father and mother. And the Russian Catechism says of icons, 'We ought to honour them, but not to make gods of them; for pictures are merely representations which serve to remind us of the works of God and His saints'. The Oriental is inclined to think that there is a savour of idolatry in those sculptured figures of saints and heroes which we erect in churches and which his own religion discourages; the Occidental is suspicious when he sees a grown-up Slav act as perhaps his own English children act towards a favourite picture of their little Jesus. Surely it is not too much to hope that each will learn to believe the other when he says that he pays divine worship to God, and to God alone.

With regard to the saints departed the Eastern Orthodox Church teaches that the invocation of them is right, if I may use the word invocation in the ordinary modern sense of the word. The English *Bishops' Book* or *Institution of a Christian Man*, published with the full authority of the Church of England in 1537 just after the breach between England and Rome, condemns 'invocation'. But by 'invocation' it means asking the saints for gifts of health and grace which God alone can give. It fully sanctions *Ora pro nobis*, for it says that it is lawful and allowed by the Catholic Church to pray to the saints 'to be intercessors with us and for us'. The theologians and the catechisms of the Eastern Church, both Greek and Russian, express themselves precisely to the same effect. Thus Macarius says, 'In venerating the saints as faithful servants, as righteous men, and as friends of God, the holy Church invokes them in her prayers, not as gods capable of affording us assistance by themselves, but as our intercessors with God, who is the only author and dispenser of every gift and every grace to all His creatures'. Khomiakoff says, 'We glorify all whom God has glorified and is glorifying; for how should we say that Christ is living within us, if we do not make ourselves like unto Christ? Wherefore we glorify the saints, the angels, and the prophets, and more than all the most pure Mother of the Lord Jesus, not acknowledging her either to have been conceived without sin, or to have been perfect (for Christ alone is without sin and perfect), but remembering that her pre-eminence, passing all understanding, which she has above all God's creatures, was borne witness to by the angel and by Elizabeth, and above all, by the Saviour himself.'

The eastern Invocation of Saints must be considered as part of the whole system of prayer both for and to the departed. Thus not only is the intercession of the Holy Virgin and all the saints directly asked, but they are prayed for in the liturgy. Some prayers to the saints are couched in an exuberant form, more like the Italian than the older Latin invocations. To balance this fact, we must remember that the saints are believed to be aided by our prayers, and it is denied that it is possible for them to have performed works of supererogation of which the merits can be applied to others. The communion of prayer is so complete that it is held that Blessed Mary and all the saints have been assisted by all the prayers of all the faithful that have lived or ever will live. All the faithful departed are prayed for; little children who sleep in Christ being prayed for more explicitly than in the West. And on the other hand, all are asked to pray for us, though they may in no wise be canonized saints. In Russia a parent will ask his departed children to pray for him, and children will ask their parents in the other world to pray for them, like the saints.

Let us link these things together. The deep belief in the Incarnation, the one single universal creed with no local additions, the one bread from heaven and cup of salvation from which the children are not barred, the church adorned not with artistic novelties but with the easily recognized portraits of one great family, the prayers in which every one helps every one living or departed, combine to strengthen a conception of the Church, that deserves our consideration. It is a conception of corporate life which seems to avoid some faults which have done much injury to religion in the West. And it is true to St. Paul's majestic doctrine of one body visible to us on earth, invisible so far as it is in Paradise, dependent upon its Head, the unseen ascended Christ. It will be found that at point after point, whether it be for instance in the authority of a Council in defining the faith, or of a bishop in ordaining, or of a priest in celebrating and absolving, emphasis is laid not upon the individuals as such, but upon the body of which they are the representa-

THE EASTERN ORTHODOX CHURCH

tives and the instruments. This is perfectly compatible with the truth that the ministry is representative of Christ and the priest an ambassador for Christ, as Christ himself in His priesthood represents God to man and man to God. It is perfectly compatible with a strongly sacramental belief. And it would lose its meaning if it were combined with the idea that any separate congregation or society could form a valid ministry for itself. On the other hand it is equally a corrective of any tendency to make the priesthood into a caste or to treat the laity as merely passive members of the Body of Christ. Ecclesiasticism in the worst sense of the word can exist quite as much in the newest sect as in the most venerable patriarchate. And its remedy is not to teach a lower, cheaper view of the Church, but one that is higher and more supernatural. And it is here that eastern theology, and more particularly that of Russia, offers to us a suggestion and a lesson.

In studying Christianity within the Turkish Empire after the date of the Council of Jerusalem, two outstanding facts immediately claim our notice. The first is the influence exercised by France, and the second is the influence exercised by the rich Greeks of the Phanar quarter of Constantinople.

France inaugurated a permanent policy in the Ottoman Empire in the time of Francis I, and early in the seventeenth century that policy was pursued with the utmost vigour. Various religious orders, Capuchins, Jesuits, Dominicans, and Carmelites, had a potent ally in Richelieu's adviser, Father Joseph du Tremblay. The near East became dotted with Latin monasteries, and even Abyssinia, Persia, and Babylon came within the sphere of French religious activities. The earlier capitulations made between the monarchs of France and the sultans of Turkey were intended to secure religious privileges for French Roman Catholics in the Ottoman Empire, and to guarantee French protection for the Holy Places owned by the Latin Church in Palestine. These rights were carefully watched and guarded by Louis XIV, who in 1674 declared the Jesuits to be 'chaplains of the King for the French in the Levant', and in 1709 authorized the Capuchins to perform parochial functions for the French embassy. But the so-called 'French apostolate' meant a great deal more than the protection of French merchants in Turkey and certain monuments hallowed by Christian tradition. It was extended to large bodies of native Christians.

The Maronites of the Lebanon, a body of Syrian Christians who had been united with Rome since the time of the Crusades, helped St. Louis himself in his Egyptian campaign, and reckoned themselves almost as vassals of the Crown of France. It was natural that they should be special objects of the pious solicitude of Louis XIV, whose name was as much revered on Mount Libanus as on Mount Carmel. He also assisted the Mirdites, the warrior clan of Roman Catholics in northern Albania.

What France did for the Maronites and the Mirdites it was possible to do for any Christians who might detach themselves from their national Churches, whether Orthodox or heretical, and unite themselves with Rome. Under Turkish law these Christians could not obtain any legal recognition as members of distinct denominations unless they obtained from the sultan a recognition of their spiritual head, and such a head must also have the recognition of the Pope. The Turks have always graciously favoured proposals for dividing the Christians in their empire. Rome saw the utility of the Turkish method and aided by French diplomacy secured a corporate separate existence for different Uniat communities which, like the Maronites, are subject to Rome but retain more or less of their national usages and rites. It often happens that western customs are introduced among the Uniats by degrees, so that we find Greek and Coptic

THE EASTERN ORTHODOX CHURCH 213

Uniat bishops wearing Italian mitres, and Maronites and even Armenian Uniats giving Holy Communion in one kind.[1]

So successful was the policy to which I have alluded, that not long before the recent war it was calculated that, excluding 100,000 Christians of the Latin rite, there were within the Turkish Empire 720,000 Christians subject to Rome and protected by France.[2] The largest defection from the Eastern Orthodox Church in the Ottoman Empire to Rome took place in Syria in the eighteenth century; and the poverty and weakness of the Christians of Syria and Palestine now that Russia is impotent to give them help will expose them to the attractions of the same propaganda.

Unhappily the Phanariot Greeks as well as the French were responsible for some of the weaknesses of the Orthodox Church. In the eighteenth century the rich and clever Greeks of the Phanar quarter of Stamboul dominated all the races of the Balkans.[3] This domination was favoured by the Turks. The Turks classified their subjects, not by their race, but by their religion. In their eyes all the Orthodox were branches of the *Rum Millet*, the Roman, that is, the Greek Byzantine community. And all the Christians, whatever their nationality might be, were ruled by Greek civil ministers and the Greek Patriarch. The effect on the

---

[1] This is done in spite of the fact that Rome officially permits the Armenian Uniats to receive Holy Communion in both kinds. *Dictionnaire de Théologie Catholique*, vol. i, col. 1956 (Letouzey, Paris, 1903): 'Toutefois, pour éviter tout scandale chez les fidèles, les catholiques ne communient plus sous les deux espèces; c'est là un privilège dont ils peuvent user, mais dont ils n'usent pas.'

[2] Joseph Aubès, *Le Protectorat religieux en Orient*, p. 43 (Paris, Bloud & Cⁱᵉ). The census of the Lebanon taken in A.D. 1922 is instructive. It included 199,000 Maronites, 81,000 Orthodox, 42,000 Melchites (Uniats of the Greek rite), 4,200 Protestants. There were also 124,000 Sunni Moslems. 104 Shia Moslems, and 43,000 Druses.

[3] For much that concerns the Phanar I am indebted to the brilliant author of *Turkey in Europe* (Edward Arnold, London, 1900). He writes under the name of 'Odysseus'.

religious life of the people was harmful, for the whole system was intended to be a means of extorting money and lent itself to other abuses which we must not conceal. It is only just to add that the Greek theologians of the eighteenth century were numerous and well educated. The most distinguished was Eugenios Bulgaris (1717–1800), a native of Corfu, who studied at Padua, knew nine languages, wrote an 'Orthodox Confession', and was called by the Empress Catherine II to occupy an archiepiscopal see in Russia.

The War of Independence which caused Greece to be detached finally from the sultan in 1830 also detached it from the rule of Phanariot officials. The hapless Patriarch Gregory V, though he had taken no share in the Greek insurrection, had to suffer from the Turks as head of the *Rum Millet*. He was hanged in his vestments on Easter Day, April the 22nd, 1822, immediately outside a door of his patriarchal church of St. George. And to this day the door remains closed, and will so remain until the Turkish rule is banished from Constantinople. When the Greeks had achieved independence, they had no desire to continue to be under any patriarch nominated by the sultan and himself an Ottoman subject. The Greek national Parliament therefore declared the Church to be autocephalous, and a Holy Synod was appointed after the Russian model.

After considerable difficulties the Patriarch in 1850 finally recognized the independence of the Church of Hellas, a Church which the Hellenic constitution affirms to be 'indissolubly united, as regards dogmas, to the Great Church of Constantinople'. At the present time it seems probable that in Greece and in other Orthodox countries an undue interference with the Church on the part of the State will have an effect analogous to that of the Tsarist régime in Russia, and this probability increases the necessity for independence and integrity in the occupants of the patriarchal throne of St. Chrysostom. The politics of to-day are not the politics of yesterday; but the history of the eighteenth and the nineteenth century shows in glaring colours the result of the patriarchate being made subservient to merely secular force and national ambition. The effect of this subservience was so paralysing that we should wonder, not that Christianity sank low, but that it did not become extinct.

The Greeks, very faithful to their religion, proud of their ancient literature, and speaking a modern Greek easily learned and well fitted to become a *lingua franca*, tried to Hellenize the Bulgarians, Rumanians, Serbs, and Arabs of the same religion. Their conduct was not wholly inexcusable. For as the Turks had ruined the native civilization of these races, of whom the Rumanians and the Serbs had exceptional mental and artistic talents, the Greeks of the Phanar might argue that where no culture existed, Greek culture might well be planted. Nor was it wrong if they wished to diminish the danger of religious schisms or even to smooth the wheels of peaceful Turkish government. But any complete Hellenization of these races was impossible, and the Hellenic influence which might have been spread by self-restraint and toleration was neutralized by rapacity and intolerance. On the shores of the Danube bickering and bitterness have been the legacy of Greece.

In Serbia the Church was deprived of its independence in 1766, when the sultan, under Phanariot influence, suppressed the Serbian patriarchate at Peć and all the Serbians in Turkey were put under the immediate authority of the Patriarch of Constantinople.[1] The next year the primatial see at Ochrida was suppressed, and all Bulgars were made immediate subjects of the same Oecumenical Patriarch. The best places of preferment were given to Greeks, Slavonic

[1] The last Patriarch in Peć was Kallinikos II, a Greek. Three of his predecessors in the eighteenth century also appear to have been Greeks.

service books were destroyed, and Greek books introduced. The Bulgarian language was written in Greek letters and the better educated Bulgarians spoke Greek. The Slavonic clergy were left uneducated. In external matters the process of Hellenization went farthest among the Rumanians, for the whole civil administration as well as the ecclesiastical was in the hands of the Greeks, headed by the Greek Hospodars who ruled Moldavia and Wallachia. The office of these Hospodars was farmed out by the Turks on a purely commercial basis, so that even when they were men of enlightened views it was inevitable that their rule was oppressive. They were accompanied by swarms of Greek adventurers and monks, and vast ecclesiastical estates were in the hands of Greek ecclesiastics. Yet during the whole period of Phanariot rule Rumanian literature was never entirely sterile, and among the Serbs the national devotion to their beautiful ancient poetry kept alive the memories of their glorious past. Everywhere a revolt was certain to come against Greek intolerance and Turkish despotism. And the ecclesiastical revolt came in its most determined form from the Balkan race which by descent and temperament is nearest to the Turks, the Bulgarians.

A Bulgarian Church, orthodox in doctrine but free from the jurisdiction of the Patriarch of Constantinople, was established in 1870 in the teeth of Greek opposition at a time when the Bulgarian State did not yet exist. The Bulgarians wanted to belong no more to the *Rum Millet* but to a *Millet* of their own, and the sultan issued the necessary firman. The Exarch, who was the head of the Church, was to reside at Constantinople, and to have jurisdiction over Bulgarians even where the Greeks were in a majority and the Orthodox Church was completely organized. The Bulgarian Church thus became 'a hostile and proselytizing sect, claiming all persons belonging to a certain race'. The exasperated

Patriarch protested against the novel doctrine that persons of a particular race are entitled to a separate ecclesiastical organization, branded it with the name of 'Phyletismos', and in 1872 held a local synod at Constantinople which pronounced the Bulgarian Church schismatic. The Churches of Alexandria, Antioch, and Athens agreed; the Church of Jerusalem took a rather less definite line, while the Churches of Russia, Rumania, and Serbia observed an attitude of non-committal. Sooner or later, when the political atmosphere is clearer, a reunion will probably be effected, a reunion rendered easier not only by identity of doctrine but by the fact that Orientals are familiar with the idea of members of different national Churches or parties in the same Church being in communion with each other when the chief officials have openly suspended official relations with one another.

Undeterred by their experience of Bulgarian national sentiment, the Greeks continued the same course in Antioch and Jerusalem. After 1724 all the Orthodox Patriarchs of Antioch were Phanariot Greeks until 1899, in spite of the fact that the great majority of the people spoke Arabic. In the latter year they elected an Arab, Meletios: he was supported by Russia and opposed by the Phanar and the French ambassador at Constantinople. The sultan wavered, then he yielded to Russian pressure, and in 1900 Meletios became Patriarch, and Arabs have since been appointed to other sees in the patriarchate. In Jerusalem the contest between the Greeks and the Arab Christians, who were formerly backed by Russia, is hardly yet concluded. The rule that the Brotherhood of the Holy Sepulchre, which recently numbered 500 members, 'must all be Greeks', was an unfortunate illustration of Greek inability to rise above the distinctions of race and language in religious matters, an inability from which some of the best educated members of the Church of England are by no means free. At the beginning of the present year, 1922, peace was very nearly restored in the patriarchate of Jerusalem, all the bishops, with the exception of the Metropolitan of Nazareth, rendering canonical obedience to the successor of St. James, Damianos, whose desire it has been to give the Orthodox Arabs of his patriarchate a greater share in ecclesiastical administration.

In Rumania, as a natural consequence of the complete national independence attained in 1881, the Church became autocephalous in 1885 with the consent of the Patriarch of Constantinople. Bitter resentment, however, was felt by the Greeks at the conduct of the Rumanian Government under Alexander John Cuza in 1864. All the monastic property in the country was secularized, and this property included estates which belonged to the monasteries of the Holy Sepulchre, Mount Athos, and Mount Sinai. The property belonging to the Rumanian Church in the recently annexed districts of Hungary is not likely to be sequestered. There, in the province of Transylvania, the Orthodox Rumanians are numerous. A vigorous Uniat propaganda was carried on among them in the eighteenth century by the Roman Church, which endeavoured to persuade the people that as their race and language were Roman, so their religion ought to be. In consequence of these activities many became so-called ' Rumanian Greek Catholics '. It is probable that large numbers of them will return to the Orthodox Church. That their attachment to Rome is not very deep may be gathered from the following complaint in a Hungarian (Roman) newspaper: 'The Catholic Union with the Roumanians lacks both expansive and intensive faculty. That explains why generally those who are converted from schism do not join the Greek Catholics, but the Catholic Church of the Latin rite, that captivates with its intensive verve, and warm, pulsating life. The Church of the Roumanian rite has nothing of this kind to offer. Nowhere has such an imperfect union proved of value. History teaches us that only a complete union is sincere and faithful, that the undulations of Catholic life reach only so far as there exists unity not only of dogma, but also of liturgy and discipline. In order to this, doctrine, rites, and hierarchy must be the same. While near the Yangtsekiang the Chinese Catholics are telling their beads and in the litany of Loretto are invoking the Holy Virgin, our neighbour the Greek Catholic Roumanian peasant knows of neither a rosary nor a litany. He is ignorant of the sublime eucharistic cult, and ignores the value of a frequent and fervent partaking of the sacraments. Catholic regeneration cannot avail with these people separated by language, liturgy, and canon law.' [1]

Serbia obtained a metropolitan united with, but almost independent of, Constantinople in 1830, and eight years later the seat of ecclesiastical government was fixed at Belgrad. In 1879, as a result of the extension of territory granted to Serbia by the Berlin Congress, the Church became autocephalous. The creation of a vast kingdom of Serbs, Croats, and Slovenes after the great war of 1914–1918 led to the incorporation of multitudes of southern Slavs who had formerly been in the territories of Turkey, Austria, and Hungary. In 1921, with the consent of the Phanar, a patriarchate was established as heir to the mediaeval Serbian patriarchate of Peć, the Metropolitan of Belgrad being elected the first Patriarch of the new kingdom. The diocese of Belgrad is for the present united with that of Sremski Karlovci (Carlovitz), which before the great war was the patriarchal see of the Serbians in Hungary and had formerly been the principal Orthodox see in the whole Austro-Hungarian Empire.[2] It lies about forty miles

[1] *The Hungarian Nation, A Monthly Review, Political, Economic, and Literary,* Buda-Pesth, January 1922.
[2] A vast migration of Serbians took place in 1690. Fleeing from the Turks these Serbians, under their Patriarch Arsenije III, settled in

north of the Serbian capital at the foot of the Fruška Gora, and the patriarchal palace is a building of suitable dignity.

The character of the Serbian Church and people is of extraordinary interest, and the spiritual problems which confront them are of extraordinary difficulty. The State of Jugo-Slavia includes large bodies of Roman Catholics in Croatia and Slovenia, and numerous Slav Moslems in Bosnia as well as Albanian Moslems farther south. The so-called 'intellectuals', even before the great war, had been infected with the atheism professed by the students of the German and Austrian universities which were frequented by the more talented young Serbians, and the Church had not had the time to adapt itself to the rapid change from Turkish oppression to infidel opposition. Moslem misrule had prevented the erection of an adequate number of parish churches, with the result that church-going had declined. Many monasteries were ruined, and others, containing as they do some of the finest churches in the Serbo-Byzantine style, were nearly empty. And yet the religion of Serbia had not degenerated into a mere stagnant fidelity to the past. It is deeply rooted in the home life and morality of the majority of the people. Some of the monasteries were never totally abandoned, even when monks had to hide in the depths of the forest and visit the churches secretly, chanting the liturgy at their peril. And round these monasteries, which kept the national life aglow, thousands of peasants encamp on great festivals to receive the sacraments and hear sermons. The religious life will certainly revive if there exists the courage that was shown, the winter before last (1920–1921), at Rakóvitza. During the war the monastery had been cruelly impoverished, the forests cut down, and the cattle stolen. Hither came the Archimandrite

Austrian dominions. In 1738 Arsenije IV headed another great band of emigrants to Austria, but they were intercepted by the Turks. The former band were granted important privileges by the Emperor Leopold I.

THE EASTERN ORTHODOX CHURCH 221

Mardarije, who had been for some years a professor in Russia and afterwards lived in Chicago. The Patriarch advised him to begin with seven students to be taught and prepared for the monastic life. He began with forty, who in the intervals of their studies set to work to repair the monastery buildings. They were reduced to such straits that they had only one potato a day with the roots and berries that they could find in the woods. At last the Archimandrite told them he could promise them no food the next week, and gave leave to any who wished to return home. Of the forty only two went away.[1] That is Serbia.

Let us now think of Russia.

Peter the Great (d. 1725) leapt over the wall between the East and the West and he returned a reforming autocrat. But he did not help Russia to develop on Russian lines. He pronounced the name of his new capital as if it were Dutch, and his architects built it after the manner of the Dutch and German barocco cities. He centralized the government of the Church in a Holy Synod which was not a real synod but an ecclesiastical committee, and this committee ruled over local consistories copied from those of the German Lutherans.[2] His immediate successors continued his germanizing policy, and the Church deteriorated as it did under German rule in England. The Tsar was in no sense a Pope, and hardly any attempt was made to interfere with the doctrine of the Church; but the new organization was equally alien to the Russian spirit and ecclesiastical tradition. The higher ranks of the clergy became the tools of an autocratic State, and this gradually had the double effect of dividing the bishops from the

---

[1] H. J. Fynes-Clinton, in *The Christian East*, December 1921 (London, Society for Promoting Christian Knowledge).

[2] His Church reforms aggravated the great schism made in 1666 by the conservative 'Old Believers'. One section has remained without priests until the present day. The other has a hierarchy.

parochial clergy and embittering the more progressive classes against the Church.

Under the Empress Elizabeth (d. 1762) the condition of the Church somewhat improved, and in the regions beyond the Volga large numbers of the heathen were converted. The Russian Church was the only Eastern Church which could possibly undertake missionary work, and as it spread eastward it gave constant proofs of fresh vitality. In the nineteenth century it produced some missionaries of the finest type, of whom three at least should not be forgotten: Bishop Innocent, who converted the savages of Kamchatka; Ilminski, who used his extraordinary linguistic gifts in converting Moslem Tartars; and above all Bishop Nicolai, whose success among the Japanese has probably had no modern parallel. During the Russo-Japanese war he was not commanded to leave but was requested to remain in Japan, and when he died in 1912 he left in Japan a Church with more than 36,000 communicants and every priest was a Japanese.

Since then has come the Revolution. The Russian Church immediately set to work to clear away abuses and to organize itself in a form which expressed its true capacities. The All-Russian Church Council which began its sessions on August the 15th, 1917, at Moscow represented every class in the Russian Church, clerical and lay, and gave full proof of its sincerity and its ability. But the atheist Jews who went from New York to Russia with the expressed intention of outdoing the French Revolution did their work rapidly, and, as they hoped, thoroughly. They held that the idea of God is pernicious, that religion is opium. In January 1918 there was issued a decree called the Decree of Liberty of Conscience, in reality a decree separating Church and State, and the harbinger of the coming persecution of Christianity and the massacre of bishops and priests. The Bolsheviks intended war to the finish against Christian doctrine, Christian morals, and Christian education. Years will probably elapse before we learn one-half of the tale of oppression and agony and woe. Facts will doubtless be denied as the promulgation of the decree for the nationalization of women was promptly denied when it was discovered that to turn men and women into animals is not a security against their rebellion.[1] To close the monasteries, to forbid the surviving bishops to travel, to prevent the training of ordination candidates, to stop the teaching of Church music in which the Russians peculiarly excel, to propagate the wildest blasphemy in parody of the 'Our Father' and the 'Hail Mary', are all parts of a vast scheme to destroy religion. And at first the poison had some effect among peasants who were hungry for land, workmen who were burdened with cruel social conditions, and demoralized soldiers who, as one was heard to say, saw no more wrong in killing a man than in killing a chicken.

Bolshevism, however, has not destroyed the faith. It has revived it. The crowded churches, the societies of men and women who protect them from injury, and such demonstrations as the vast procession in Petrograd on May the 8th, 1921, when some 150,000 people marched with banners to the Kazan cathedral, testify that the Church is more, and not less, living. And it has a leader. In November 1917, the Council of the Church having determined to revive the Russian patriarchate which Peter the Great had abolished, lots were drawn after the apostolic fashion in the cathedral of the Saviour at Moscow. A venerated hermit drew the name of Bishop Tikhon who had laboured among the numerous Russians in the United States and was a firm friend of the Anglican Church.

[1] I was well acquainted with a keen and cultured Serbian student, Mr. D. S. Marić, a B.Litt. of Oxford, who was in Samara when the decree was issued. He assured me that it was also issued in the government of Saratov. A Bolshevik lecturer who advocated the measure in Petrograd was mobbed by women, and the plan was dropped in consequence.

Pious Russians saw in this choice the hand of God. Tikhon's simplicity, patience, and heroic courage made them realize that Tikhon represented Russia in a way that Lenin and Trotzky never can and never will, and as no Russian who is a renegade from Christ either can or will. For if Christ does elicit and consummate all that is worth anything in our character, if it is true that He makes himself ours, He does this in the East as well as in the West. And if we Englishmen suppose, not altogether unjustly, that we obey some of the ten commandments more easily than some other nations whose opportunities have been poor and scanty when compared with our wealth of opportunities, there is no room for boasting about our merits. Self-examination is better than self-congratulation. The Orthodox Slav may be a great saint, or he may be a great sinner. But in his heart he believes in the Beatitudes which are sung at the celebration of his liturgy. And so long as any man has that belief, he can believe in his own future.

VIII

ASPECTS OF CHRISTIAN THOUGHT SINCE 1815

St. John xvii. 21 : That they all may be one; as thou, Father, art in me, and I in thee, that they also may be one in us: that the world may believe that thou hast sent me.

THE downfall of Napoleon, the Colossus whose feet had trampled on freedom and religion, was followed by a religious revival which was like a spring after a long winter. But it was like an English spring. There were days that were so warm that they appeared unseasonable, and there were days of driving rain and unexpected frost. For twenty years after the battle of Waterloo we can trace the checks, the conflicts, the signs of change and progress. In England the Evangelicals and Evangelical books, such as those by Scott, Venn, and Wilberforce, did much for religion, but in 1822 there were only twelve Evangelical clergymen in London. The older school adhering to the principles of the Caroline divines was not extinct; words, doctrines, and practices which were afterwards attributed to the Tractarians had, as a matter of fact, never been entirely forgotten. The piety of this older school was not dead. One of the most striking instances of integrity in high places is that of Archbishop Howley when he visited King George IV in his last illness. It is recorded that the King ' turned round to the Arch-Bishop to receive the Host '. The archbishop ' declined administering the same until such time as His Majesty was more calm and free from anger '. The King, who had quarrelled with an attendant, sent for the man, shook him by the hand, sincerely forgave him, and after a few moments of solemn devotion received the sacrament.[1] But on the whole forgetfulness, ignorance, and aimlessness

---

[1] For this, see J. Wickham Legg, *English Church Life from the Restoration to the Tractarian Movement*, p. 46 (Longmans, London, 1914). This

were prevalent, and the slackness of the clergy did nothing to save their popularity.

In France the opposition to religion was most bitter and determined. The circulation of infidel and immoral books was enormous: in less than eight years more than two million two hundred thousand such volumes were printed in Paris and hawked through the country districts. The official recognition of the Church and the laws passed to support it, so far from strengthening religion, made it suspected. In 1830 priests hardly dared to show themselves in the streets of Paris, and two years later during the visitation of cholera they were insulted even in the exercise of their heroic devotion to the sick. In Germany the new political grouping of the different States made it necessary for each State to make a separate concordat with the Pope. But a concordat did not always bring concord even in Bavaria or in Köln, where the vast majority of the people were Roman Catholic. There was continual friction between Church and State, a friction which was inflamed by the imprisonment of the Archbishops of Köln and Posen in 1837, an act of tyranny which produced an inevitable reaction in favour of Rome. In the meantime religion was not only retarded by these dissensions but numbed by the frigid individualism and scepticism which blew from the Protestant districts of Prussia.

And yet a change was coming. In France a pleiad of distinguished writers were devoting all their great abilities to the defence of Christianity. They included Chateaubriand, de Maistre, de Bonald, and Lamennais, whose names cannot be forgotten either in the history of French

---

use of the word *Host* was doubtless extremely rare in the English Church at that period. The rule of receiving the Holy Communion fasting had never become extinct. As an instance of this the Rev. G. C. Berkeley, vicar of Southminster, Essex, told me that when he was a boy at Charterhouse, *c.* A.D. 1824, his 'dame', an elderly Evangelical lady, observed this rule, not breaking her fast till some time after midday.

literature or in the annals of this revival of religion. They, and some of their immediate successors, such as the great preacher Lacordaire, are sometimes described as the prophets of a Liberal Catholicism, but it would be more accurate to say that they wished to Catholicize Liberalism, political Liberalism. 'People tremble before Liberalism,' said Lamennais, 'Catholicize it and society will be born again.' Germany, on the other hand, produced teachers of philosophy and religion who were too anxious to adapt Christianity to the new intellectual transformation of the period, and had to encounter the massive but enlightened conservatism of John Adam Möhler (d. 1838) and later of Döllinger, the greatest figure of modern Catholic Germany.

Interwoven with a definitely religious thought and life was Romanticism. The men of the Romantic movement burnt what their teachers had worshipped and worshipped what their teachers had burnt. We have previously noticed some of the characteristics of Romanticism. It was not a mere attempt to walk back into the Middle Ages. On the contrary, the literature of the time proves that it was deliberately modern. It disliked the grey tones and the stiff outlines of a false classicism. It craved for colour. The dissolution of the Napoleonic empire brought into play a love of home, of fatherland, and national traditions. The Romantics were tired of individualism. They had learnt that brotherhood and freedom are not to be attained by a violent dislocation of society. They recognized the existence of mystery, of something more than meets the eye. That is why they preferred a ruined abbey to a church which was just an oblong room adorned outside with a Doric portico and inside with three galleries resting on tubes of cast iron. Among the charming letters of Sir Walter Scott is one to George Crabbe in which he makes the modest confession that to his own 'Gothic ear, the *Stabat Mater*, the *Dies Irae*, and some of the other hymns of the Catholic

Church, are more solemn and affecting than the fine classical poetry of Buchanan!'[1] These words correspond with his liking for mediaeval Scottish architecture and for episcopacy, and they bring us very close to the heart of the religious side of the Romantic movement.

Individualism and isolation in philosophy and religion, with the doubt which they engendered, were met by their opposite extremes. There came in time certain ideas concerning development and evolution which, whether they led to positivism or to an exaggerated socialism, taught an extreme anti-individualism. Comte, the philosopher who made humanity an idol, taught that 'the individual is only an abstraction'; sociologists made the State man's providence and his proprietor; and scientists, teaching men to realize the antiquity and the vastness of the universe, chilled them with the thought of the pettiness and the fragility of the individual life. Something was needed, something distinct from the mania of egoism and from the paralysis of believing oneself to be too paltry to matter. Was it not then right that men should think more about the Christian Church? And, as a matter of fact, the idea of the Church made a great appeal to some of the finest minds in Europe, who believed that man is truly a social being and that nevertheless the individual human person has an eternal and not a merely ephemeral value.

What is the Church and what ought to be the relation of the Church to society? Joseph de Maistre and Lamennais in France, Schleiermacher and Möhler in Germany, John Henry Newman and John Frederick Denison Maurice in England, tried to grapple with the question. Some of these writers had to encounter a storm

---

[1] *Memoirs of the Life of Sir Walter Scott*, vol. iii, p. 25 (Cadell, Edinburgh, 1837). Among the many precious pieces of history in this volume is the story that the inhabitants of the island of Egg laughed at their neighbours of Rum as *Protestants of the yellow stick*, as having been converted to Protestantism by the malacca cane of their chieftain.

of opposition, and doubtless no one of them was infallible. But they all believed in Christ and all believed that there is a kingdom of Christ, a supernatural society, the depositary of those laws which alone can guide men to brotherhood and happiness, and that the collective experience and witness of the Church are God's remedy against anarchy and doubt. This renewed belief in the kingdom of God, visibly manifested in the Church, has been fruitful in philanthropic heroism at home and missionary heroism abroad. But what this belief meant for the inner life of the Christian can nowhere be discovered more truly than in a study of the beginning of the Oxford Movement.

The Oxford Movement became an effective force at the end of 1833 when it was joined by Edward Bouverie Pusey, who had been made Regius Professor of Hebrew in 1828. His solid learning, impressive sermons, and Spartan loyalty to the Church of England kept the movement from disintegration. But the author of it was John Keble, manly, unaffected, true gentleman and poet, whose verses had been published in 1827, the year before John Henry Newman[1] became vicar of this parish. It is nearly one hundred years ago, and the time has come when we can calmly estimate the verdict passed upon the Tractarians by their opponents, neglecting the verdict of the mob and the infamous insinuations which were conveyed year after year in the cartoons of *Punch*. The criticisms made by Mark Pattison and Dean Stanley deserve more serious attention. Pattison's own words of acid disappointment unconsciously reveal to us why he was not a competent critic of the movement. He had been a blind disciple of Newman and Pusey, but quite correctly says that his Anglicanism had been a ' garment '

---

[1] The name was then pronounced 'Nooman', the 'ew' being sounded like the 'oe' in 'shoe'. I learned this from one of the very last persons who remembered Newman in his Oxford days, Dr. James Bellamy, President of St. John's College, Oxford.

and his Catholicism a ' husk '.[1] Under that garment and that husk he had remained at heart a Calvinist who had never consecrated his intellect to the ' reasonable service ' of grasping the theology of the Church as a whole. And it was that very fact which made him disdainfully discontented with the lesser Tractarians whose intellectual abilities were smaller than his own. Newman was a far greater man than Pattison, but he could, as we shall see, find room for the ordinary Christian, the 'little ones' of Christ.

Dean Stanley, in his essay entitled ' The Oxford School ', pays a sincere tribute to the learning of Pusey, saying, ' He was deeply learned in all the learning of the Germans '.[2] We may easily believe that if Newman had thoroughly known the German language he would have employed with telling effect the works of the great German Roman Catholics who exposed the unbelief of their compatriots. Pusey, however, was well acquainted not only with German books but also with some of the leading German Protestant scholars, and Stanley does not call in question Pusey's wisdom in abandoning the too optimistic views which he once entertained with regard to German religion. Keble is faintly praised by Stanley, who, in words that to a modern reader appear grotesque, says concerning Newman, ' it may be doubted whether in the whole range of historical or theological thought there is a single subject in which he has left his permanent mark '.[3] That, indeed, is a strange judgement to pass upon the man who taught half the thoughtful minds in Christendom to ask themselves in what sense they held that there has been, and ought to be, any development in Christian theology. But behind the

---

[1] Mark Pattison, *Memoirs*, pp. 327, 328 (Macmillan & Co., London, 1885). Pattison, however, testifies to the intense hatred with which 'Puseyites' were regarded: 'If you were able to describe a man as a Puseyite, he became, *ipso facto*, unfit for any public appointment ', p. 230.
[2] *Edinburgh Review*, April 1881, p. 316.
[3] *Loc. cit.*, p. 313.

verdict of these two critics, and that of Dr. Arnold,[1] there is one great fundamental error. It is the error of not recognizing the religious importance of the Tractarians.

The Oxford Movement of the nineteenth century, like the Oxford Movement of the eighteenth, was concerned with religion, the relation of the soul to God. We cannot dismiss Wesley and Whitefield, or even St. Peter and St. John, by pointing out that they did some foolish actions. Nor have we disposed of the Tractarians by saying that they had their follies. The real fool is the man who is so afraid of making mistakes that he will do nothing for God. 'A man's error', said Newman, 'may be more acceptable to God than his truth.' The Tractarians tried to call men back to the Christian character. And they were right, as the Continental theologians were right, in seeing that this character was threatened by excessive individualism. The intellectual life, the moral life, and the devotional life were all threatened: the intellectual life by arbitrary and self-willed theories about religion, the moral life by a Christianity which Pusey called 'Christianity without the Cross', and the devotional life by a growing irreverence in worship. What was to be the remedy? The Tractarians saw a remedy in the Church, not as a substitute for Christ but as the body of Christ. The Church, in Newman's beautiful phrase, is 'a home for the lonely',[2] and the Christian must realize himself as a member of that body, an inmate of that home.

---

[1] *Edinburgh Review*, April 1836. Dr. Arnold poured torrential abuse upon the 'Oxford Malignants', whose 'fanaticism' he describes as 'the fanaticism of mere foolery'. Some excuse for his words may be found in the fact that they were written during the heat of the controversy concerning Dr. Hampden, whose latitudinarian views were assailed by the Tractarians. Hampden little deserved such a vigorous defence. His hatred of Tractarianism led him in 1842 to require a candidate for the degree of B.D. to write in support of a low doctrine of the Eucharist. For an impartial account of this 'high-handedness and shabbiness' see R. W. Church, *The Oxford Movement* (Macmillan, London, 1891).

[2] *Parochial and Plain Sermons*, vol. iv, p. 185 (Rivingtons, London, 1882).

This spiritual society had been guided by the Spirit of God. Guided by Him the Church had been able slowly to carry forward a process of selection, and to assimilate the thoughts and arguments which she derived from different systems but which contributed to her own development. The individual teacher who by taking part in this process of selection helps Christianity to advance must exercise his talent under a sense of grave personal responsibility. He has to bear in mind his duty to all who like himself are members of the mystical body of Christ. If he has any real belief in the Church, he will consider and calculate the probable effect of what he says and writes, he will pray that none of those who seek God will be confounded through him. He contributes to a common store. He strengthens the brethren while he advances knowledge.

But what is the position of those Christians who have neither the time nor the learning nor the penetration to read much or think much or argue much about the truths of religion? Are they to be regarded as having no claim to wisdom, is their judgement of no value, are they necessarily ignorant, narrow-minded, and without any comprehension of the world of thought? No. The case is far otherwise. Not only have the simple and unlearned at their service the contemplation, the diligence, the erudition of the learned defenders of the faith, so that when they hear that faith assailed, they do not feel alone, but are conscious that they have on their side men whose intellectual distinction cannot be questioned. Newman has something more to say than that. Simple Christians can show in a marked and unmistakable degree the refining elevating influence of religion, because, though their powers of reasoning may be small, their faith 'fits them to be the instruments and organs, the voice and the hands and the feet of Him who is invisible, the divine wisdom in the Church—who knows what they know not, understands their words, for they are His own, and directs their efforts to His own issues, though they see them not, because they dutifully place themselves upon His path'.[1] How remote is this doctrine from Mark Pattison's inept denunciation of 'the mere mechanical association of the unthinking members of the Catholic Church'.[2] It is the doctrine of a vital, spiritual, organic unity in which the highly educated intellectual men and women have not a monopoly of truth, because life is deeper than thought and the divine Reason is deeper than man's reasoning. The fact that God chose the foolish things of the world to confound the wise, and the weak things of the world to confound the things that were mighty, is no disparagement of learning and philosophy. It really gives us a broader view of both.

And just as in the intellectual life the richer must help the poorer and all draw wisdom from Him in whom all wisdom is centred, so it is in the moral life. The weaker members of the Church have a right to some of the resources of the stronger. The writings of the saints and the great devotional books of Christendom help to neutralize the effect of the evil that is in the world. But the saints are not dead. To a generation that was ceasing to call Mary blessed, Keble spoke of the 'blessed maid' as Bishop Ken had spoken. And every soul in the Church, while retaining that true individuality which Newman emphasized to the very last,[3] is brought near to the spirits of the just, and, as he says, 'if we would be worthy to hold communion with believers of every time and place, let us hold communion duly with those of our own day and our own neighbourhood'. The sanctity of the Christian is not an isolated sanctity.

---

[1] 'Wisdom, as contrasted with Faith and with Bigotry', in *Sermons Preached before the University of Oxford*, 2nd edition, p. 300 (London, Rivington, 1844).

[2] *Op. cit.*, p. 210.

[3] *Op. cit.*, iv, p. 80, and the meditation on 'God the blessedness of the soul' in *Meditations and Devotions*, p. 442 (Longmans, London, 1893).

We can support each other, help each other to live in an atmosphere which is frequently a poisoned atmosphere. We do not help each other simply by what is most common and fundamental in us all, but by something, however small it may be, which is distinctive. Every one whose life is a protest against evil helps to save others from moral loneliness. The Tractarians did not build these theories in the clouds. They laid the utmost stress upon the principle that intellectual truth must be reached by moral character. Since their day some advance has been made in the study of social problems and something has been done to lessen human misery. But who is there among us who could surpass the piercing eloquence with which Pusey denounced the Poor Law of early Victorian times and depicted the Christian who had neglected the destitute, standing for judgement before the Son of Man? [1]

And in worship the Church is also the home for the lonely. The Tractarians exhorted men to be reverent even in the meanest church and before the poorest altar because reverence is simply an acknowledgement of the presence of God. It is not solitary, it is in company with angels and archangels and all God's saints. By baptism we were incorporated into a Church far wider than the English alone or the Roman alone or the Greek alone, and by the very institution of that visible rite Christ indicated that the Church was to be 'one visible association of Christians, and only one; and that permanent'.[2] Just as the unlimited sway of private judgement had tended to destroy the sense of responsibility for truth, so it had tended to destroy and disown the duty of reverence. Newman, speaking in this church, spoke of professing Christians who 'considered awe to be superstition and reverence to be slavery', who

---

[1] *Christianity without the Cross a Corruption of the Gospel of Christ*, p. 27 (Parker, Oxford, 1875).
[2] Newman, *op. cit.*, vol. vii, p. 236.

had learnt to be 'familiar and free with sacred things, as it were on principle'.[1] It is well that the Tractarians rebuked that spirit and taught that the reverence due to God from human persons cannot be only mental reverence. It is paid to an incarnate Saviour, and it must embrace man's entire personality, including outward actions and touching outward things. And had not outward forms and words and rites, appealing to the heart and to the imagination of the worshipper, kept alive a knowledge of God's mysteries and served to unite men with that great society which even in time has looked into eternity? That society extending through earth and heaven around the throne of the Lamb is in its worship the home of every lonely soul. For we are, when we worship, taken out of ourselves, out of the toil and fretfulness of daily life, into that stillness which reigns in heaven by the sea of glass. You may remember how in one of the most famous of his sermons Newman speaks of heaven as 'home' and how the thought comes back in the poem, 'Lead, kindly light.'

The belief of the Tractarians in the Church must be studied from the beginning if we would understand their relation to the European thought of their period and to the history of the English Church since Newman's historic surrender to the Church of Rome. Newman clung to the Church of England almost with desperation, he left it with agony. And his heartbroken complaint uttered at Littlemore is so pathetic because in a great measure it was true. The Church of England, which had been losing so heavily for two generations, seemed to him unlike a home, unlike a mother to her children. 'Thou sellest them for nought to the stranger that passes by.'[2] The existing authorities and organs of the Church seemed to repudiate, and even to repudiate as

[1] *Op. cit.*, vol. viii, p. 6.
[2] Sermon on 'the Parting of Friends' in *Sermons bearing on Subjects of the Day*, 2nd edition, p. 462 (London, Rivington, 1844).

dishonest, a position which was a logical adjustment of the teaching of the great English divines of the seventeenth century. He saw, in the main correctly, that if that position were abandoned, Englishmen must either betake themselves to Rome or to a Protestantism which Rationalism would certainly destroy.[1] The treatment of the Tractarians by the authorities of the Church of England simply played into the hands of Cardinal Wiseman, a true child of Seville and of Rome, a man of fashion and a man of letters, ostentatious but tactful, florid in his language and expansive in his sympathies. After the Oxford converts had gone and accepted an Ultramontane form of Roman Catholicism, it was the massive weight of Pusey which gave the Church of England time to recover. 'Cunctando restituit rem.' Newman recognized what the common people recognized when they adopted Whately's word 'Puseyite'. In addressing Pusey in 1866 he wrote, 'You more than any one else alive, have been the present and untiring agent by whom a great work has been effected. . . . There is no one anywhere—among ourselves, in your own body, or, I suppose, in the Greek Church—who can affect so large a circle of men, so virtuous, so able, so learned, so zealous, as come, more or less, under your influence.'

Newman, after he joined the Church of Rome, was regarded as suspect. To Roman theologians who believed in the immutability of dogma his celebrated *Essay on the Development of Christian Doctrine* seemed tainted with a heterodox liberalism. When the Jesuit Perrone attacked the teaching of this book Wiseman had the generosity to give Newman his support, but the ordinary dispensers of official doctrine were on the other side. Newman's philosophic insight had taught him to proclaim the principle of evolution in the realm of theology before it was definitely proclaimed in the realm of natural science. He saw that

[1] See app. note 25, p. 281.

the doctrines of the Church had been 'evolved' with 'effort, hesitation, suspense, interruption, swayings to the right hand and to the left'. He believed that dogmatic formulae represent to us the truths confided by God to the Church. They represent them 'economically', to use a word familiar in Greek theology, in an outward form, as the ideas conveyed by the senses represent the external world, imperfectly indeed, but in a way suited to our practical needs. They are fashioned in accordance with the time and the persons concerned, and the task of developing them in a manner suited to other times and other people is divinely given to the Church as it is gradually influenced by advancing culture and knowledge.

It is remarkable that, a few years before Newman, a Bohemian priest, Anthony Günther (1783–1863), had been grappling with the same problem with no little ability and originality. Günther held that the dogmatic formulae of the Church, being adapted to the requirements of this or that particular epoch, give to the faithful the best possible approximation to the truths in question, but may be capable of revision and improvement in the future as knowledge advances. Therefore the decisions of the Church in matters of faith may only have a provisional value. Günther unfortunately fell into such grave errors with regard to some of the fundamental doctrines of Christianity that any similar theories were certain to meet with distrust and opposition. And Newman was suspected although he fell into no such errors as Günther and firmly held the teaching of the creeds. He presented his theory of the evolution of dogma as a hypothesis and carefully sought to lay down the conditions under which this hypothesis can be entertained without in any way impugning the integrity of the Christian revelation. There is a stationary principle as well as a principle of progression included in a genuine development, and Newman lays down careful tests for distinguishing a true from a false development, though his historical knowledge was not always enough to enable him to use his own tests, and he was not fully alive to the importance of historical evidence when the genesis of a particular doctrine is under consideration. The famous passage in his Anglican sermon on Development, where he compares dogmatic theology with the science of the musician, has a double application. For while it suggests that the dogmatic formulae which convey to the soul divine truths can never adequately represent these truths as they are in themselves, it also suggests the necessity of strictly preserving the formulae. The musician does not despise his technique, though he knows that the mechanism is not identical with the ideas that it conveys. To Newman's mind musical sounds brought 'echoes from our Home', and the theology of the Church, if it is to speak, like music, to the soul, must be preserved from error and distortion.

Newman established once for all the fact that if we believe the Gospels, we must admit that the principal dogmatic definitions of the Church were the alternatives to the corruptions which they excluded, and that they protected and did not supersede the original ideals of Christianity. But it cannot be denied that his apologetics were sometimes reckless. His defence of the doctrine of Transubstantiation in his *Apologia*[1], where he maintains that nobody knows anything about substance, and that the 'Catholic doctrine leaves phenomena alone' and 'deals with what no one on earth knows anything about', is like an attempt to build faith upon a foundation of agnosticism.

Let us return to 1835, a year which marks an epoch in the history of theology. In that year Dr. Pusey published his elaborate treatise on Baptism, and became at once the head and centre of the Tractarian movement. The same

[1] See app. note 26, p. 281.

year appeared in Germany Strauss's *Life of Jesus*, and a work on the Pastoral Epistles of St. Paul by Ferdinand Christian Baur, the chief of the Tübingen school. Strauss made no pretension to have applied the processes of literary criticism to the sources of the life of Jesus. But the Tübingen school attempted to bring the somewhat vague results of literary criticism into connexion with historical processes, and at the same time 'to force Christian history into the Hegelian *tripudium* of thesis, antithesis, and synthesis'. The Tübingen view of the New Testament was injured by false spectacles; one eye of the critic was blurred by the old Lutheran opposition between faith and good works, the other eye by the doctrines of eighteenth-century Rationalism. The original 'thesis', Jewish Unitarianism, represented by St. Peter, was to be found in certain sections of the Synoptic Gospels. St. Paul represented the 'antithesis'; he quarrelled permanently with St. Peter, and being convinced that the Gentiles would not come to Christ by way of circumcision, he proclaimed salvation by faith. Four Epistles, those to the Galatians, Romans, and Corinthians, reveal his antithesis, and they only are genuine. The Apocalypse denounces St. Paul under the name of Balaam and emanates from the Petrine side. The two parties, Petrine and Pauline, continued their struggle until both were threatened by a common enemy, the essentially pagan Gnosticism of the second century. They were then forced to unite. The necessary synthesis took place. And of the twenty-seven books of the New Testament, twenty-two were either revised or written in the second century to obliterate the ugly feud of earlier days.

No more brilliant attempt has ever been made to explain Christianity, and to explain it away. It was in harmony with the philosophy of the time, it was a natural reaction against the undue sentimentalism of Schleiermacher, and it had the merit of forcing students to notice the individuality of the different sacred writers and to ask themselves what was the real relation of St. Paul to the Saviour whose bond-servant he proclaimed himself to be. But it is false. Even the four Epistles to which Baur appealed do not really support his view of the relation between St. Paul and the original apostles. And every addition of an epistle to Baur's list of genuine epistles made his theory weaker. If we turn to early Christian literature outside the New Testament the same principle holds good. It was vital to Baur's theory that no book of a Catholic character should have existed in the early years of the second century before the alleged reconciliation of the Petrine and Pauline parties. But in the letters of St. Ignatius, now proved to be genuine, we find a Catholic Christianity, name and thing, existing at that very period. Thus the Tübingen theory in its original form, and that was its only consistent form, has tumbled like a tower of sand. It had begun to tumble when Renan, a flippant pagan, presented to the world in his *Life of Jesus* (1863) German infidelity in a magical French disguise, and was hailed by Strauss as an ally across the Rhine. Baur was the forerunner of 'Modern Protestantism', and Renan the forerunner of Modernism.

With regard to the date of the books of the New Testament, there has been a retreat to tradition along almost the whole front.[1] There are indeed some critics, mostly Dutch, who have insisted that we must deny the authenticity of even those writings which Baur treated as genuine. And it is not without some reason that such critics urge that if we assume that miracles never happened and that there was nothing supernatural in the life of Jesus, time must have elapsed before Christianity could assume the coherently supernatural form which it takes throughout the New Testament. But they themselves, like Baur, attempt to make Catholic Christianity the creation of a period later

[1] See app. note 27, p. 282.

than the apostolic age, and in so doing make the second century responsible for the first. That is a wild impossibility, and it is on the same intellectual level as the old Keltic legend that St. Patrick swam the Irish Channel carrying his own head between his own teeth.

It is not my purpose to give any complete picture of the present state of New Testament Criticism, but there are two points which force themselves upon our attention. They are both closely connected with the plan of making the evidence support views about our Lord derived from Deists and Rationalists of the eighteenth century. The first is the strong prejudice that exists in 'Modern Protestantism' against admitting the possibility that the Fourth Gospel is, what it professes to be, the work of a personal eyewitness of the ministry of our Lord. The second is the attempt to lay at the door of St. Paul the guilt of radically altering and indeed perverting the Christian religion. With regard to St. John's Gospel, the internal signs of an exact acquaintance with the historical and religious environment of our Lord are so numerous, and the author's knowledge of small details is so evident, that to deny that it is the work of one who knew Christ in the days of His flesh leads us only into a blind alley. Those who do deny it have sometimes plainly been influenced by presuppositions which they have not cared to disguise, while English scholarship has already done so much to put the question on the basis of ascertained facts that those who are willing to be convinced can find more than sufficient reasons for a favourable verdict.[1]

With regard to St. Paul, the rehabilitation of the

[1] For the most careful sifting of the linguistic evidence, see Professor C. F. Burney, *The Aramaic Origin of the Fourth Gospel* (Oxford, Clarendon Press, 1922). Dr. Burney's investigations strongly confirm the opinion that the author of the Fourth Gospel, if not the son of Zebedee, was an actual eyewitness of the events which he describes. Almost the whole of Modernist theology is allied with the rash assumption, common to German Rationalism, that the author was *not* an eyewitness.

authenticity of nearly all his Epistles, even in the eyes of non-Christian critics, has produced the most startling results. The task which Baur set himself was to prove where St. Paul differed from the original apostles. But he never showed what was equally important, namely, in what essential points he did agree with those apostles. Readers who allow the texts to speak for themselves would affirm that with regard to the incarnation, the resurrection, redemption, and the sacraments, there is no vital difference between St. Paul's Epistles, St. Peter's First Epistle, and St. John's Gospel. All give us real aspects of primitive Christianity. To escape the inevitable conclusion, we must either copy the Tübingen school and pronounce spurious every document which we find inconvenient, or we must say that St. Paul recast the Gospel in the moulds of pagan thought. Whether he began the process of recasting when he was meditating in the deserts of Arabia or became infected with it when in company with the citizens of Antioch and Corinth, the defenders of this theory have not yet decided. The bolder advocates of it say quite simply that St. Paul constructed his own theory of salvation and of the Person of Christ, making Him a saviour god like Adonis, Osiris, and Attis.[1] The more cautious, like Harnack, deny that St. Paul corrupted Christianity, but find themselves forced to admit what they have previously denied, and to deplore, as Harnack does, the wrong direction of St. Paul's 'speculative ideas'.[2] Only good is done to history and theology by

[1] So Alfred Loisy, *Hibbert Journal*, October 1911, p. 51.
[2] In his famous *What is Christianity?* Harnack strongly criticizes the critics who either maintain that St. Paul corrupted Christianity or call him the real founder of that religion. But a few pages later he admits that St. Paul did corrupt it by his speculative ideas. A little later we find an explanation of these words. He says: 'Paul became the author of the speculative idea that not only was God in Christ, but that Christ himself was possessed of a peculiar nature of a heavenly kind.' *Op. cit.*, English trans., pp. 176, 184 (Williams & Norgate, London, 1901). In plain words St. Paul invented the doctrine of our Lord's Deity.

a candid recognition of the different manners in which the apostles apprehended Christian truth, or by noting the points of contact between Christianity and the pagan religions which were feeling after God. Genuine Christianity gains by genuine criticism. But it is mere vanity when students, regardless of time and space, seek for the origins of Christian beliefs and institutions anywhere from Memphis to Mesopotamia, from Elam to Eleusis,[1] origins which might be found in the nearest London synagogue. But they can be discovered in the synagogue only on one assumption: I mean the well-grounded assumption that the New Testament does not misrepresent the teaching which our Lord gave to His immediate followers, and that these followers and worshippers gave to St. Paul the right hands of fellowship. A divine Christ, and only a divine Christ, explains the transition from Judaism to the religion of the early Church in Corinth. 'Modern Protestantism' is betraying St. Paul with a kiss. Modern Roman Catholicism is wont to pass him by. In the meantime let it be our happiness to follow in the steps of Robertson and Lightfoot, of Liddon, and of Sanday also when he was still unconquered by the Germans, and let ourselves be guided by St. Paul to the life of the risen and ascended Christ and the life in Christ.

The reaction against irresponsible criticism.is unreflecting credulity, and widespread scepticism is always followed by superstition. So it was that the Vatican Council of 1870, not content with asserting the central truths of

[1] One of the pioneers in this eccentricity was Professor Percy Gardner in his pamphlet, *The Origin of the Lord's Supper* (Macmillan & Co., London, 1893). According to this learned writer, St. Paul, during his stay in Corinth, was so much impressed with the Eleusinian mysteries that he thought it would be good for the Church to have a similar institution. St. Paul therefore 'asserts that such a sacrament was sanctioned by a special communication from his Lord'. The professor eulogizes the apostle for his action and says, 'Surely there is nothing in all this to pain or shock a modern Christian'.

Christianity in opposition to contemporary infidelity, was persuaded to declare the Pope to be infallible and his 'definitions' to be 'irreformable of themselves, and not of the consent of the Church'. By this definition of the dogma of the infallibility of the Roman Pontiff, a dogma declared to be 'divinely revealed', the Pope was clearly made superior to the Church, and Ultramontanism secured its decisive triumph over Gallicanism and, we must add, over history and truth.[1]

The Vatican Council opened on December the 8th, 1869, a day of heavy rain and threatening clouds, a date purposely selected that the immense concourse of prelates should do honour to the Immaculate Conception of the Blessed Virgin which the Pope, Pius IX, had previously defined. The bishops met in the north transept of the basilica of St. Peter. On a throne before them sat the aged pontiff, his highest hopes in the balance; near them were pictures which falsified Church history; and above them were the words of Christ, 'I have prayed for thee that thy faith fail not', placed there in order to suggest, in defiance of patristic interpretation, the infallibility of every Pope in faith and morals. The Council closed on July the 18th, 1870, when amid peals of thunder and flashes of terrific lightning five hundred and thirty-three bishops shouted *placet*, and only two, one Italian and one American, refused assent.

The full inner story of the Vatican Council is never likely to be known. But it is known that on the winning side were the bishops of Southern Europe and Southern America, men who in their seminaries had been fed upon the teaching of Liguori; and that on the other side had been the majority of the German, Austrian, and Hungarian bishops, together

---

[1] See *Edinburgh Review*, July 1871, article 'The Vatican Council', and E. S. Purcell, *Life of Cardinal Manning*, vol. ii (London, Macmillan & Co., 1895).

with the very flower of the French episcopate; that tumult, invective, and intrigue prevailed to a degree which would be impossible in any ecclesiastical assembly in this country; that the minority, apparently numbering eighty-eight, disputed every inch of the ground; that some of them in so doing committed the fatal mistake of protesting against the threatened definition as 'inopportune', a mere strategical move to screen their conviction that it was false; that all but the courageous two left Rome rather than face their enemies; and that among the foremost champions of the new dogma was Archbishop Manning who was well supported by *The Times* newspaper,[1] a paper which later, in the days of Leo XIII, supported the papal condemnation of Anglican Ordinations.

The true meaning of the dogma remains unsettled. On the one hand, we find minimizers who assure us that the Popes have hardly ever spoken infallibly, declare that they cannot act apart from the Church, and suggest that it can only be seldom and slowly that a decision can be made as to when the Pope has finally settled a dispute on faith or morals. On the other hand, the more extreme supporters of the dogma desired an oracle whose daily utterances on religion could not lawfully be disputed by any Christian. The majority of the bishops who voted *placet* were probably a little nearer to the second of these two opinions than to the first. They wanted neither an infallibility which settles no disputes, nor one that is the mouthpiece of novel revelations to mankind; but they wanted to render impossible that appeal to 'a future Council' which had sometimes qualified men's professed submission to the Papacy, they wanted prompt and definite answers to difficult questions, more prompt than could be given by a Council, and

---

[1] English secular newspapers provided Manning with his trump card by their assertions that the Ultramontanes alone were consistent and straightforward. Purcell, *op. cit.*, p. 456.

therefore they intended to include in the definition all papal decisions which affect 'such acts as are derived from faith and morals'. The determination, the energy, the fever, which marked the action of the papal party can only be explained by the fact that they regarded the dogma as one of vital moment, indispensable and practical. At the time of the Council the English Roman Catholic laity were, according to Manning's own statement, 'averse and impatient'. And Newman, whom the Pope of set purpose omitted to summon as a consultor to Rome, had expressed intense anxiety lest the doctrine should be defined and 'an aggressive, insolent faction be allowed to make the heart of the just sad, whom the Lord hath not made sorrowful'. But when the deed was done Newman acquiesced, so did the vigorous Bishop Strossmayer, the friend of Slavonic nationalism, so did the learned Bishop Hefele, Dupanloup the zealous pastor of souls, and even Archbishop Kenrick of St. Louis who marshalled the strongest arguments to prove the doctrine to be untenable. It is tempting to conjecture what might have happened if Manning had remained within the Church of England, and if the see of Westminster had been occupied by an hereditary Roman Catholic.

In the midst of the lamentable surrender one great man stood firm. It was Ignatius von Döllinger. Döllinger was born within a year of Newman's birth and he died at a great age within a few months of Newman's death. He had long been the pillar of German Roman Catholicism, one of the most active and enlightened branches of the Church. He was a power in Church and State, his influence was commanding. If he had not Newman's skill in accumulating brilliant arguments, he had far greater skill in accumulating a knowledge of historical facts. The better historian a man is, the better Christian he ought to be, and Döllinger's Christianity was put to a severe test. The progress of Ultramontanism in the middle of the nineteenth century could not fail to arouse alarm among German Catholics who were in the first rank of theological learning. Of these men Döllinger was the acknowledged chief. He foresaw the downfall of the Pope's temporal power, and as early as 1861 he delivered a series of lectures in Munich, in which he maintained that the secular kingdom of the Popes was not necessary for the discharge of their spiritual functions. In this matter the Ultramontanes were peculiarly sensitive, and the papal nuncio, who attended one of the lectures in deference to the lecturer's great reputation, did not remain until the end. When the Vatican Council drew near Döllinger published a series of letters, not Protestant or heretical, but forming an indictment of the policy which had converted the Papacy into an autocracy inconsistent with the rights of the episcopate. Himself a friend of the King of Bavaria, Ludwig II, he suggested that several European States should present to the Holy See a declaration that the definition of the new doctrine was against public policy. This plan was frustrated, largely by the skill of Manning and his clever and not too scrupulous Protestant ally Odo Russell, who was practically, though informally, British minister at the Vatican.

After the Council was over, the Archbishop of Munich, who had accepted the dogma which he had previously denounced, demanded Döllinger's submission. Döllinger then had to decide whether he could or could not endure to be excluded from that communion of which he had been one of the most renowned defenders, and which he had ever regarded as the true Church of Christ. He replied, 'As a Christian, as a theologian, as a historian, as a citizen, I cannot receive this doctrine'. He said with truth that the dogma was founded upon a novel interpretation of the texts of Scripture, and that to assert it would be a breach of his oath as a priest to interpret Scripture 'according to the unanimous consent of the Fathers', and that the bishops who had assented to the doctrine had been educated in seminaries which employed the false proof-passages in the books of Liguori and Perrone. He was excommunicated.[1]

Döllinger and his friends then found themselves in the position of being without a Church. He was unwilling to form a new body but associated himself with the newly formed Old Catholic Church which quickly allied itself with the old Church of Holland. Unfortunately the German-speaking Old Catholics, alike in Germany, Switzerland, and Austria, have shown little of the caution of their Dutch allies. In Holland nearly two hundred years after their separation from Rome the Old Catholics had kept the Mass in Latin, a celibate clergy, and the doctrines of Trent. But the rapid changes made in worship and discipline, especially the too hasty permission of clerical marriage, ruined the opportunities of this new German reformation. It was the work of scholars, and it was supported by adherents who were more anxious to protest against Rome than to live as practising Catholics. It left the ordinary people unmoved; and whereas schemes in favour of a Catholic system free from Rome were expected to attract Teutonic races, this expectation has been signally falsified. For the present it is among the Slavonic subjects of Rome that the revolt is most serious and most popular. It began among the numerous Poles in the United States, where the National Polish Church now numbers some 80,000 people. It has assumed larger proportions in Poland itself, where the religious order of the 'Mariaviten' revived the original Franciscan rules and was excommunicated by the Pope. The Mariaviten have shown great religious fervour and zeal for social service. In 1910 they were so numerous as to be already under three bishops who were consecrated by Archbishop Gul of Utrecht.[2] More recently has come the huge defection

[1] See Döllinger, *Erklärung an den Erzbischof von München-Freysing* (Munich, 1871).

[2] Bishop Kowalski, the General of the Order, was consecrated in 1909;

among the Czechs, people who never forgot John Hus and chafed under the rule of Austria and Rome. They have effected a union with the Serbian Orthodox Church, while retaining rites of the Western type to which they have been so long accustomed.[1]

What fate is in store for these Churches we can hardly forecast. They may make mistakes; the German-speaking Old Catholics have made serious mistakes. But they are free to occupy a position which is doctrinally and morally tenable unless the position of Döllinger and Kenrick and Strossmayer, and indeed that of the Church of England, is fundamentally wrong. And they may, if they will, help Eastern and Western Christendom to join hands in a day when a Christianity which called itself Pauline and was not, and a Christianity which called itself Petrine and was not, will learn better and unite in Christ.

In my first lecture it was suggested that a study of the Reformation and the Counter-Reformation proves the need and the importance of maintaining a middle path between two contrasted hostile movements. The need for that path, the oldest and yet the most progressive, has never been more serious than it is at present. Our relation to Rome and our relation to Geneva and Berlin are not dead questions of the seventeenth century; they affect our own intellectual and religious life and our whole attitude towards the reunion of Christendom. Sound learning and earnest reflexion will persuade us that others cannot drive us from our place, and that some of the unwise concessions which

Bishops Golembiowski and Próchniewski were consecrated at Lowicz in 1910. See Arthur Rhode, *Bei den Mariaviten* (E. Runge in Gr.-Lichterfelde-Berlin, 1911); *Kalender 1912 für das alt-katholische Haus* (Kempten im Allgäu, 1911); *Kalendarz Maryawicki*, 1914 (Lodz, Drukarnia Biskupa Maryawitów).

[1] The first bishop of the Czecho-Slovak Church, united with the Eastern Church, was consecrated at Belgrad, September the 25th, 1921. The service was described in the next day's issue of the Belgrad paper *Politika*.

we have been advised to make would hinder the very union which they are intended to promote. Our living authority is the whole Church of past and present days, and our freedom is limited by the laws made by Christ for His mystical bride. The use of ambiguous and equivocal formulae, like a lax hold upon things which have behind them the sanction of the whole Catholic Church, such as confirmation, episcopacy, and the sacramental system, would deprive the Churches in communion with the see of Canterbury of their unique capacity for reconciling the true but separated elements of Christianity which exist outside that communion. Doubtless the first condition of reunion is a thorough moral renovation, and in the true form of the Creed the holiness of the Church is affirmed after its unity and before its Catholicity, for the unity and the Catholicity of the Church largely depend upon the holiness of her children. But a moral renovation will necessarily strengthen opposition to any kind of make-believe or pretence in what we say, just as it will strengthen fidelity to that stationary element in revealed religion which is essential for the progress and formulation of Christian thought.

It is here that we touch the question of Modernism.

Modernism first in France and then in England has tried to meet the difficulties of faith in a novel manner. It endeavours to disarm doubt by dissolving truth. It has not been quite the same in France [1] and in England. The French form is nearer to Newman and Oxford, the English is nearer to Harnack and Berlin. And it is an interesting fact that though French Modernism showed a wider and more varied intellectual outlook than English Modernism, the French Modernists attacked those whom they called 'Intellectualists', while the English name the objects of their hostility 'Traditionalists'. But on both sides of the

[1] For Modernism in France see Albert Houtin, *Histoire du Modernisme catholique* (Paris, 1913).

Channel the Modernists have emphasized the weak elements in Newman's theory of the development of doctrine and the function of dogmatic formulae; they have leaned consciously or unconsciously upon a one-sided philosophy which denies the intervention of God in history; and they have recklessly assimilated many of the most dubious conclusions of German criticism.

These three mistakes led them to the strange opinion that it is right to worship Christ while not believing in His Deity; that it is right to receive the Holy Communion and declare in the most solemn of all prayers that Christ instituted this sacrament and commanded it to be continued, while doubting whether He ever intended it to be repeated;[1] and that it is right to declare that He rose again while holding that His body rotted in the grave. I submit that if it be right to employ words 'symbolically' so that they cover exactly what they were intended to exclude, and plainly do exclude, there is no superstition that cannot be condoned. If it be moral for an Englishman to assert that our Lord was born of the Virgin Mary when he holds that Christ was the Son of Joseph, then it is moral for a Frenchman to assent to the doctrine of the infallibility of the Pope when he believes the old Gallican doctrine of the Papacy, and it is moral for an Italian to recite the collect in honour of the holy house of Loretto when he is sure that it was not carried by angels from Nazareth to Loretto. Therefore Modernism is not, what it sometimes claims to be, a means of establishing a *modus vivendi* between Catholicism and Evangelicalism, but rather, as was wisely said several years ago by the present Dean of St. Paul's, an attempt to deal with the crisis of faith ' by establishing a *modus vivendi* between scepticism and superstition'.[2]

[1] 'He may be even uncertain whether Christ intended to institute a service which should be repeated.' *The Modern Churchman*, December 1920, p. 483.

[2] Dr. W. R. Inge, 'The Meaning of Modernism', *Quarterly Review*,

Nor can I see any fundamental difference between the Roman Catholic Modernists whom at that moment he was describing and the Protestant Modernists who have accepted the same standard of truthfulness.

The gravity of this crisis of faith is sometimes greatly exaggerated. I impute no unworthy motives to those who imagine that Christianity is being crucified by natural science and desire to save it from such a fate. But as a matter of fact no discoveries of science, not even the Copernican system or the truths of evolution, require us to abandon one single clause of the authoritative statement of the Christian faith, the Nicene Creed. The intelligent Greek bishops who composed it, and all the great Fathers of the Church, believed that their task was not one of innovation but of interpretation; and that the Holy Spirit was given to guide the Church in determining her creed, not to add to what was apostolical, but to express it in view of new intellectual situations. Above all, it was their transparent purpose to keep before the eyes of men that picture of God's nature which is gradually revealed to us in the Old and in the New Testament, and to enable them to find in Jesus Christ all that was found in Him by the apostles and the evangelists.

The problem which most concerned them is the problem which most concerns us. The doctrine of the Person of Christ is again the centre of discussion. 'What think ye of Christ?'

The question, 'What think ye of Christ?' is no obsolete question. It can never become superannuated. If we can be sure that there is a moral meaning in the universe and in our self, if we can make that supreme act of faith which is

---

April 1909. The same essay reappears under the two different titles of 'Catholic Modernism' and 'Roman Catholic Modernism' in Dr. Inge's *Outspoken Essays* (Longmans, London, 1919). The reason for these changes would appear to be the fact that after 1909 the name 'Modernist' became commonly adopted by a party of English Protestants.

equally the supreme act of reason, and say, 'I believe in God', I believe because this belief strengthens, settles, makes me more perfect, fits me for life, then we cannot ignore Jesus Christ. Nor can we think it right to divide our manhood, and say that we are willing to affirm as believers what we deny as thinkers. Christ meets us not as believers only nor as thinkers only, but as men. And He meets us as one Christ, not as a naturalistic Christ born in Judaea and as a supernatural Christ created by the Church. The Christ of history cannot be separated from the Christ of dogma, for both in history and in dogma we find the Christ of experience.[1]

There is still, as in the early nineteenth century, a theology which tends to the doctrine, or even teaches the doctrine, that Jesus was a human person, only with a much more perfect filial submission to God and confidence in God than we have known in other men. Some would say that each man may become all that Jesus was. And when the objection is raised that this view of the Founder of Christianity cannot be reconciled with the evidence of the New Testament, we are told that this evidence, and therefore the whole subsequent teaching of the Church, is deeply coloured by misunderstandings which were inevitable in the mental conditions of the period when the New Testament was written. Christ, we are told, was a genius, but the claim that His life was supernatural must be set aside. We are told to see in Him a combination of piety with talent and experience, talent which owes its origin to causes which are entirely natural though ordained by God, and experience which was conditioned in a manner wholly and solely normal.

Verse after verse in the New Testament proves that our Lord attributed to himself a significance for humanity far exceeding the limits imposed by such a theory. These

[1] For some words of Dr. T. B. Strong on the 'Jesus of History' see app. note 28, p. 284.

passages cannot all be wrong. They are too early in date, too coherent in character. And consequently we must conclude either that He was a deluded dreamer, as some indeed would tell us, or that He was and is infinitely more than an important link in the chain of human history. The evidence demands a clear decision in favour of the supernatural estimate of His Person. That estimate is from the point of view of historical exegesis unassailable. He interpreted His life, His death, His resurrection as the work of divine interposition. And if we, like Him, do not reject but admit supernaturalism in the sphere of the spirit, we cannot say 'Thus far and no farther' and, unlike Him, proscribe supernaturalism in the sphere of the physical.

This is not a question only for the learned and the intellectual. The simplest Christian can see a difference between the assertion that the risen Christ is a divine Person with a human nature, human though changed, and the assertion that He is a human person without a body. Even children raise the question. Not very long ago I was taking a country walk with a little boy about seven years of age. Suddenly he asked me, 'Had they churches before Jesus came?' I answered briefly as well as I could. Instantly the child said, 'Could Jesus hear them?' You may be sure that I answered 'Yes'. He would not have understood such words as 'Deity' and 'pre-existence'. But it meant something to him that the Jesus of the manger and the cross always cared for the world into which He came. That has not been the conviction of one man, one school, one epoch, but the Christian conviction of all ages, as it has been the Christian conviction of all ages that 'Christ died for our sins, and that He was buried, and that He was raised on the third day'. If St. Paul and the disciples who taught him that confession of faith had only believed that the spirit of Christ had been raised to heaven after death, the mention of His burial would have been totally superfluous and the mention of the third day would have been obviously misleading.

Just as nothing less than Deity can satisfy the language in which our Lord advanced His claims, so nothing less than resurrection from a tomb left empty can satisfy the language of the apostles and the evangelists. On those two truths the Christian Church was built. They are the foundation of a home of freedom, hope, and joy, not a prison for the confinement of slaves; and it is false to teach that fidelity to these truths is a mark of obscurantism and stagnation. The life of Jesus on earth is but the manifestation in human form of those attributes which have been His from all eternity; and we comprehend His human character, we learn its value for our own development, when we can say with all our heart, 'Thou art the everlasting Son of the Father, When thou tookest upon thee to deliver man, thou didst not abhor the Virgin's womb, When thou hadst overcome the sharpness of death, thou didst open the kingdom of heaven to all believers'.

It is this Christ, and no other, that binds us with the past and the future, with the good and holy of all periods since the world began, this Christ who alone at this moment is able to save. And if the scattered children of God are again to be made one, unity can only be secured from Him and through Him and in Him. The prospect of a united Christianity is distant, but the vision of peace is a little nearer than it was. What consolation, what courage, what energy, what progress this unity would bring, 'eye hath not seen nor ear heard, neither have entered into the heart of man'. But of this we may be certain. Those who believe that He is 'God of God, Light of Light', and believe that Jesus hears them, will beyond the possibility of doubt grow in the discernment of what that truth implies and of what is really inconsistent with it in thought or practice. If they do not live to see the accomplishment of their prayers for unity, they know that their work is not in vain. God is on their side, and in the unclouded presence of their Saviour they will find their reward. In the meantime let each one of us in looking at the image of our Redeemer crucified, not only see in His face the reflection of eternal love, but also see in His arms outstretched to both horizons a token of our duty to the world and a call to join with Him in His present and perpetual intercession.

APPENDED NOTES

LECTURE I

NOTE 1. See p. 10

The Council of Trent on Indulgences. The *Decretum de indulgentiis* passed at Sessio XXV decrees as follows: 'Quum potestas conferendi indulgentias a Christo ecclesiae concessa sit, atque huiusmodi potestate divinitus sibi tradita antiquissimis etiam temporibus illa usa fuerit, sacrosancta synodus indulgentiarum usum, Christiano populo maxime salutarem et sacrorum conciliorum auctoritate probatum, in ecclesia retinendum esse docet et praecipit, eosque anathemate damnat, qui aut inutiles esse asserunt, vel eas concedendi in ecclesia potestatem esse negant. In his tamen concedendis moderationem iuxta veterem et probatam in ecclesia consuetudinem adhiberi cupit, ne nimia facilitate ecclesiastica disciplina enervetur.' Then follows a mention of 'abuses' and 'base profits' which are to be abolished.

Richter, *Canones et Decreta Concilii Tridentini*, p. 468 (Typis Bernhardi Tauchnitii, Lipsiae, 1853). J. Waterworth, *Canons and Decrees of the Sacred and Oecumenical Council of Trent*, p. 277 (Burns & Oates, London, no date). The haste with which this decree was prepared is shown by Waterworth, who says, 'as a general wish had been expressed that something should be defined in regard of Indulgences, it was resolved to use the few hours that were left in preparing a brief statement of doctrine on that subject' (pp. ccxl, ccxli). A hurried consideration was therefore given to a matter which had been of transcendent importance. The decree betrays this haste by totally ignoring the difference both in theory and in practice between the remissions of penalty granted in ancient times and the 'pardons' which led to the Reformation.

NOTE 2. See p. 11

The Council of Trent on Episcopacy. Sessio XXIII, canon vi, enacts, 'Si quis dixerit, in ecclesia catholica non esse hierarchiam divina ordinatione institutam, quae constat ex episcopis, presbyteris et ministris: anathema sit.'

Canon viii enacts, 'Si quis dixerit episcopos, qui auctoritate Romani pontificis assumuntur, non esse legitimos et veros episcopos, sed figmentum humanum: anathema sit.'

The former of these two canons, in stating that the hierarchy 'was instituted by divine ordinance', says what would be accepted without hesitation by Ultramontanes, Gallicans, and Anglicans, not to mention Orthodox Orientals. But it avoids the precise point which the Spanish bishops wished to emphasize, viz. that it was Christ himself who instituted the hierarchy and that a bishop is what he is and acts as a bishop by virtue of Christ's ordinance, and not because either (i) jurisdiction has come to him through the Pope or (ii) the power to exercise jurisdiction received by him from Christ has come through the Pope. Both these latter theories imply that St. Peter possessed powers which were different in kind from those of the other apostles, and that these powers are possessed by the Pope.

The second of the two canons and the decree of the same session concerning the residence of ecclesiastics leave undecided the exact nature of the Pope's authority. Bishops whom the Pope 'assumes' are real bishops and all who have the care of souls must tend their sheep. But whether residence was necessary by virtue of the power of the Pope, or by a divine law binding on all to whom Christ gave episcopal jurisdiction, was left a matter of speculative interest. (The practical importance of the question was vividly illustrated in 1801 when nearly all the French refugee bishops in England refused to resign their sees at the demand of Pope Pius VII acting at the instance of Napoleon. See p. 123.)

Richter, *op. cit.*, p. 174.

Waterworth, *op. cit.*, p. 174. Waterworth regards 'assumed by authority of the Roman pontiff' as equivalent to 'created by the Roman pontiff', *op. cit.*, index, p. 313.

In addition to the actual canons of the Council it is useful to study documents such as those contained in I. v. Döllinger's *Ungedruckte Berichte und Tagebücher zur Geschichte des Concils von Trient*, Zweite Abtheilung, Nördlingen, 1876. The tension between the episcopal and the papalist parties is clearly illustrated, pp. 194 ff.

NOTE 3. See p. 20

The hymn attributed to St. Francis Xavier. The hymn was written neither in Latin nor in Portuguese, though it was translated into Latin verse and in Goa is known in

LECTURE I

a Portuguese prose translation. One Latin version is as follows:

> O Deus, ego amo te,
> Nec amo te ut salves me,
> Aut quia non amantes te
> Aeterno punis igne.
> Tu, mi Jesu, totum me
> Amplexasti in cruce;
> Tulisti clavos, lanceam
> Multamque ignominiam,
> Innumeros dolores, sudores
> Et angores et mortem;
> Et haec propter me
> Et pro me peccatore.
> Cur igitur non amem te,
> O Jesu mi amantissime?
> Non ut in caelo salves me
> Aut ne in aeternum damnes me
> Nec proemii ullius spe,
> Sed sicut tu amasti me,
> Sic amo et amabo te,
> Solum quia Rex meus es,
> Et solum quia Deus es.

This is based upon a Spanish sonnet; see *Revue Hispanique*, 1895, p. 120 (A. Picard, Paris):

> No me mueve, mi Dios, para quererte
> El cielo que me tienes prometido;
> Ni me mueve el infierno tan temido
> Para dexar por esso de ofenderte.
>
> Tu me mueves, Señor; muéveme el verte
> Clavado en essa cruz, y encarnecido;
> Muéveme el ver tu cuerpo tan herido;
> Muévenme tus afrentes, y tu muerte.
>
> Muévesme al tu amor en tal manera,
> Que aunque no hubiera cielo, yo te amára;
> Y aunque no hubiera infierno, te temiera.
>
> No me tienes que dar, porque te quiera;
> Que aunque quanto espero no esperára,
> Lo mismo que te quiero te quisiera.

The author of these beautiful lines is quite unknown.

Note 4. See p. 21

St. Francis Xavier's exposition of the creed. A full translation of the original as given by Teixeira is printed by Stewart, *op. cit.*, pp. 242 ff. It is interesting to compare this with a modern Portuguese expansion of it printed at Nova Goa in 1878 in a book entitled *O Devoto de S. Francisco*

Xavier, pp. 139 ff. In the former it is said that 'We are obliged to believe such of the holy canons and councils as are ordered by the Church, and the ordinances made by the Pope, Cardinals, Patriarchs, Archbishops, and Bishops, and Prelates of the Church'. In the latter it is said that 'We owe a profound respect, an unwavering faith, a prompt submission to the canons of the Holy Fathers, to the decrees of the councils, to the decisions pronounced and directed by the Sovereign Pontiff to all the Church, and which are transmitted to us by the intermediary of the Cardinals, Patriarchs, Archbishops, Bishops, and other Prelates'.

NOTE 5. See p. 27

The Five Condemned Propositions attributed to Jansenius. These prepositions condemned by Pope Innocent X in his Bull *Cum Occasione* of May the 31st, 1653, are as follows:

1. Aliqua Dei praecepta Hominibus iustis volentibus, et conantibus secundum praesentes, quas habent vires, sunt impossibilia, deest quoque illis Gratia qua possibilia sunt.

2. Interiori Gratiae in statu Naturae lapsae nunquam resistitur.

3. Ad merendum, et demerendum in statu Naturae lapsae non requiritur in Homine libertas a necessitate, sed sufficit libertas a coactione.

4. Semipelagiani admittebant praevenientis Gratiae interioris necessitatem ad singulos actus, etiam ad initium fidei, et in hoc erant Haeretici, quod valent eam Gratiam talem esse, cui posset humana voluntas resistere, vel obtemperare.

5. Semipelagianum est dicere, Christum pro omnibus omnino mortuum esse, aut sanguinem fudisse.

Bullarum Privilegiorum ac Diplomatum Romanorum Pontificum Collectio, tom. vi, pars 3, p. 248 (Romae, 1760).

NOTE 6. See p. 28

A moral reason for supporting the Jansenists. The following passage from a letter (number 737) of Madame de Sévigné, written from Nantes May the 17th, 1680, shows the attitude of a cultivated woman who was a shrewd judge of character: 'Ma consolation, c'est d'être à mes Filles de Sainte-Marie; elles sont aimables; elles ont conservé une idée de vous, dont elles me font leur cour; elles ne sont point folles, ni prévenues; comme celles que vous connoissez, elles ne croient point le pape d'aujourd'hui (Innocent XI) hérétique;

LECTURE I

elles savent leur religion; elles ne jetteront point par terre l'Écriture sainte, parce qu'elle est traduite par les plus honnêtes gens du monde; elles font honneur à la grâce de Jésus-Christ; elles connoissent la Providence; elles élèvent fort bien leurs petites filles; elles ne leur apprennent point à mentir, ni à dissimuler leurs sentiments; point de *coquesigrues* ni d'idolâtrie: enfin je les aime. M. de Grignan les croira jansénistes, et moi je pense qu'elles sont chrétiennes.'

LECTURE II

NOTE 7. See p. 34

The First Prayer Book of Edward VI and the Canon of the Mass. Professor A. F. Pollard, in his chapter on 'The Reformation under Edward VI', in *The Cambridge Modern History*, vol. ii, p. 485, says in regard to the First Prayer Book of Edward VI that 'the "abominable canon" was removed because it shut the door on all but the Roman doctrine of the Mass'. The canon was not 'removed' but carefully revised. The doctrine of the real presence was taught even more distinctly than before, by the insertion of a phrase from the Greek liturgy of St. Basil. Certain sacrificial terms were removed. These terms originally referred to the unconsecrated bread and wine and not to the body and blood of Christ as offered in the Mass. The single exception was the phrase *sacrificium laudis* which Cranmer retained, connecting it with the 'holy gifts' which have already been consecrated to be the body and blood of Christ. It is derived from the Old Testament, where it is applied to the peace-offering. Cranmer expanded it into 'sacrifice of praise and thanksgiving', which is the precise phrase which the mediaeval party in 1546 compelled Shaxton, Bishop of Salisbury, to apply to 'the oblation and action of the priest' in the Mass, as one of the proofs that he rejected the Protestant doctrine of the Eucharist. See my *History of the Book of Common Prayer*, p. 99 (Longmans, London, 1905), and for the sources of the Prayer Book see F. E. Brightman, *The English Rite* (Rivingtons, London, 1915). In regard to Edward VI's Second Prayer Book there is a good deal of truth in the words of Professor F. C. Burkitt that Cranmer, influenced by St. Augustine, 'was not abolishing the Sacrifice, but only transforming it', *Eucharist and Sacrifice*, p. 22 (Heffer, Cambridge, 1921).

NOTE 8. See p. 40

The excommunication of Queen Elizabeth. The Bull *Regnans in excelsis* was signed by Pope Pius V on February the 25th, 1570. The following is the important passage in which the Pope accuses the Queen of Calvinism: 'Missae sacrificium, preces, ieiunia, ciborum delectum, coelibatum, ritusque Catholicos abolevit, libros manifestam haeresim continentes toto regno proponi, impia mysteria, et instituta ad Calvini praescriptum a se suscepta, et observata, etiam a subditis servari mandavit.' *Bullarum Privilegiorum ac Diplomatum Romanorum Pontificum Collectio*, tom. iv, pars 3, p. 98 (Romae, 1746). Professor F. W. Maitland, in his chapter on 'The Anglican Settlement and the Scottish Reformation', in *The Cambridge Modern History*, vol. ii, p. 588, interprets this to mean that the Pope accused Elizabeth of 'participation in "the impious mysteries of Calvin", by which, no doubt, he meant the *Cène*'. I doubt the correctness of this interpretation. The Bull with its subtle exaggerations betrays a mind too clever to be guilty of such a gross falsehood as accusing Elizabeth of participating in a Calvinistic Eucharist. 'Mysteria' no doubt means 'sacraments'. But 'Instituta' means 'ordinances', and the Pope probably took the word deliberately from the title of Calvin's famous book, though he carefully avoids saying that Elizabeth had accepted Calvin's own institutes.

In this connexion it is of some importance to understand the attitude towards the English Book of Common Prayer taken by John Knox, who, unlike Elizabeth, was a Calvinist. Professor F. W. Maitland, *loc. cit.*, p. 591, seems to under-estimate the opposition of John Knox to the English Prayer Book. He says, ' To that book in 1559 Knox had strong objections; he detested ceremonies . . . but there was nothing doctrinally wrong with the book.' Now Knox's statements show an antipathy to something more serious than ceremonies. Not only does he denounce as ' Diabolicall inventions ' the singing of the 'Letanie' and ceremonies properly so called, even those in the semi-Puritan *Second* Prayer Book of Edward VI. He also takes up a doctrinal ground, maintaining that 'wher Christ is not preached (marke well that I say, preached), that there hath the Sacrament neither life nor soule'. Therefore in opposition to the teaching of the English Reformers, Knox makes the efficacy of the Sacraments depend upon the doctrine preached by the minister; and the Scottish Con-

LECTURE II

fession of Faith shows that this doctrine must agree with that of Calvin's *Institutes*, the Genevan Confession, and the works of John Laski. See B. J. Kidd, D.D., *Documents Illustrative of the Continental Reformation*, pp. 691 f., 703 (Oxford, Clarendon Press, 1911).

NOTE 9. See p. 44

British Calvinism. The following passages show the nature of the Calvinism taught by the Presbyterians and by the Congregationalists in Great Britain and in America. The passages which the Congregationalists took over from the Westminster Confession are printed in Roman type, the parts added by them at the Savoy in blacker type.

'*Of the Perseverance of the Saints*

'They whom God hath accepted in his beloved, effectually called and sanctified by his Spirit can neither totally nor finally fall away from the state of grace, but shall certainly persevere therein to the end, and be eternally saved.

'II. This Perseverance of the Saints depends not upon their own free-will, but upon the immutability of the Decree of Election, from the free and unchangeable love of God the Father, upon the efficacy of the merit and intercession of Jesus Christ, **and union with him, the oath of God,** the abiding of **his** Spirit, and of the seed of God within them, and the nature of the Covenant of Grace, from all which ariseth also the certainty and infallibility thereof.

'III. **And though** they may through the temptation of Satan, and of the world, the prevalency of corruption remaining in them, and the neglect of the means of their preservation, fall into grievous sins, and for a time continue therein, whereby they incur God's displeasure and grieve his holy Spirit, come to **have** their graces and comforts **impaired,** have their hearts hardened, and their consciences wounded, hurt and scandalize others, and bring temporal judgements upon themselves; **yet they are and shall be kept by the power of God through faith unto salvation.'**

Further light is thrown upon this by a previous statement about the non-elect. It is, 'Others not elected, although they may be called by the Ministry of the Word, and may have some common operations of the Spirit, yet **not being effectually drawn by the Father, they neither do nor can** come unto Christ, and therefore cannot be saved.'

The verbal differences between the Presbyterian and the Congregationalist forms make no doctrinal difference.

And the American divine Cotton Mather describes the 'Congregational Churches' in New England as 'Reform'd Churches, nothing in Doctrine, little in Discipline, different from that of Geneva'. *Magnalia Christi Americana, or The Ecclesiastical History of New England from 1620 to 1698*, Book i, p. 1 (London, 1702).

The kindness which the early colonists received from certain Indians, especially one named Squanto, must have seemed hard to reconcile with the Calvinistic doctrine of the total depravity of man. Mather, however, compares the tongue of Squanto with that of the dog who licked the sores of Lazarus.

A most valuable and complete account of the whole doctrinal position of the Congregationalists is given in Williston Walker's *The Creeds and Platforms of Congregationalism* (Charles Scribner's Sons, New York, 1893).

NOTE 10. See p. 44

The Pope as Antichrist. The British Calvinist teaching as to the Pope is as follows: 'There is no other Head of the Church but the Lord Jesus Christ, nor can the Pope of Rome in any sense be Head thereof; but is that Antichrist, that man of sin, and son of perdition, that exalteth himself in the Church against Christ, and all that is called God.' Williston Walker, *op. cit.*, p. 396.

It is said that the first person in Oxford in the seventeenth century who publicly denied that the Pope is Antichrist was Dr. Gilbert Sheldon, afterwards primate of all England, when reading his academical exercise for a degree in divinity, 1628. 'The doctor of the chair (Dr. Prideaux), wondering at it, said, *Quid, mi fili, negas Papam esse Antichristum?* Sheldon answered, *Etiam nego.* Dr. Prideaux replied, *Profecto multum tibi debet Pontifex Romanus, et nullus dubito quin pileo cardinalitio te donabit!*' H. J. Todd, *Life of Brian Walton*, vol. i, p. 291 (Rivington, London, 1821).

LECTURE III

NOTE 11. See p. 70

The Position of the Church of Sweden. At the Lambeth Conference of 1920 the Anglican episcopate took definite steps towards a partial intercommunion with the Lutheran Church of Sweden. The position of that Church is so ambiguous that greater caution would not have been unwise. On behalf of the admission of Swedes to holy communion at our altars it can be urged that the Swedish Church has retained (i) the three ancient creeds retained by the Church of England and that the Augsburg Confession, which the Swedish Church also accepts, need not be regarded as inimical to these creeds; (ii) an episcopal succession, it being practically certain that at the time of the Reformation at least a tactual succession was preserved through the consecration of Archbishop Laurentius Petri by Petrus Magni, Bishop of Westerås, who was consecrated at Rome May the 1st, 1524; (iii) edifying Catholic rites and ornaments, among which the episcopal mitre and staff and the priest's chasuble would in a special degree indicate the intention of keeping orthodox views of the Church and the sacraments.

On the other hand it is certain that the Swedish Church has tolerated, and still tolerates, Lutheran innovations of a pronounced character. For (i) it is in full communion with other Lutherans, such as those in Denmark who have only nominal bishops, and those in America who have no bishops. This fact alone is enough to cause serious misgivings as to the doctrine of the Swedes concerning the Church, and as to their intention in ordaining their priests; (ii) there is no order of deacons in any strict sense of the word; (iii) the doctrine and practice with regard to confirmation are seriously insufficient, and the Swedish bishops have openly stated that they regard the laying on of the bishop's hand for the purpose of confirming as among things that are indifferent; (iv) the liturgy lacks a definite prayer of consecration and the celebrant is not obliged to communicate: these two facts are in harmony with the Lutheran view that the presence of Christ is effected at the distribution of the sacrament rather than at the words of consecration spoken by the celebrant.

The establishment of sacramental intercommunion should not be regarded as one of the first steps, but as the ultimate step, in reunion. And therefore the administration of the holy communion at our altars to Swedes ought, in view of the possibility of a complete reunion, to be postponed until their Church as a body has forsaken such causes of estrangement between us as have been indicated above.

For the Swedish attitude towards the Lambeth Conference of 1920 see 'The Reply of the Bishops of the Church of Sweden' in *Theology*, July 1922 (Society for Promoting Christian Knowledge, London).

NOTE 12. See p. 94

The languages spoken by the Sephardic Jews in Amsterdam and London. It is well known that in the seventeenth century Amsterdam was a great centre of the important division of the Jewish community known as *Sephardim*, a word which originally meant 'people of Sardis', but became adopted by the Jews of Spain and Portugal, distinguishing them from the *Ashkenazim* of Russia, Poland, and Germany. From Amsterdam and elsewhere many of the Sephardim came to London, a fact which accounts for the numerous Portuguese names found in the Denizations and Naturalizations of Aliens published by the Huguenot Society of London in 1911. Here we find names like Fonsequa and Pinheiro side by side with Huguenot names like Du Quesne and Bouverie.

The languages spoken by these Jews are a matter of both historical and philological interest. It is clear that in both Amsterdam and London the Sephardic synagogues were usually called Portuguese. The oldest official vernacular records in the London synagogue (for which see p. 267) are in Portuguese. But the language of the majority of the Sephardim in both cities was Spanish. So far as I can judge from books in my own possession and others which I have found mentioned, the vernacular prayer books were all in Spanish, though I believe that a prayer for the government of the Netherlands, and later of England, was read in Portuguese. The following short list of books is enough to prove the use of Spanish:

Orden de Benediciones, Amsterdam, 5447 (A. D. 1687), Hebrew and Spanish. *Orden de las Oraciones Cotidianas*, David Tartas, Amsterdam, 5452 (A. D. 1692); another edition was published in Amsterdam in 5477 (A. D. 1717), and another in London by the noted Rabbi Ishac Nieto in A. D. 1771. The same Nieto published a new translation of the Prayers for *Ros-ashanah y Kipur*, Londres, En casa de Ricardo Reily, Año 5500 (A. D. 1740). The introduction is in good Spanish and claims to be free from the old and inappropriate words found in other translations. The author condemns 'Castellano-Hebraico; que no es ni Hebraico, ni Castellano'. Another Spanish book of prayers is *Orden de los Cinco Ayunos*, David Tartas, Amsterdam, 5455 (A. D. 1695). There seems to be no Portuguese book exactly corresponding with the above mentioned, though a Hebrew Order of the Daily Prayers with Portuguese notes was published in

LECTURE III

Amsterdam by S. L. Maduro in 1768. And early in the nineteenth century sermons in the London synagogue were in Spanish, the first English sermon being on March the 26th, 1831. Some light is thrown upon the question by a work on the Psalms by Yahacob Yehuda Leon, published in Amsterdam in 5431 (A. D. 1670–1671). It is called *Alabanças de Santidad*. The psalms are printed in Hebrew and the translation and paraphrase are in Spanish. But the official imprimatur and report of the censors of the book are in Portuguese, and the author even speaks of 'our Portuguese nation'. The explanation seems to be that by the end of the sixteenth century the strictly Spanish Jews had been all expelled from Spain or converted to Christianity. Those in Turkey kept, and still keep, the fifteenth-century dialect which Nieto calls 'Castellano-Hebraico'. In the seventeenth century the Jews in Spain were mostly of Portuguese origin except in Majorca. These Portuguese Jews retained Portuguese as an official language but acquired a knowledge of Spanish. Spanish being easier to learn, and being the vernacular of the Jews who came to Holland and England from North Africa, prevailed over Portuguese.

It may be added that until the nineteenth century marriages between the Sephardim and the Ashkenazim were almost unknown. Also that there was a decided drift of the old Sephardic families towards Christianity. Descendants of several such families have been personally known to me.

LECTURE IV

NOTE 13. See p. 98

Roman Catholicism in Amsterdam. In 1716 the Roman Catholic churches in Amsterdam outnumbered all the rest: 'Het getal der Roomsche Kerken is in deze Stadt vry groot, en overtreft in meenigte, die van alle de overige gezintheeden met malkander. . . . Alle de Roomsche Kerken zyn zodanig gebouwd, dat men van buiten geen hoedanigheid van een Kerk zien kan.' *Wegwyzer door Amsterdam*, p. 211 (Nicolaas ten Hoorn, Amsterdam, 1716).

NOTE 14. See p. 98

The Sephardic (Spanish and Portuguese) synagogue in Bevis Marks, London. This synagogue, the oldest in London, was dedicated in 1702. The builder was a Quaker named Avis, who incorporated in the roof a beam given by Queen Anne. The last-known organization of Jews for worship in Spain was discovered at Madrid in 1720. An organization for Moslem worship was discovered at Cordova in 1727 and at Cartagena as late as 1769. But the Inquisition had done its work so thoroughly that Judaism and Islam were almost extinct by 1700. See H. C. Lea, *A History of the Inquisition of Spain*, vol. iii, pp. 308, 406 (Macmillan Company, New York, 1907).

NOTE 15. See p. 113

Medals commemorating the suppression of the Jesuits. On the suppression of the Society of Jesus two medals were circulated in Rome. The first represents the Pope with the inscription *Clemens XIV Pontifex Max.*, and on the reverse shows our Lord accompanied by two apostles driving before Him three Jesuit priests wearing birettas; and the inscription *Nunquam novi vos discedite a me omnes.* A specimen of this medal has been kindly shown to me by Dr. W. H. Hutton, Dean of Winchester. The second medal represents the Pope with the inscription *Clemens XIV. Pont. Max. A.V.*, and on the reverse shows the Church seated on a globe, holding in one hand a cross and in the other an olive-branch and the Holy Dove inspiring her, the inscription being *Salus generis humani.* Below are the words *Jesuitarum societas deleta* MDCCLXXIII.

NOTE 16. See p. 118

The Protestation of the English Roman Catholics in 1789. This Protestation has been printed in full by Bernard Ward, *The Dawn of Catholic Revival in England 1781–1803*, vol. i, pp. 139 ff. This most important document brought about the Relief Act of 1791 which released English Roman Catholics from persecution. It is of a pronounced Gallican type separated by an immense gulf from the English Roman Catholicism of the present day. In accordance with Gallican teaching it contains 'a vehement protest against the existence of any authority of the Pope which could interfere directly or indirectly with the government of the realm' (*loc. cit.*, p. 144). Its language is irreconcilable with the Bull which excommunicated Queen Elizabeth. The following extract illustrates its tenor:

' We have been accused of holding as a principle of our Religion that Princes excommunicated by the Pope and

Council or by authority of the See of Rome may be deposed or murdered by their Subjects or other persons.

'But so far is the above-mentioned unchristianlike and abominable Position from being a Principle that we hold, that we reject, abhor and detest it, and every part thereof as execrable and impious.'

. . . . . .

'We have also been accused of holding as a principle of our Religion that implicit Obedience is due from us to the Orders and Decrees of Popes and General Councils and that therefore if the Pope or any General Council should for the good of the Church command us to take up Arms against Government, or by any means to subvert the Laws and Liberties of this country, or to exterminate persons of a different Religion from us, we (it is asserted by our accusers) hold ourselves bound to obey such Orders or Decrees, on pain of eternal fire.

'Whereas we positively deny that we owe any such obedience to the Pope and General Council, or to either of them; and we believe that no act that is in itself immoral or dishonest can ever be justified by or under colour that it is done either for the good of the Church, or obedience to any Ecclesiastical Power whatever. We acknowledge no infallibility in the Pope, and we neither apprehend nor believe that our disobedience to any such orders or decrees (should any such be given or made) could subject us to any punishment whatever.'

All the Roman Catholic bishops then resident in England signed this Protestation. And though one of them, Dr. Matthew Gibson, afterwards withdrew his name, he does not appear to have done so on the ground of belief in the Pope's infallibility.

The action of these bishops is the more remarkable inasmuch as they were 'Vicars Apostolic', and therefore peculiarly dependent upon Rome. The Rev. Joseph Berington, a Roman Catholic clergyman and writer of this period, gives a scathing description of this method of governing a Church as ' an economy in its obvious nature, most extraordinary and dependent, in which they who styled themselves bishops, were but the delegated agents or stewards of another, while that other, the Roman pontiff, was himself the ordinary or immediate bishop of the English Catholic Church. This bishop apportioned out to his delegates the *quantum* of jurisdiction, it should seem expedient they should exercise, which he could recall, limit, or modify, as his own will or their conduct might direct. The agents were independent of each other in their respective offices (which did but more evince the nature of the link that bound them to the Roman chair) "moving equally abreast", it has been said with some wit, "without any mutual relation, coherence or order among themselves"'. *The Memoirs of Gregorio Panzani, translated from the Italian Original with an Introduction and a Supplement*, Supplement, pp. 373–4 (Swinney & Walker, Birmingham, 1793).

NOTE 17. See p. 126

The cultus of the hearts of Jesus and Mary. The worship of the Sacred Heart of Jesus was advocated in St. James's Chapel, London, in the time of Charles II by a chaplain of Mary of Modena, Father De la Colombière. But until 1814 it remained almost unknown to English Roman Catholics. This is shown by the fact that there are no prayers to the Sacred Heart in the *Garden of the Soul* by Bishop Challoner and none in the excellent *Manual of Devout Prayers* which was employed in this country before his time. The present devotion to the Sacred Heart owes its realistic form and wide popularity to certain visions affirmed to have been seen by the French sister, Margaret Mary Alacoque of Paray-le-Monial (1647–1690), who was canonized by the late Pope Benedict XV.

Some discussion has taken place as to the more remote genesis of the devotion. On the one hand it has been urged that whether the form of it was supernaturally revealed to Margaret Mary or not, its antecedents were Catholic. Among them was the mediaeval devotion to the Five Wounds of our Lord. The latest English mediaeval art depicted the Five Wounds arranged on a shield, the wounded Heart being in the centre. Such a shield is painted on one of the two rare banners of the time of Queen Mary at St. John's College, Oxford. On the other hand, it has been urged that Father De la Colombière, who was Margaret Mary's director, recommended it to her, and that he was influenced by a popular treatise *The Heart of Christ in Heaven towards Sinners on Earth* written by the well-known English Congregationalist, Thomas Goodwin, who had been Oliver Cromwell's chaplain.

It is not necessary to regard the two theories as mutually exclusive. Father De la Colombière was in England from 1676 to 1678, and there is no difficulty in believing that he was acquainted with Dr. Goodwin's treatise. The two

LECTURE IV

divines were exercising their ministry in London at the same time. Pietism had in it something that was international (see p. 95), and both were probably acquainted with some of the same mystical books. De la Colombière was at Paray-le-Monial for some time before, and for a brief time after, his stay in London. If the most important visionary experiences of Margaret Mary were, as is alleged, earlier than 1676, there is little likelihood of her having imbibed from her director the teaching of Thomas Goodwin. The coincidences in their teaching are remarkable and the dates of her visions are uncertain, but the evidence seems in favour of a period before 1676.

Although this devotion entered upon a new phase through the efforts of Margaret Mary and her director, it had been already anticipated in part.

1. Before the sixteenth century there seems to have been no actual worship of the Sacred Heart, but simply a mystical exercise of affection for Christ connected especially with meditation on the Five Wounds.

2. In the sixteenth century Louis de Blois and others gave this mysticism a new turn by invoking the Heart of Jesus.

3. About 1640 Father Eudes of Caen promoted a veneration of the ' Most loving Heart [*sic*] of Jesus and Mary ', and congregations were founded in honour of the 'Heart of Jesus and Mary'. The extraordinary use of the singular rather than the plural suggests that *heart* was regarded primarily as a metaphorical word for *love*.

4. The devotion which originated with Margaret Mary and her director and spread rapidly after 1685 is the worship of the material physical Heart of Jesus Christ. It was regarded with caution and encountered considerable opposition within the Roman communion, but received the complete sanction of Pope Pius IX when he beatified Margaret Mary in 1864. He also gave his definite approval to the practice of paying the worship of *hyperdulia* or extra-servitude to the material physical heart of the Blessed Virgin. In 1793 this devotion was described by Berington as 'a modern *devotion*, and which, with many others, to the disgrace of real religion, has been invented in our church from sordid and superstitious views' (*op. cit.*, p. xxxii).

Although the worship of the Sacred Heart of Jesus is defended as a safeguard against Docetism, the theologians of the eighteenth century who believed that it savoured of heterodoxy showed more intelligence than their opponents care to admit. Rome has already had to condemn the phrase 'Penitent Heart of Jesus', and explain that Mary has 'no empire properly so-called, no authority, over the Heart of Jesus'; but has left uncondemned praises and prayers which adore a deified humanity rather than an incarnate Deity. (For the history of the devotion see *Dictionnaire de Théologie Catholique*, articles 'Cœur-Sacré de Jésus', 'Cœur de Marie', Letouzey, Paris, 1906; and *The Edinburgh Review*, January 1874. For a criticism of the implied theology see A. Nicholson, *The Adoration of Christ*, The Blackfriars Printers, London, 1897.)

LECTURE V

NOTE 18. See p. 145

The Wesleyan Methodist and Calvinistic Methodist Schisms. The circumstances attending Wesley's 'ordination' of ministers for America can be read in Townsend, Workman, Eayres, *A New History of Methodism*, vol. ii, pp. 92 ff. (Hodder & Stoughton, London, 1909). Thomas Coke, D.C.L., who was already a priest, demurred at first to being 'consecrated'. His conscientious scruples were overcome and Wesley, 'assisted by other ordained ministers', 'set him apart as a Superintendent'. This was in 1784, the year before Bishop Seabury's arrival in America. Wesley excused his action on the ground that large numbers of people in America were without clergymen to administer the sacraments. For this fact the British Government was entirely responsible on account of its refusal to send bishops to America. Francis Asbury was 'ordained' in America by Coke, assisted by Whatcoat and Vasey, who were 'ordained' by Wesley and James Creighton, a priest. Wesley called Coke and Asbury 'joint Superintendents'. But they both called themselves 'bishops', as is shown in their letter to the President of the United States (Washington) dated May the 29th, 1789.

George Whitefield was not a great organizer such as Wesley was. But as early as 1743 the Welsh Calvinistic Methodists were carefully organizing their societies within the Church, and Whitefield was chosen as their Moderator, the title being borrowed from Scotch Presbyterianism. He resigned the office. But under Thomas Charles (1755–1814) elaborate rules for the government of the sect were drawn up, and in 1811 Charles took the final step of 'ordaining' lay preachers to administer the sacraments. See W. Williams, *Welsh Calvinistic Methodism* (Publishing Office of the Presbyterian Church of England, London, 1884).

NOTE 19. See p. 152

Political Principles of the Scottish Episcopalians in the time of George I. Many acute remarks on the social and religious customs of the period are to be found in Burt's *Letters from the North of Scotland* reprinted by William Paterson, Edinburgh, 1876. In vol. i, pp. 222 ff., the writer speaks of the 'Episcopalians' and says, 'Their Ministers here are all Nonjurors, that I know, except those of the Chief Baron's Chapel in Edinburgh, and the Episcopal Church at Aberdeen; but whether there is any qualified Episcopal Minister at Glasgow, St. Andrews, &c., I do not know.

'The Nonjuring Ministers generally lead regular Lives; and it behoves them so to do, for otherwise they would be distanced by their Rivals.

'I saw a flagrant Example of the People's Disaffection to the present Government in the above mentioned Church of Aberdeen, where there is an Organ, the only one I know of, and the Service is chaunted as in our Cathedrals.

'Being there, one Sunday Morning, with another English Gentleman, when the Minister came to that Part of the Litany where the King is prayed for by Name, the People all rose up at once, in Contempt of it, and Men and Women set themselves about some trivial Action, as taking Snuff, &c., to show their Dislike, and signify to each other that they were all of one Mind; and when the Responsal should have been pronounced, though they had been loud in all that preceded, to our Amazement there was not one single Voice to be heard but our own, so suddenly and entirely were we dropped.'

The following short passage shows that the Jacobitism of the Episcopalians was combined with a somewhat democratic assertion of the right of self-determination: 'The Nonjuring Ministers have made a kind of Linsey-Woolsey piece of Stuff of their Doctrine, by interweaving the People's civil Rights with Religion, and teaching them that it is as Unchristian not to believe their Notions of Government as to disbelieve the Gospel.'

NOTE 20. See p. 155

Early American Church Architecture. Three of the finest American churches of the eighteenth century still remaining are Christ Church, Philadelphia, begun in 1727; St. Michael's, Charleston, begun in 1751; St. Paul's, New York, opened in 1766. King's Chapel, Boston, mentioned in this lecture as the only Anglican church that became Unitarian, was begun in 1749 and has a fine interior with double columns supporting the galleries and roof. St. Philip's, Charleston, begun in 1710, was considered superior to them all, but it was destroyed by fire and rebuilt in the same style in 1835.

The early churches in the vast country now comprised in the United States deserve a careful study. Many are of architectural merit and of historical and religious interest. It is not possible here to touch upon those erected by the French in Louisiana, and those erected by the Spaniards in Florida, Texas, New Mexico, and California from the sixteenth to the early nineteenth century. Those built by the English colonists fall into certain distinct categories. The Anglican colonists in the seventeenth century built churches which recall the Gothic churches of English country villages. Such are St. Luke's, Smithfield, Virginia, 1632, and St. Peter's, New Kent County, in the same State, 1700, somewhat less Gothic. The Puritans built 'meeting-houses' which are simply large wooden rooms, the exteriors of which display at least some of the picturesqueness of the domestic architecture of the period. Such are the meeting-house at Hingham, Massachusetts, 1681, and the Quaker meeting-house at Flushing, New York, 1692.

In the eighteenth century we find a strong influence exercised by the art of Wren and his pupil Gibbs. It is shown in a rough, simple form in Christ Church, Boston, 1723, and Trinity Church, Newport, 1726. Far more elaborate examples of the same style are the churches mentioned at the beginning of this note. St. Paul's, New York, bears a rather close resemblance to Gibbs's masterpiece, St. Martin-in-the-Fields, London, but, unlike Gibbs, the architect has not placed the exquisite spire immediately behind a huge portico. Later in the same century, near the time of the separation of the United States from Great Britain, the American Dissenters began to adopt Anglican architecture. This was many years before the English Dissenters changed the form of their meeting-houses. The Baptist meeting-house at Providence, Rhode Island, 1775, is of an Anglican type from its Renaissance spire to its shallow sanctuary. The same influence is shown, though rather less strongly, in the Congregationalist 'Center Church' and 'North Church' at New Haven, Connecticut—two beautiful buildings erected in 1814. The former of these two shows a fine example of the American device of placing the lowest storey of the spire within the portico, between and near the two central columns. The Congregationalist 'Center Church' at Hartford in the same State has no structural sanctuary, but resembles some of the best English work of that date—1806. The double row of Ionic columns gives to the interior a dignity which is quite lacking in some of our late Georgian churches. By this time the Roman style of Gibbs was blending with that of the Greek revival, and the Anglicans in the United States were returning to the use of Gothic. An early example of this is Trinity Church, New Haven, consecrated in 1816.

The Roman style, however, died hard. St. John's, New York, built in 1807 and barbarously pulled down within the last few years, was probably the last Anglican church of this type, and it was but little inferior to its elder sister, the church of St. Paul, in the same city.

The Americans have given the name 'Colonial' to the architecture of their classical Georgian churches. The name is convenient, but not rigorously correct. The most distinctively American type of classical architecture was developed, as we should expect, after the separation from the mother country. It lingered till about 1830, the year in which George IV died. One of its best examples is the Independent Presbyterian church at Savannah, designed by an Englishman and built in 1800 (burnt and rebuilt later). Here there is Gothic detail in the windows. And in Trinity Church, Newark, New Jersey, we find a building erected in 1805 with a pseudo-Gothic nave, and a portico and spire of good Colonial Roman design.

NOTE 21. See p. 158

The Lapse of American Congregationalism into Unitarianism. In 1800 there were within the limits of the city of Boston two Episcopal (Anglican) churches, two Baptist churches, and one small Methodist society. In these a belief in the Holy Trinity was maintained. One Congregational church, the 'Old South church', where Whitefield had preached in 1740, had a minister whose orthodoxy was suspected. On the other hand, the 'Liberal' or Unitarian party had ten churches—eight were originally Congregationalist, one was Universalist, and the remaining one was King's Chapel. The apostate churches in Massachusetts included the most historic churches of the Pilgrim Fathers; the first church of Plymouth, founded 1620, the first church of Salem, founded 1629, the first church of Boston, founded 1632. The schism between the two Congregational parties, the Unitarian and the Trinitarian, became definite in 1815, the Unitarians still usually keeping the name 'Congregational'. Forty years later the tide had begun to turn against Unitarianism, and the evaporation of all definite Christianity among the American Unitarians has caused a large number to forsake their sect for the Protestant Episcopal (Anglican) Church. Minute statistics relating to Unitarianism and Universalism are given by Daniel Dorchester, *Christianity in the United States*, revised edition (Hunt and Eaton, New York, 1895). The Unitarian side can be read in J. W. Chadwick, *Old and New Unitarian Belief* (G. H. Ellis, Boston, U.S.A., 1894).

LECTURE VI

Note 22. See p. 178

Goethe on the Sacraments. The following passage is a valuable illustration of the truth that Goethe could prefer the better while he followed the worse.

'The sacraments are the highest part of religion, the symbols to our senses of an extraordinary divine favour and grace. In the Lord's Supper earthly lips are to receive a divine Being embodied, and partake of an heavenly under the form of an earthly nourishment. This sense is just the same in all Christian churches; whether the Sacrament is taken with more or less submission to the mystery, with more or less accommodation as to what is intelligible; it always remains a great holy thing, which in reality takes the place of the possible or the impossible, the place of that which man can neither attain nor do without. But such a sacrament should not stand alone; no Christian can partake of it with the true joy for which it is given, if the symbolical or sacramental sense is not fostered within him. He must be accustomed to regard the inner religion of the heart and that of the external church as perfectly one, as the great universal sacrament, which again divides itself into so many others, and communicates to these parts its holiness, indestructibleness, and eternity.

LECTURE VI

Here a youthful pair give their hands to one another, not for a passing salutation or for the dance; the priest pronounces his blessing upon them, and the bond is indissoluble. It is not long before this wedded pair brings a likeness to the threshold of the altar; it is purified with holy water, and so incorporated into the Church, that it cannot forfeit this benefit but through the most monstrous apostasy. The child in the course of life practises himself in earthly things of his own accord; in heavenly things he must be instructed. Does it prove on examination that this has been fully done, he is now received into the bosom of the Church as an actual citizen, as a true and voluntary professor, not without outward tokens of the weightiness of this act. . . . In the infinite confusion in which he must entangle himself, amid the conflict of natural and religious claims, an admirable expedient is given him, in confiding his deeds and misdeeds, his infirmities and doubts, to a worthy man, appointed expressly for that purpose, who knows how to calm, to warn, to strengthen him, to chasten him likewise by symbolical punishments, and at last by a complete washing away of his guilt, to render him happy and to give him back, pure and cleansed, the tablet of his manhood. Thus prepared and purely calmed to rest by several sacramental acts which, on closer examination, branch forth again into minuter sacramental traits, he kneels down to receive the host.' The passage continues with a defence of extreme unction and the 'spiritual heirship' of apostolic succession. 'It is not he, the priest, whom we reverence, but his office; it is not his nod to which we bow the knee, but the blessing which he imparts, and which seems the more holy, and to come the more immediately from heaven, because the earthly instrument cannot at all weaken or invalidate it by its own sinful, nay, wicked nature.' *Dichtung und Wahrheit*, Book VII, vol. xi, pp. 284 ff. (Stuttgart, 1866).

LECTURE VII

NOTE 23. See p. 192

The Greek Rite in Italian Churches. The Greek rite still survives in certain Albanian communities of southern Italy and Sicily, but is no longer regularly celebrated in any church existing among the remnants of the Byzantine Greek population. These remnants, still speaking Greek and then numbering about twenty thousand, are described by

H. F. Tozer in the *Journal of Hellenic Studies*, vol. x, 1889. He concludes that they are descendants of Greeks who migrated thither not later than the eleventh century, but that their numbers were reinforced at a later date. He describes them as forming two separate groups, one in the 'heel' of Italy or Terra d'Otranto, the other in the 'toe', a mountain region in and around the town of Bova in Calabria. The language, which had evidently lost ground before the advance of Italian, was unmixed with Albanian. In all the Greek villages the church services seem to have long been in Latin. They were formerly in Greek, and Tozer quotes Barcio as writing in 1571 to the effect that the Greek rite was used from Leucopetra to Bova.

Rossano, about midway between the two districts mentioned above, is a city where the Greek rite was peculiarly tenacious. In it there were seven Greek Basilian monasteries in the fifteenth century. In the cathedral the Greek rite was maintained until 1571, and in other churches of the city it lingered some fifty years longer. This district was visited in 1889 by P. Vincenzo Vannutelli, O.P., who gives a brief account of the Greek rite in Italy in his work *Le Colonie Italo-Greche* (Roma, 1890). He says that the Greek rite was abolished by a Franciscan bishop, Matteo Saraceno, but is maintained at Rossano on certain days of the year 'per richiamare il tempo passato'. He found the Italian Albanian villages depressed and poverty-stricken; in Calabria about thirty had adopted the Latin rite, about eighteen had kept the Greek, Lungro being the place where it was best preserved. His notes show plain marks of haste, as he elsewhere in the same book says the Greek rite is kept in about twenty-five villages. All were under the authority of the Roman Church. In Sicily he found numerous Albanians under Rome using the Greek rite, notably at Mezzoiuso, La Piana, and Palazzo Adriano. At the last he specially noted the use of leavened bread and the Western rite of Benediction after the liturgy. He emphasizes the fact that in Sicily the faithful are permitted to avail themselves of the sacraments of Penance and the Eucharist according to either the Latin or the Greek rite, except at the time of their Easter communion or their Viaticum. Of this practice he approves, and also, to some extent, of the toleration of a married clergy among Orientals, instances of which he found in Sicily (*ibid.*, p. 89). See also articles 'Italo-Greeks' and 'Rossano' in *Catholic Encyclopedia*.

LECTURE VII

NOTE 24. See p. 203

Constantinople and Anglican Ordinations. The following is a translation of the Official Encyclical of the Oecumenical Patriarch Meletios to the Presidents of the Orthodox Churches of the East. It is reprinted from the *Church Times* of September the 8th, 1922.

'The Most Holy Church of Constantinople, kindled from the beginning with zeal for universal union, and always keeping in mind the Lord's words prayed by Him to His Heavenly Father just before His Saving Passion, has always followed with keen interest every movement in the separated Churches, and has examined with care and study their every and any expression of faith which might point towards a *rapprochement* with Orthodoxy. Further, it has concluded with real joy that amongst them the Church which has manifested the most lively desire to remove the obstacles towards a *rapprochement* and indeed to full union with the Orthodox Church is the Episcopal Anglican Church, which herself having first received the light of Christianity from the East, has never ceased to remember the East and to account as an important end a sincere *rapprochement* towards a full union in Christ Jesus with the Orthodox in the East.

'Therefore the great Church of Christ (now) under our presidency, necessarily honouring the readiness of this Church in former periods, especially in the last twenty years, has entered into many sincere brotherly relations with it, and recently established a special committee, with instructions to report upon the still existing points of difference on the basis of a scientific inquiry, and on the method of their removal, with a view to accomplishing a full union of the two Churches in the same Orthodox Christian spirit.

'Perceiving in its labour that on an important question —namely, the validity of Anglican Ordinations—the Holy Orthodox Church had not yet officially delivered any opinion either as a whole or through any of the particular Holy Synods, although there have been many discussions (on the matter) from time to time among her theologians, and that an authoritative and canonical solution of this important question would greatly facilitate the desired union by removing one of the most serious obstacles that oppose the objective of reunion which is sought on either side and is dear to God, the committee brought under the judgment of our Holy Synod a special report treating scientifically the above-named question. Our Holy Synod studied this report of the committee in repeated sessions, and took note:—

'1. That the ordination of Matthew Parker as Archbishop of Canterbury by four bishops is a fact established by history.

'2. That in this ordination and those subsequent to it there are found in their fullness those Orthodox and indispensable visible and sensible elements of valid Episcopal Ordination—namely, the Laying-on of Hands and the *Epiklesis* of the All-Holy Spirit, and also the purpose to transmit the *charisma* of the Episcopal Ministry.

'3. That the Orthodox theologians who have scientifically examined the question have almost unanimously come to the same conclusion and have expressed themselves as accepting the validity of Anglican Ordinations.

'4. That the practice in the Church affords no indication that the Orthodox Church has ever officially treated the validity of Anglican Orders as in doubt in such a way as would point to the re-ordination of the Anglican clergy being regarded as required in the case of the union of the two Churches.

'5. That expressing this general mind of the Orthodox Church the most Holy Patriarchs at different periods, and other hierarchs of the East, when writing to the Archbishops of the Anglican Church, have been used to address them as "Most Reverend Brother in Christ", thus giving them a brotherly salutation.

'Our Holy Synod, therefore, came to an opinion accepting the validity of the Anglican priesthood, and has decided that its conclusion should be announced to the other Holy Orthodox Churches in order that occasion might be given them also to express their opinion, so that the mind of the Orthodox world on this important question might be known.

'Accordingly, writing to your . . . well-beloved . . . and informing you of the considerations which, in this question, prevail with us, we have no doubt that your . . . also having investigated this question with your Holy Synod, will be pleased to communicate the result of your consideration to us, to the end of a further improvement of our relations in regard to union with the Anglican Church: in the hope that the Heavenly Ruler of the Church will supply that which is lacking through His All-Power-Inspiring Grace, and will guide all who believe in Him to a full knowledge of the truth and to full union, in order that there may be of them one flock under One Chief Shepherd—the true Shepherd of the sheep, our Lord Jesus Christ, to Whom be the glory for ever.—Amen.'

LECTURE VIII
NOTE 25. See p. 236

Newman on the Anglican Position. As early as 1837 Newman said, 'It still remains to be tried whether what is called Anglicanism, the religion of Andrewes, Laud, Hammond, Butler, and Wilson, is capable of being professed, acted on, and maintained on a large sphere of action and through a sufficient period, or whether it be a mere modification of Romanism or of popular Protestantism, according as we view it.' *Lectures on the Prophetical Office of the Church*, p. 21 (Rivington, London, 1837). He then strongly supported the first view. When we remember the frequent accusation directed against the Tractarians that they appealed simply to Antiquity, it is worth noting that Newman in this work expressly repudiates any such notion. He says, 'The mere Protestant, indeed, and the Romanist may use Antiquity. . . . We, on the contrary, consider Antiquity and Catholicity to be the real guides, and the Church their organ' (p. 322). The whole passage is important.

NOTE 26. See p. 238

Newman on Transubstantiation. 'People say that the doctrine of Transubstantiation is difficult to believe; I did not believe the doctrine till I was a Catholic. I had no difficulty in believing it as soon as I believed that the Catholic Roman Church was the oracle of God, and that she had declared this doctrine to be part of the original revelation. It is difficult, impossible to imagine, I grant—but how is it difficult to believe? Yet Macaulay thought it so difficult to believe, that he had need of a believer in it of talents as eminent as Sir Thomas More, before he could bring himself to conceive that the Catholics of an enlightened age could resist "the overwhelming force of the argument against it". "Sir Thomas More", he says, "is one of the choice specimens of wisdom and virtue; and the doctrine of transubstantiation is a kind of proof charge. A faith which stands that test, will stand any test." But for myself,

I cannot indeed prove it, I cannot tell *how* it is; but I say, "Why should not it be? What's to hinder it? What do I know of substance or matter? just as much as the greatest philosophers, and that is nothing at all;"—so much is this the case, that there is a rising school of philosophy now, which considers phenomena to constitute the whole of our knowledge in physics. The Catholic doctrine leaves phenomena alone. It does not say that the phenomena go; on the contrary, it says that they remain: nor does it say that the phenomena are in several places at once. It deals with what no one on earth knows anything about, the material substances themselves.' *Apologia*, pp. 374-375 (Longman, London, 1864).

NOTE 27. See p. 240

The Return to the traditional Dates of many Books of the New Testament. The most significant, not to say sensational, return to views which placed most of the books of the New Testament well within the first century of the Christian era, occurred in Professor Adolf Harnack's 'Chronologische Tabelle' at the end of the first part of volume ii of his *Geschichte der altchristlichen Litteratur bis Eusebius* (Leipzig, 1897). Since that time the learned author has adopted even more conservative views, especially as to the date of the Acts of the Apostles.

The following extract from Professor Adolf Jülicher's *Einleitung in das Neue Testament*, p. 12 f. (Tübingen, 1906), illustrates the views now held by German 'Liberal' theologians of the work of Baur and the older Tübingen school:

'Ein grosser Teil der Tübingischen Thesen hat sich als unhaltbar erwiesen. Schon innerhalb der Schule, mit Entschiedenheit zuerst durch Hilgenfeld, wurde erkannt, dass von den Briefen mit paulinischer Etikette aus inneren Gründen I Th., Phl. und Phm. keinem anderen Verfasser zugesprochen werden können als Gal. und Cor., und dass eine Annäherungstendenz ihnen nur aufgedrängt wird. Dass schon äussere Zeugnisse uns hindern, eine grosse Zahl NTlicher Schriften so tief ins 2. Jhdt. herabzurücken, konnte auch auf die Dauer nicht geleugnet werden. Und was noch wichtiger ist, durch Holsten's Verdienst wird jetzt von den meisten Tübingern zugegeben, dass es nicht angeht, Petrus und die Urapostel überhaupt als die Vorkämpfer des radikalen Judaismus zu betrachten, dass vielmehr Petrus einen im Verhältnis zu den von Paulus schroff bekämpften judaistischen Agitatoren freieren, milderen, nur eben nicht prinzipiell klaren Standpunkt vertritt, dass auch hier in gewissem Sinne der Gegensatz das Spätere ist, eine — relativ weitherzige — Einheit das Ursprüngliche. Aber hierbei stossen wir auf die Hauptfehler der Geschichtskonstruktion Baur's. Er überschätzt die Bedeutung des Judaismus in der ältesten Christenheit, weil er mit dem Judentum jener Zeit nicht ausreichend bekannt ist, er übertreibt die antijüdischen Elemente in der Gedankenwelt des Paulus und isoliert diesen, als hätte er allein universalistische Tendenzen vertreten und heidenchristliche Gemeinden gegründet, er behält für die Persönlichkeit Jesu kaum einen Raum übrig. So einseitig paulozentrisch ist seine Auffassung von der Geschichte des Urchristentums orientiert, dass er diese eigentlich von den Anfängen bis tief ins 2. Jhdt. hinein von dem einzigen Interesse an dem durch Paulus angeregten Kampf beherrscht sein lässt, dem Kampf um die Fortdauer des Gesetzes und die Prärogative der Juden, während dieser Kampf doch nur ein geschichtebildender Faktor neben anderen gewesen ist, und zahllose Christen der ersten beiden Generationen nicht bloss kein Verständnis für diesen Streit gehabt, sondern nicht einmal etwas von ihm gewusst haben werden. Es sind ja nicht Gedanken und Grundsätze in erster Linie, von denen eine neue Religion lebt, sondern Stimmungen, Empfindungen, Hoffnungen sind das ausschlaggebende; Baur's Vorstellung · von der Entwicklungsgeschichte der apostolischen und nachapostolischen Zeit ist eine zu sehr logisch korrekte und an Farbentönen arme, um wahrscheinlich zu heissen. Trotzdem bleibt es dabei, dass Baur eine neue Epoche der NTlichen Wissenschaft eröffnet hat, schon durch eine Menge von neuen und unangreifbaren Einsichten betreffend Fragen der Einleitung wie der Exegese und NTlichen Theologie, vornehmlich aber dadurch, dass er den Betrieb unsrer Wissenschaft auf eine höhere Stufe gehoben, die subjektivistische Vereinzelung in der Untersuchung beseitigt, die literarkritische Detailarbeit in den Dienst der Geschichte der Ideen genommen hat: seit Baur kann die Literaturgeschichte des NT's nicht mehr ausserhalb des Zusammenhangs mit der Gesamtgeschichte des Christentums, ja der Religion und überhaupt der Menschheit behandelt werden; er hat uns gelehrt, die Bücher des NT's wahrhaft geschichtlich, als Erzeugnisse des religiösen Geistes einer bestimmten Zeit und als Zeugnisse für denselben zu würdigen.'

NOTE 28. See p. 253

The 'Jesus of History'. The following words of Dr. T. B. Strong, Bishop of Ripon, are applicable to all forms of modern Rationalism except those which deny that our Lord had any existence.

'I do not quarrel with the attempt to disentangle the "Jesus of History" from the existing records. But I think we have a right to ask that the figure which results should account for the existence of the Church and the development of its thought and practice. I venture to think that this condition is not fulfilled. There is one fact written large over the New Testament as a whole, which is that the new movement in religion, whatever it was, dated from the presence in the world of Jesus Christ. None of those to whom it fell to spread the movement were in the smallest doubt about this. St. Paul was not a man to accept dictation or to conceal his own part in the movement; but, though he tells us nothing new of the life of the Lord, there is no doubt that his whole mind and will are prostrate in abasement before the Lord. The same is true of the other New Testament writers: there is not the slightest vestige of a suggestion that any of them were acting in any other capacity than as servants of His. It is difficult to see how if Christ were merely a prophet of the Second Coming with an "interim ethic", if He were merely a preacher of righteousness and charity, with no message of Salvation, if He had succeeded after His death in convincing His followers of immortality, but did not rise from the grave—it is difficult to see how His followers can have held and retained the opinion of Him which they express in their works. . . . You may study the Apocalypses and the mystery religions and the current philosophy, and show, probably quite truly, how various elements in the doctrine of the New Testament fit on to elements in pre-Christian and non-Christian thought; but this will not explain the figure of Christ—the impression He made upon His followers. What is called the "Jesus of History" will not, I think, displace the Jesus of the New Testament, of the New Testament as a whole and not merely of the Gospels.' *The Gospel and the Creed*, pp. 10 ff. (Oxford University Press, 1922).

INDEX

A.

Aberdeen, 57, 273.
Absolution, 2, 89, 104, 129.
Acceptants, 105.
Adam, fall of, 7, 49, 54, 78, 141.
Advertisements, book of, Grindal's, 40; Parker's, 46.
Alacoque, St. Margaret Mary, 270.
Albert of Brandenburg, 4.
Alphonsus Liguori, St., 125.
Amsterdam, 92, 94, 98.
Anabaptists, 42, 76, 157 n.
Andrewes, Lancelot, Bishop, 50, 130.
Angelus Silesius, 85.
Anne, Queen of England, 132, 150.
Antinomianism, 8, 138, 147.
Antiquity, the appeal to, 47, 65, 87, 103, 281.
Anti-Trinitarianism, 65, 81, 137, 157.
Apostles' Creed, 71.
Apostolic succession, 34, 159.
Appellants, 105.
Architecture, English, 66, 274; Rococo, 108; American, 155, 274.
Arianism, in England, 137, 139; in America, 158; in Switzerland, 174.
Arminianism, 93, 138, 143, 145.
Arminius, Jacobus, 92.
Arnold, T., Dr., 231.
Arpafeelie, 154.
Articles, the thirty-nine, 39.
Atonement, doctrine of, 65, 81, 138.
Augsburg, confession of, 163.
Augustine, St., 26, 103, 107, 127.
Augustinus of Jansenius, 27.
Austria, Church reforms in, 110.

B.

Bahrdt, K. F., 171.
Bajus, M., 26.
Balliol College, Oxford, 200.
Baptismal regeneration, 64.
Baptists, or Anabaptists, 42, 58, 76, 157 n.

Barrowe, Henry, Congregationalist, 43.
Baumgarten, S. J., 167.
Baur, F. C., 186, 239, 282.
Baxter, Richard, 63.
Bayly, Lewis, Bishop, 95.
Bellarmin, R. F. R., 42, 50, 91.
Benedict XIV, Pope, 107.
Benedict XV, Pope, 270.
Benedictines, 118.
Benediction, rite of, 195.
Berlin, 84, 168, 169, 182, 189, 249.
Berthelsdorf, 84, 162.
Bethlehem in Pennsylvania, 161.
Bickerdike, Robert, 41.
Bismarck, 73.
Boehme, Jacob, 86, 143.
Bohemia, 162; *see also* Czecho-Slovak.
Bonaparte, 121 ff.
Booth, W., 18.
Borromeo, St. Charles, 13.
Bossuet, J. B., Bishop of Meaux, 25, 29, 102.
Boston, U.S.A., religion of, 158, 275; old churches of, 157, 274.
Bousset, W., 172.
Brandenburg, Albert of, 4; John Sigismund of, 83.
Breda, 62.
Brightman, F. E., 45 n., 261.
Browne, Robert, founder of Congregationalism, 43.
Bucer, Martin, 35.
Bulgarian schism, 216.
Bunyan, John, 95.
Burnet, G., Bishop, 130, 135.
Burney, C. F., 241 n.
Burning for heresy, 37.
Busenbaum, his moral theology, 112.

C.

Cajetan, Cardinal, 5.
California, Franciscan missions in, 113.
Calissen (Calixtus), George, 87.
Calvin, John, 42, 77 ff.
Calvinism, in Great Britain, 42 ff., 63, 141; on the Continent, 81 ff.;

in America, 44, 158, 263; its connexion with learning, 89; reaction against, 81, 89, 92, 138, 158.
Calvinistic Methodism, 145, 272.
Canon of the Mass, 34, 36, 85, 261.
Canonical Scriptures, 72.
Carlovitz, *see* Karlovci.
Carstares, William, 62.
Cartwright, Thomas, 42.
Casaubon, Isaac, 90.
Casuistry, degeneration of, 28.
Chalice, denial of the, 69; permitted to Uniats, 213.
Challoner, R., Bishop, 116.
Channing, W. E., 158.
Charles I, King, religious policy of, 56.
Charles II, King, religious policy of, 60, 62.
Chasuble, Anglican retention of, 38; Lutheran retention of, 84, 265.
Chateaubriand, 226.
Choir Office, 18.
Clarke, Samuel, 139.
Clement XIV, Pope, 112, 268.
Clitheroe, Margaret, 41.
Cocceius, J., 175.
Collegia philobiblica, 96.
Commonwealth, the, religion under, 58.
Communion, frequent, 16, 36; under both kinds, 35, 69, 213.
Confession, auricular, retained by Lutherans, 82, 85; by Calvin, 79; by Anglicans, 95 n., 132.
Congregationalists, 43, 58, 62, 137.
Connecticut, Congregationalism in, 156 ff.; the Church in, 156 ff.
Consalvi, E., Cardinal, 125.
Constantinople, the Church in, 192, 211 ff.
Consubstantiation, 72.
Contarini, G., Cardinal, 9.
Convocation, suppression of, in 1717, 142.
Counter-Reformation, 1 ff.
Cranmer, Thomas, Archbishop, 36.
Cromwell, Oliver, 58.
Cutler, Timothy, 156.
Czecho-Slovak Church, 249.

D.

Dale, R. W., on Evangelicalism, 148.
Dead, indulgences for, 4.

Decretals, False, 68, 109.
Deism, 133 ff., 167, 173, 241.
Depravity of human nature, Protestant doctrine of, 7, 49, 54, 93, 141.
Devonshire, rising in, against the prayer-book, 36.
Directory, French, 121.
Discipline, Book of, 54.
Discipline, in the ancient church, 2.
Dissenters, in eighteenth century, 137.
Doddridge, Ph., 139.
Döllinger, I., 246, 258.
Donne, John, 49.
Dort (Dordrecht), Calvinistic synod at, 93.
Douai, seminary at, 116.
Dresden, 162.
Dupanloup, F. A. Ph., Bishop of Orleans, 246.
Dutch, Reformed Church, 92 ff., 174.

E.

Eastern Orthodox Church, the, 192 ff.
Eckhart, 86.
Edinburgh, religious riots in, 57; Episcopacy in, 150.
Edward VI, King, 41.
Einsiedeln, Zwingli at, 74; church at, 74, 108.
Elders, Congregationalist, 43; in Calvin's polity, 79.
Election, Calvinistic doctrine of, 78, 93, 263.
Elgin, 151.
Elizabeth, Queen, 37 ff.; excommunication of, 40, 262.
Ephrata in Pennsylvania, 161.
Episcopacy, in England, 34, 63; in Scotland, 55 ff., 60, 150 ff.; in America, 155 ff.; in Sweden, 70, 265.
Ernesti, J. A., 170.
Erudition for any Christian Man, 34.
Eschatology of the Gospels, 169, 284.
Eucharist, doctrines of, 72, 76, 78, 204.
Eudes, J., teaches worship of the Sacred Heart, 271.
Evangelical Church, German, 181 ff.
Evangelical movement, 147.
Extreme unction, 35.

INDEX

F.

Faith, nature of, 6, 70.
Fall of Adam, effects of, 7, 49, 54, 78, 141.
Farel, Guillaume, 54.
Fathers, appeal to the, Anglican, 35, 46, 50, 64; Gallican, 32, 103.
Fawkes, Guy, 41.
Fénelon, F. de S. de la M., Archbishop, 25, 99.
Filioque, 203.
Fletcher, J., of Madeley, 148.
Florence, Council of, 205.
Forbes, Robert, Bishop, 153.
Francis de Sales, St., 23.
Francis de Xavier, St., 20.
Frederick II, King of Prussia, 166.
Frederick William I, King of Prussia, 166.
Frederick William III, King of Prussia, 181.
Free Grace, 146.
'Free Protestantism', 187.
Freewill, 7, 65, 92.

G.

Gaelic language, 57, 151, 152 n.
Galle, church at, 94.
Gallicanism, 29, 32, 101 ff., 124, 244, 268.
Gardner, P., 243.
Geddes, Jenny, 57.
Geneva, 42, 89, 174.
Genevan Bible, 46.
George I and George II, Kings, the Church under, 132 ff.
George IV, King, 225.
Gerhardt, P., hymn-writer, 85.
Germany, Protestantism in, 1 ff., 69 ff., 162 ff.; Roman Catholicism in, 108, 247; Rationalism in, 169 ff., 240 ff.
Glasgow, English Prayer Book at, 55; Presbyterian Assembly at, 55, 57.
Glencoe, 131, 151.
Goethe, J. W., 167, 178, 276.
Gomarus, F., 92.
Goodwin, Thomas, 59, 270.
Grabe, J. E., Lutheran convert, 87.
Grace, divine, 12, 26 ff., 93, 103, 260.
Gratry, A., 16; on Liguori, 126 n.
Greek Church, Orthodox, 192 ff.
Greek rite in Italy, 192, 277.
Grégoire, H., 'Constitutional' Bishop, 119.
Grindal, Edmund, Archbishop, 40.

Grotius, Hugo, 93.
Grou, J. N., 121.
Guadalupe, Our Lady of, 99.
Günther, A., his resemblance to Newman, 237.

H.

Halle, Pietists at, 96, 166.
Harnack, A., 187, 242, 250.
Hawley, General, 152.
Hearne, T., 131.
Heart, the Sacred, worship of, 59 n., 126, 270.
Henke, H. Ph. C., 87 n.
Henry VIII, King, 45, 122.
Herrnhut, 84 n., 162.
Highlands of Scotland, 150, 154.
Hoadly, B., Bishop, 140, 142.
Hogarth, W., 140.
Holdsworth, W. S., 49 n.
Holland, Protestantism in, 92, 174, 189; Jansenism in, 107; Roman Catholicism in, 93, 98, 190 n.; Old Catholicism, in 248.
Hontheim, Nik. von, Bishop, 108.
Hooker, Richard, 47, 64.
Horsley, S., Bishop, 141.
Huguenots, 90, 99.
Hus, John, 249.

I.

Icons, veneration of, 206.
Idealism, German, 179.
Ignatius de Loyola, St., 17.
Illumination or Aufklärung, 167.
Immaculate conception, 127, 244.
Independents, *see* Congregationalists.
Indulgences, origin of, 2 ff.; Council of Trent on, 10, 257.
Infallibility of the Pope, repudiated by English Roman bishops, 118, 269; supported by Liguori, 126; made a dogma, 127, 244.
Inge, W. R., 251.
Innocent XI, Pope, 102.
Innocent, Bishop of Kamchatka, 222.
Inquisition, 10, 15.
Inverness, 54, 151 ff.
Invocation of saints, 32, 69, 209.

J.

Jablonsky, D. E., Moravian bishop, 163.
Jablonsky, P., 162.
Jacobi, F. H., 179.
Jacobites, 150, 273.

288 INDEX

Jaffna, church at, 94.
James I and VI, King, 55.
James II and VII, King, 62, 130.
Jansenists, 29, 102 ff.
Jansenius, C., Bishop, of Ypres, 27, 260.
Jerusalem, synod of, in 1672, 202 ; patriarch of, 218.
Jesuits, 18, 27, 32, 45, 106; suppression of, 112, 268.
' Jesus of history ', the, 253, 284.
Jews, in Spain, 16, 98, 266 ; in Holland and England, 94, 98, 266, 267.
John, St., Gospel of, in modern criticism, 183, 241.
John, St., of the Cross, 17.
Johnson, S., of Yale, 156.
Johnson, Samuel, Dr., 135.
Joseph II, Church reforms of, 110.
Justification, doctrine of, 6, 11, 70, 87 n.

K.

Kant, I., his relation to Christianity, 172.
Karlovci, Serbian see, 219.
Keble, J., poems of, 229.
Kelpius, J., 164.
Keltic Church, 3.
Ken, T., Bishop of Bath and Wells, 131.
Kenrick, P. R., Archbishop of St. Louis, 246.
Kettlewell, J., 131.
Kidd, B. J., 5 n., 263.
Klopstock, 176.
Kneeling at communion, 53.
Knox, John, work of, 53 ff.
Köln, 69 n., 109, 226.
Königsberg, 87.

L.

Lacordaire, H. D., 227.
Lainez (Laynez), J., defends papal absolutism, 11.
Laity, chalice given to, 69, 213 ; position in Eastern Church, 211.
Lambeth, 45.
Lamennais, F. de, 226.
Lamettrie, J. O., materialist, 168.
Latitudinarian party, 142.
Laud, William, Archbishop, 51, 56, 65, 92.
Laurentius Petri, Archbishop, 265.
Law, W., mystic, 86, 135, 142.
Learning, in seventeenth century, 42, 89.

Leavened or unleavened bread at the Eucharist, 193.
Lebanon, 212.
Leibniz, G. W., 166.
Leighton, R., Archbishop, 62.
Leipzig, University of, 96.
Leo X, Pope, 1.
Leo XIII, Pope, 245.
Lessing, G. F., 169.
' Liberal Protestantism ', 158, 187, 189.
Lightfoot, J. B., Bishop, 243.
Liguori, St. Alphonsus Maria, 125 ff.
Lippe, 83.
Loisy, A., 242 n.
Lola Montez, 179 n.
Loofs, F., 173.
Louis XIV, King of France, 99, 101, 212.
Louis XV, King of France, 106, 112.
Louis XVI, King of France, 107.
Lowlands of Scotland, 153.
Lucaris, Cyril, Patriarch, 199.
Luther, Martin, 1 ff., 22, 26, 70 ff., 187.
Lutheranism, 6, 32, 69 ff., 161 ff. ; in America, 85 ; in Sweden, 70, 264.

M.

Mackenzie, Hector, 151.
Maistre, J. de, 228.
Maitland, F. W., 262.
Major, G., 70.
Manning, H. E., Cardinal, 245.
Marcion, 72.
Maria Theresa, Empress, 110.
Mariana, J., 42.
Mariaviten, Old Catholic Church of the, 248.
Maronites, 212.
Mary, blessed Virgin, 126, 270.
Mary, Queen of England, 37.
Mary, Queen of Scots, 39.
Mass, the, 16, 34, 36, 85, 261.
Massachusetts, 43, 156, 159, 276.
Maxwell, John, Bishop of Ross, 56.
Mazarin, J., Cardinal, 58.
Melanchthon, Philip, 6, 199.
Melchites, 213 n.
Meletios, Patriarch of Constantinople, 203, 279.
Melville, Andrew, 55.
Methodists, 141, 145, 272.
Mexico, 13, 99, 114.
Michael Caerularius, Patriarch of Constantinople, 192.
Michaelis, J. D., 170.
Milan, 13.

INDEX

Miller, P., 165.
Milne, W., 53.
Missions, 20, 97, 99, 113, 134, 148, 161, 222.
Modernism, 81, 250 ff., 284.
'Modern Protestantism', 190, 240, 243.
Mogila, Peter, 201.
Mohawk language, 165.
Molina, L., 27.
Molinos, M. de, 95.
Montaigne, M. E. de, 30.
Montfaucon, B. de, 25.
Montreal, 154 n.
Moravians, 97, 162.
Morone, G. de, Cardinal, 9.
Mosheim, L., 167.
Mosques, 199.
Mysticism, 70, 82, 86, 95, 143.

N.

Nag's Head Fable, 45.
Neri, St. Philip, 15.
Nestorianism, 76.
New Haven, Connecticut, 275.
Newman, John Henry, 16, 229 ff., 281.
New York, 155, 159, 274.
Nicene Creed, 71, 157, 252.
Nitschmann, D., Moravian Bishop, 161, 163.
Noailles, L. A. de, Cardinal, 106.
Nonconformists, 42, 63, 137.
Nonjurors, 130, 150, 273.

O.

Ochino, B., 9.
Oldenbarnevelt, 93.
Orange, Maurice, Prince of, 93; William, Prince of, 131, 149.
Oratorians, 16.
Orders, Anglican, 35, 45, 63, 245, 279; Swedish, 265.
Ordinal, 34.
Organs, 76, 94.
Orthodox Church, 192 ff.
Oxford, Magdalen College, 59, 91: Wadham College, 66; Trinity College, 66; St. John's College, 131; Balliol College, 200.
Oxford movement, 229 ff.
Oxfordshire, recusants in, 41.

P.

Parker, Matthew, Archbishop, 45 ff.
Parker, Theodore, 159.
Pascal, B., 28 ff.
Pater, W., 167.
Paterson, M., on Catholicism, 229, 233.
Paul III, Pope, 10.
Paul of Samosata, 81.
Paul, St., his doctrine of Justification, 6, 70.
Pearson, J., Bishop, 89.
Pelagianism, 26.
Penance, 2 ff., 35.
Perfectionism, 146.
Perrone, 236, 248.
Perthshire, 151.
Peter the Great, Tsar, 221.
Petrograd, 223.
Philip II, King of Spain, 40.
Philip Neri, St., 15.
Photius, Patriarch of Constantinople, 193.
Picart, 133.
Pietism, 95 ff., 161.
Pistoia, synod of, 112.
Pius IV, Pope, 13, 39.
Pius V, Pope, 39, 40, 262.
Pius VI, Pope, 121.
Pius VII, Pope, 122 ff.
Pius IX, Pope, 244, 271.
Poland, 81, 98, 162, 248.
Pole, R., Cardinal, 6.
Pollard, A. F., 261.
Pombal, 113.
Pompadour, Mme. de, 113.
Pope, authority of, 2, 11, 34, 49, 51, 68, 102 ff., 258; infallibility of, 126, 244; as Anti-Christ, 264.
Port-Royal, 28, 104.
Prague, 69 n., 111.
Prayer Book of 1549, 34, 53, 85; of 1552, 36, 38; of 1662, 63, 66.
Prayer Book, Lutheran, 85.
Predestination, doctrine of, 44, 50, 54, 75, 78, 92, 263.
Presbyterianism, 42, 54 ff., 62, 137 ff., 150 ff.
Priestley, Joseph, 141.
Primer, 34.
Probabilism, 29, 126.
Puritanism, 42 ff., 65, 156.
Pusey, E. B., Dr., 168 n., 172, 229, 231, 236.

Q.

Quebec, 99.
Quesnel, P., 104, 112.

R.

Rationalism, in America, 157; in Germany, 166 ff., 241 ff.
'Rationalist', defined by Kant, 173.

INDEX

Ratisbon, 6.
Rawlinson, R., Bishop, 131.
Recusants, 41.
Reformation, beginning of, in Germany, 1 ff., 69 ff.; in Great Britain, 34 ff.; in Switzerland, 74; in Holland, 92.
Reformed, the differences between Lutherans and, 81.
Reimarus, H. S., 169.
Remonstrants, 93.
Renaissance, 1, 8.
Renan, E., 240.
Reserved sacrament, 36.
Restoration, in England, 62; in France, 128.
Revolution, the English, 131, 149; the French, 118 ff.
Ricci, Sc. de', Bishop, 112.
Ritschl, Albr., 184.
Robertson, F. W., 243.
Rodriguez, A., 17.
Roman Catholics, English, under Elizabeth, 41; in the eighteenth century, 115, 268; in the nineteenth, 118, 246.
Romantic movement, 180, 227.
Rome, local Church of, 15.
Rossano, 278.
Rousseau, J.-J., 174.
Rumanian Church, 216, 218.
Russian Church, 221.

S.

Sacraments, as retained in English Church, 35, 63; Lutheran doctrine of, 71, 85; Zwinglian doctrine of, 76; Calvinist doctrine of, 63, 78; considered invalid apart from preaching, 262; Goethe on, 178, 276.
Sadoleto, J., Cardinal, 9.
Sales, St. Francis de, 23.
Sancroft, William, Archbishop, 130.
Sanday, W., Dr., 188, 189, 243.
Savoy conference, 63.
Savoy declaration, 44, 138, 263.
Scheffler, J. (Angelus Silesius), 85.
Schiller, J. Chr. F., 176.
Schlegel, F., 180.
Schleiermacher, F. D., 182, 185.
Schweitzer, A., 188.
Scotland, reformation in, 52 ff.; Church in eighteenth century in, 150 ff.
Scott, Sir Walter, on Episcopacy, 155; on mediaeval hymns, 227.
Scripture, authority of, 10, 68, 72, 80; verbal inspiration of, 172; rationalist criticism of, 186, 239, 284.
Seabury, S., Bishop, 155.
Semler, J. S., 170.
Separatists, 43.
Serbia, Church of, 198, 215, 219, 249.
Serra, Junipero, 113.
Shaftesbury, A. A. C., Earl of, 134.
Sheldon, G., Archbishop, 264.
Sinan, Armenian architect, 199.
Socinianism, in Holland, 138, 174; in England, 138 ff.; in America, 159.
Socinus, Faustus, 81.
'Solitary', Order of the, 164.
Spain, Counter-Reformation in, 16 ff.; missions of, 20, 113.
Spanish bishops, at Trent, 11, 258.
Spener, Ph. J., 96.
Spinoza, B., 94, 169.
Squanto, American Indian, 264.
St. John's College, Oxford, 131.
St. Paul's church, London, 66.
St. Peter's church, Rome, 1, 12, 244.
Staupitz, 70.
Stolberg, F., 180.
Stone, Darwell, 206 n.
Strauss, D. F., 135, 186.
Strossmayer, J. G., Bishop, 246.
Supremacy, papal, 2, 11, 34, 101, 109, 123 n., 258.
Supreme Head, title of, 38.
Swedish Orders, question of, 265.
Switzerland, reformation in, 74 ff.; rationalism in, 174.
Synagogue, in Amsterdam, 94; in Bevis Marks, London, 98, 267.

T.

Tauler, J., 86.
Taylor, John, Arian, 140.
Teellinck, W., 96.
Teresa, St., 21.
Tetzel, J., 2, 4.
Theatines, 9.
Tikhon, Patriarch of Moscow, 223.
Tindal, W., 134, 136.
Toland, J., 134, 136, 166.
Toleration, in Holland, 95.
Tractarians, 230 ff.
Tradition, 10.
Transubstantiation, 204.
Trent, Council of, 10 ff.
Trinity, doctrine of the, 65, 81, 160.
Trinity College, Oxford, 66.
Troeltsch, E., 191.
Tübingen school, 239 ff., 282.
Turks, 1, 196.

INDEX

U.

Ultramontanes, 32, 102, 244.
Uncas, Mohican, 161 n.
Unction of the Sick, 35.
Uniat Churches, 99, 201, 212.
Unitarians, Socinian, 81, 138, 141; modern, 65, 158, 253, 275.
Universalists, 159, 276.
Ursulines, 9.
Utrecht, 248.

V.

Vatican Council of 1870, 244 ff.
Venice, 9, 91, 94.
Venn, H., 147.
Verbal inspiration, 172.
Vernacular, services in the, 68.
Vestments, Eucharistic, 38, 84, 265.
Vienna, Congress of, 125.
Virgin birth of Christ, 183, 251.
Virginia, the Church in, 155 ff.
Voet, G., 95, 175.
Voltaire, in Prussia, 168.

W.

Wadham College, Oxford, 66.
Wake, W., Archbishop, 105.
Waterland, 133 n., 139 n.
Watters, 145.
Watts, Isaac, 139.
Wedderburn, James, Bishop of Dunblane, 56.
Weinel, H., 188.

Wesley, John, 84, 85, 144 ff., 16 272.
Westminster Confession, 44, 138, 263.
Whately, R., Archbishop, 236.
Whitefield, George, 144 ff.
Wieland, Chr. M., 176.
William III, King, 62, 95, 130, 150.
Wilson, Thomas, Bishop, 131.
Winkworth, C., 86.
Wiseman, N. P. S., Cardinal, 236.
Wittenberg, reformation at, 5, 7.
Wolfenbüttel Fragments, 169.
Wolff, Chr., 166.
Woolston, Th., 135.
Wrede, W., 188 n.
Wren, Sir Chr., 66, 274.

X.

Xanten, church at, 4.
Xavier, St. Francis de, 20.

Y.

Yale, 156.
York, persecution of recusants at, 41.

Z.

Zinzendorf, N. L., Count, 161 ff.
Zürich, 42, 75.
Zwiefalten, monastery church at, 108.
Zwingli, Huldreich, 74 ff.

www.ingramcontent.com/pod-product-compliance
Lightning Source LLC
Chambersburg PA
CBHW062001220426
43662CB00010B/1191